Sparkle: Bright Reflections on Life

Laura Nashman

Sparkle: Bright Reflections on Life, 4th edition

© Laura Nashman 2023

ISBN: 9798367781120

Edited by Colin Eatock and Slava Kovalsky

Cover art by Michael Moon

Published independently

Contents

Chapter One: My Flutopia 1

Chapter Two: My Two Families 29

Chapter Three: Ito, Kito and Tigger, My Furry Friends   47

Chapter Four: Loving the Animals . . . 68

Chapter Five: Joyous Journeys and Celebrity Sightings   88

Chapter Six: Adventuring Life 122

Chapter Seven: Friends and Lovers . . . 147

Chapter Eight: Mystical Moments . . . 196

Chapter Nine: Healing and Reflecting . . . 222

Chapter Ten: My Life as a *Lebenskünstler* . . 239

Chapter Eleven: My *Sparkle* Wisdom . . . 254

Appendix 286

Foreword

I never planned on writing a book. It kind of wrote me.

It happened during the Covid-19 pandemic. While in lockdown at home, practising my flute, painting, and doing online courses, one particular course really nourished my spirit: Soulo Theatre with Tracey Erin Smith. On Zoom, a small group of us delved deeply into our souls, and the transformational moments in our lives. We wrote, we listened to each other's stories, we laughed, we cried, we shared, and more.

It was a safe, private space to share our deepest life's moments and experiences. These sessions were remarkably fortifying, rich with writing, sharing, and candidly telling our life stories openly and honestly to one another. At the end of each course, we got to perform our one-person shows as personal and intimate monologues for an online audience.

I participated in three of these remarkable Soulo intensives with Tracey Erin Smith over the course of the pandemic. Unexpectedly, I developed a penchant for writing: free-flow, stream-of-consciousness, authentically, unapologetically. It became a daily exercise in deep personal reflection. I got into such a good habit of writing with spontaneity that I was more often "in the flow" than not. Tracey encouraged us with her "first thought, best thought" technique, borrowed from improv theatre.

At the end of each of these intense and personal sessions, I often felt primed to write more. I was inspired to recall the most memorable moments of my life; then, I committed them to paper. There was no time for writer's block – or any blocks, for that matter. I wasn't at all interested in shaming myself or engaging my inner critic. Instead, I soared through my thoughts, turning them into words on the page with effortless bliss. They naturally bubbled up from my unconscious, full and overflowing, like never before. The quality of timelessness that the lockdown provided offered me a once-in-a-lifetime opportunity to zero in on my life without a sense of pressure or deadline.

I guess it also helped to be a flutist, using my "flutist's fingers" to type rapidly at the keyboard, much like playing rapid technical passages on my flute. It felt like the words were flying out of my fingertips!

I began to remember the most significant and unforgettable moments of my life. I found them coming to my awareness naturally. And in less than a year, I found myself remembering over 250 lived experiences. From them, I've learned many very powerful lessons. I also realized that I could share them with others, perhaps to shed light on their own life experiences, the challenging and the sublime.

With the pandemic lasting over three years, we may have experienced a strange unplugging of our individual sparks. With *Sparkle*, it is my hope to help us access and regain the sparkle we all had and hope to retrieve. Our lives can become living sparkplugs, offering us the inspiration and motivation to go out and live even more magical stories.

Sparkle is my living diary or journal, for you, the reader, to open on any page that speaks to you, inviting you in. The purpose of this book is to encourage you to visit and experience your own life with renewed gratitude and appreciation. It isn't until we reflect upon the outcomes of events in our lives that we gain the wisdom and courage to move forward to our next lived stories.

At the end of end of each *Sparkle* story, there are questions for you to consider, ponder, and reflect upon to bring your own stories to life.

Thank you for the opportunity of sharing some of my life's most precious moments with you.

It's an honour and privilege.

Laura Nashman
Toronto, Canada
January 1, 2023

How to Use This Book

Sparkle can be opened anywhere, thumbed through, or read from cover to cover. Since it's an exploration of life's lessons, viewed through the lens of many short stories, you can decide what appeals to you, and simply open *Sparkle* to any page you choose. Your personal connection to each story will bear fruit in any order or sequence!

Acknowledgements

I would like to thank Colin, my beloved partner, for his time and love, and for encouraging me to continue and finish the book.

I'd also like to thank Tracey Erin Smith, whose exceptional creativity and bold teaching in her Soulo intensives helped catapult me into being a writer who loves to write from my heart and soul.

There are so many other people to thank: all my friends, family, lovers, and random yet special people who have had a profound impact on me – and have become the very fabric of this memoir.

Testimonials for *Sparkle*

Keith Whiting, music producer, author, entrepreneur:
"Laura Nashman's first book of meditations, reflections and life lessons learned is sure to both inspire and motivate."

Marnie Woodrow, comedian and author of *Heyday* and other works:
"Your pieces are just fabulous, Laura. Delicious, brief sparks of experience meet insight. I love the takeaway food for thought at the end of each! Each one is touching in different ways. And the way you recognize the deep magic in everyday life that is there if one has eyes to see it. You make the spiritual applicable to daily events. Thank you so much for sharing these."

Michael Gelb, author of *How to Think Like Leonardo da Vinci*:
"If you're lucky enough to hear Laura Nashman play the flute then you'll be moved by her mellifluous, enchanting and rich sound. In *Sparkle* she translates the soul-impulses behind those exquisite tones into words that will uplift, enlighten and inspire."

Mary Hughes, publisher of *SpaLife* and *Inns Magazine*:
"When you look at all the people that you've met in your life there's probably just a handful of them who really have made an impression and are very special. Laura Nashman is one of those people. Her musical talent ignites wonderful inspiration

in all those that have been in her audience. If you get the great pleasure to meet her and speak with her you will see her inspiration, enlightenment and her positive spirit that exudes through everything she touches and does. *Sparkle* is the perfect word to describe Laura and anything she sets her mind to! I am forever grateful for her in my life."

Jeff Zook, flutist, Detroit Symphony Orchestra:
"*Sparkle* is eclectic, dynamic and creative! Whether she is playing her flute soulfully, painting her pictures beautifully, or writing her words thoughtfully, Laura's artistry is always striking, inspiring and amazing!"

David Roche,
speaker and author of *Love at Second Sight* **and** *The Church of 80% Sincerity***:**
"Laura Nashman's writing offers us delicious bite-sized pieces of life. At the end of each piece, she offers comments that are always supportive and encouraging, never lecture-y. In sum, these little truffle episodes reveal Nashman's life and her vibrant persona. You will enjoy meeting her in this book; she offers consistent delight."

Chapter One

My Flutopia: A Life with Music

Let's begin with the flute – my flute! The sound of the flute, the feel of my fingers on the flute, playing the flute – always such an otherworldly yet totally natural and innate experience for me. From relieving my headaches and stress to uplifting my own and others' moods, my flute has always been one of my life's all-time best companions. Deep breaths, deep longing, and always exhaling music – my flute has been a most unusual, harmonious soulmate.

1. My Soul's Calling, Early in Life

I was only eight years old when I was captured and moved by the soulful sound of the flute. A simple Bach *Flute Sonata* played by my cousin Corine with her harpsichord accompanist caused in me an unexpected downpour of emotion. It wasn't subtle. You know those big, non-stop tears? This type of emotional flow ran down my face, curving around my chin and trickling all the way down my neck.

The sound of the flute was sheer beauty. It reached my heart and soul directly, evidenced by my overflowing tears. Suddenly, I heard a voice inside my head say, "Laura, look at how you're reacting. These tears must really mean something. See how deeply moved you are by the haunting and beautiful sound of the flute." How very strange to witness my soul talking to myself!

I chose to follow the nudging of this wise voice within. When band classes were offered in grade school, I competed for the flute. Because it was such a popular instrument, we all had to tell the band teacher why we wanted to play the flute. I told my mystical story, about hearing that inner voice, my soul, speak to me at my cousin's concert. It worked – and I was given a flute.

I started private flute lessons at age twelve, went to the Royal Conservatory of Music in Toronto at sixteen, participated in many flute masterclasses in Canada and abroad, and recorded many CDs. I also performed many chamber music recitals with exceptional musician friends: pianist John, guitarist Bill, and many others over the years.

I took that inner voice very seriously. What was it anyway? Was it the voice of my soul? This may sound strange, but sometimes I feel like I am not only a flutist, but a flute itself. It really seems this way, since I really feel the flute in my heart when I play. The flute seems to merge seamlessly with my soul.

Soul, spirit or essence are all words for your inner wisdom, and your divine, authentic self. Have you been called to something: a certain art form, vocation, personal expression that feels so real to you and makes your soul sing? What are these expressions? What do they mean to you? Listen closely for the signs and respond with your life.

2. Discovering Synesthesia: My Forest Flute

I had only been playing flute for just under a year. As member of a concert band, I was invited to play a solo at one of our upcoming community concerts. I felt a little bit nervous standing up in front of the entire band, since I had never done this before. Feeling a bit emotionally naked and awkward, I surrendered to my vulnerability and the moment at hand.

I took a deep breath and simply closed my eyes, playing my solo from memory. I didn't plan or expect what was about to happen next. What I saw in my mind's eye was not only spectacular but exceptionally beautiful. Was I dreaming? I had suddenly become suspended and immersed in a lush green forest. For the entire time I played the piece, I was surrounded by green – it was so vivid. As I heard the applause, I opened my eyes and the forest disappeared. It dissolved into the present moment, and the thunderous ovation enveloped me.

I never quite understood what had happened, but I've heard about altered states and meditative moments. Was this one of them? I was completely in awe.

Altered states can be unnerving, but also fun and mind-altering. Often, these states sneak up on us when we least suspect them. Have you ever experienced altered states, through meditation, listening to music, dreaming, in the shower, bathtub, upon waking, falling asleep or at other times? How did you feel?

3. Winning the Silver Medal

Preparing for the Kiwanis Music Festival Ontario Finals was an intense process. I prepared the Cécile Chaminade *Concertino for Flute*, with Susan, my friend and accompanist. A romantic piece, it was written by a woman, and rarely had I played any repertoire by female composers. This was one of my all-time favourites. For two-to-four hours a day, I rigorously practised, did Alexander Technique for body and mind awareness in classes at the Royal Conservatory, and also practised visualization techniques – tirelessly yet enthusiastically. These visualization exercises have been used by Olympic athletes to train their brains in advance of the competition. They also work for musicians learning and memorizing music.

Memorizing music has always been a challenge for me. With the Kiwanis Music Competition, it was mandatory. It seems that violinists and pianists are more accustomed to memorizing their music. Plus, they have the advantage of looking at their fingers on the fretboard or piano keys. Flutists can't. In any event, there I was, having advanced to the Ontario Finals of the Kiwanis Music Competition. I was so relieved that I had made it this far!

As I prepared to go on stage, I believed God was there with me, and I prayed to play beautifully and without the jitters. I vividly remember doing self-affirmations in the washroom mirror, sliding down the wall to gain good spinal alignment, and then going out and playing my flute from memory. I felt confident. I felt divinely supported – transported into a state of ease and flow.

I got through the performance as flawlessly as I could, and to my utter amazement, ended up winning Silver Medal at the Kiwanis Provincial Finals! It was a true honour.

Have you ever been in a competition and consciously planned to be the very best version of yourself? Have you visualized yourself winning, while giving gratitude to God/Source? Did you then go on to do what was needed to be your best and win? What happened for you?

4. Discovering Keys to My Winning Formula

I will always remember my grade six music exam at Toronto's Royal Conservatory of Music. My adjudicator was Gordon Kushner, the Vice-Principal of the Conservatory at the time. A sweet, short, Jewish man, always showing appreciation and giving compliments where compliments were due. As I entered the examination room, I felt a bit nervous, trying to mentally tame the butterflies in my stomach. I took a few deep breaths and focused. Then, I played my Telemann *Flute Sonata* for him along with some other pieces, and it all went unbelievably well. He seemed very impressed. I felt relieved. I got through the exam with flying colours!

My patient mom sat outside ready to pick me up and take me to McDonald's across the street for a snack. She was so supportive and very kind, my biggest cheerleader. I found a paper placemat and got out a pen. It was there that I mapped out all the positive aspects that I could repeat in the future when doing another flute performance. In effect, I was writing out my "winning formula" and strategy to follow to repeat this peak performance in the future.

Thinking in Neuro-Linguistic Programming terms, (before I even formally studied NLP, ten years later), I analyzed my winning strategy for a polished performance. I realized that I spoke kind words in my head, (positive self-talk with a kind tonality), and used affirmations to encourage my performance to go well. I reminded myself to allow my body to be at ease, *allowing* rather than forcing it. I guess I have always had scientist and teacher genes in me, curious to discover the best ways of doing things most effectively.

Do you have winning formulas or strategies you use? Have you documented them for yourself, and do you apply them to your life often? When have you used these strategies most?

5. Learning How to Make Mistakes

In my mid-teens, I was a flutist in a community orchestra. Our conductor was intense, yet always wise and insightful. He really empowered us musicians to do our best, always. He also encouraged us to be confident performers.

On one occasion, the principal clarinetist made a big mistake, playing the wrong note boldly and loudly. There was no hiding this mistake: It was a very pronounced error, and all members of the orchestra noticed it. He shuddered with embarrassment as the rest of us went silent.

I was surprised when I heard how our conductor responded. He said, "If you are going to make a mistake, you might as well make a big one! Don't pussyfoot around. Play with confidence, *always*." I guess this was his way of excusing the mistake, due to the bold intention behind it.

This profound lesson has remained with me throughout my life. In a nutshell, it's better to approach life with confidence and boldness than to be timid and pussyfoot around. I have found this approach works best for me. Boldness trumps timidity, even if we sometimes end up making huge mistakes!

Has there been a time when you made a mistake and were applauded for it? What "miss-takes" have you learned most from?

6. Delivering My Best Flute Performance Out of My Treasure Chest

This is a story about my best flute jury performance ever!

I used to get very nervous doing end-of-year juries at the University of Toronto's Faculty of Music. The scene was always the same; a long table with stern professors sitting side by side, along with a clear glass jug of water, paper and pencils, poised and ready to adjudicate my flute performance. I was always so intimidated by their officious faces, and even the room had an intimidating smell of fear to me. I never liked these juries, yet I loved playing my flute.

It was the second year of my bachelor's degree in flute performance, and I really didn't want to ruin my performance with jittery nerves. I decided to create and visualize a fantasy situation in my mind's eye. I imagined that rather than being *judged*, I was being *invited* to play a piece that I had discovered deep down in the ocean, in a treasure chest. My performance at this jury today would be the first time it had been performed in thousands of years. My imagination was primed to deliver my best flute performance ever. I saw a beautiful treasure chest, open halfway, bubbling away with pearls, jewels, various treasures and the most important one of all, a perfect flute manuscript. Somehow, imagining this literally took the intimidation out of the performance process. I was creating a new reality that would help my flute performance.

Along with this visualization, I positioned the jury in my mind's eye as *real people* I felt compassion for. Rather than seeing them judging me, I saw them as people stuck at a table for eight hours, relentlessly listening to musicians all day, and having very few breaks.

Internally, I decided to offer my performance as a gift to them, something to cheer up their day. And I rejected my own mental image of them as a scary-monster group of professors, resembling music critics with stern looks and unforgiving attitudes.

Astonishingly, it turned out to be my best jury performance ever. Since then, I have used my imagination and visualization to bring about many positive outcomes in my life. I am no longer terrified by situations that used to intimidate me. Reframing and visualizing really works!

When have you called upon your imagination to overcome or reframe something terrifying? How did it help you? Have you used this visualization again? How have you harnessed your creativity to solve a challenge? What else have you applied this strategy to?

7. Musically Merging with a Master Flutist in My Sleep

As classical music students, we often put on earphones to listen to a recording of a master musician, to hear how the piece we're studying should *really* sound. For this reason, I remember putting on a recording by the legendary flutist James Galway.

I closed my eyes, surrendering and letting his beautiful flute tone penetrate my ears, heart and soul. Semi-awake and semi-asleep, this was an unusual in-between sate of consciousness. I felt the music throughout my body, and very strongly in my heart. The intensity of the sound felt so close and inside me: I was both listening and feeling, moment to moment, like I myself was making the very music I was feeling so moved by. Was this me playing this beautiful flute music? It sure felt this way.

When I woke out of this immersive sound dream, I felt fortified by both the music and the unusual experience. Satiated by the music, I felt as if I had just played a concert with Galway's beautiful sound and seamless technical agility. Clearly, it wasn't me, but a recording of the legendary James Galway! I had never had such a surreal experience with a recording in my life.

Definitely, I was in an altered state: a delicious sound-memory I would cherish forever.

How does this happen when we seem to have a "merging experience" like this? Have you had any merging and immersive experiences you will never forget? What happened? Has anything like it happened since then?

8. Shawnigan Lake: Making Music in a Magical Place and Time

Attending Canadian flutist Robert Aitken's Summer Chamber Music School at Shawnigan Lake, British Columbia, in my early twenties was one of the most magical summers of my life. It was a remarkable chamber-music summer school hidden away in a beautiful, forested resort on Vancouver Island. We were privileged to have world-class musicians and master teachers from all over the world on the faculty, including pianist Greta Kraus, composer R. Murray Schafer, flutists Robert Aitken and Douglas Stewart, and many others. Somehow, combining the studying of chamber music with nature was the perfect mix of joy, serenity, and magical connections.

I especially remember the lesson I learned at lunch, sitting across the table from R. Murray Schafer. An acclaimed Canadian composer, he believed that musicians should go to school for other subjects, like art, literature or philosophy, to broaden their scope of being. He was such a wise and talented man, and I felt so honoured learning from him and others in such a musical paradise.

Our Shawnigan Lake schedule was broken down into our instrumental masterclasses, chamber music practising in the afternoon, and concerts in the evening. One evening, after hearing the astounding "Dumky Trio" by Dvořák, a German flutist and I took a canoe and paddled under the astonishing midnight, star-studded sky. It was like being in our own private oasis, gazing up at the bejewelled sky. Everything was so still. Peace was palpable there.

My mom had just died a few years before, and I was starting to gradually feel accustomed to this profound change in my life. Along with it came acceptance, fond memories and a certain level of peace. Suddenly, as we were slowly paddling in the still lake, I experienced an altered state of pure bliss and quietude. I was overcome by a deep feeling of calm. I felt my mother's presence, along with all others who had lived and left this Earth, dwelling peacefully in the trees, the stars, the lake. I felt and found peace. I will never forget this transcendent moment. To this day, when I think back to that canoe ride at midnight, I feel such tranquility, and know all is well.

Have you experienced a moment of true connection and tranquility with life itself? What do you remember about it? How has it affected your life since?

9.   My Master Teacher, "Wibb"

I have never had a guru, but the closest thing to it was my British master flute teacher, William Bennett, a.k.a. "Wibb." I have been transported, inspired and blissed out in his presence. I have been his student, his audience and one of his biggest fans.

He would speak of "tasting the air" in the back of our throats, as we flutists inhaled air to play a musical phrase. He would speak of "painting the tone with royal blue" at the opening of the Bach *Flute Sonata in E Major*. I loved his use of synesthesia, that blending of the senses.

Most of all, he was a hilarious, insightful, sometimes irreverent, but deeply patient and devoted teacher. The technical exercises I didn't have the desire or patience to do alone in my practise room came to life in Wibb's flute masterclasses. He would easefully demonstrate something on his flute, and then have us students echo back the teaching. What a totally inspiring, mesmerizing and immersive experience. Time would fly by, but since it was packed with such presence and joy, it was always time well spent.

Wibb was childlike, playful, and very entertaining. He would make funny faces and noises and was filled with a keen British wit and sense of humour. He seemed invincible to me – boundless and without limitations. I fondly remember our spirited leisure times after lunch at the "water hole," as Wibb put it. We flute students enjoyed swimming just as much as Wibb's classes. He loved his daily swims, even if the water was freezing. He seemed just as enthusiastic about swimming as playing the flute!

Wibb exuded that rare sense of genius. And I've noticed this quality in other highly gifted people: they have a type of genius "gene." It could be subtle too, as in the way he seemed so fascinated by things most people find ordinary, like going for a swim in a lake. Such a sense of joy and sheer celebration, moment to moment – that child-like nature that combines with their art form to distinguish geniuses' way of being.

The seemingly simple becomes elevated to another level of consciousness – that joyous inquisitiveness a lot of brilliant people seem to have. And I wonder if this phenomenon exists because their attention is on some challenging endeavour, most of the time. Yet even when they do a simple activity, they exude a sense of strange fascination. Ordinary things seem captivating to them.

Wibb was like this: very curious about life in all its intricacies, from playing flute, teaching and inspiring students, to being so joyfully absorbed in simple pleasures of life, like swimming and doing interesting yoga positions. I loved watching his fascination and curiosity about all things. Such a true inspiration, that Wibb.

William Bennett was one of the biggest influences in my life. Now, more than forty years since I studied with him, I look back at those formative flute years in my teens and early twenties in masterclasses with him with deep gratitude.

We are all both students and teachers throughout our lives. Have you been impacted at the soul level by any of your teachers – formal or otherwise – and followed a life path a certain way because of them? If you could identify a teacher that most impacted your life, what would you say to him/her today? How have you continued their legacy, if they are no longer alive?

10.   Serendipity, Coincidence, or Simply "Perfect Timing"?

Most of my life, I have had moments of synchronicity and perfect timing. One example happened when I was studying with master flutist William Bennett – or "Wibb," as he was known – in a summer masterclass at Mount Orford, Quebec, in

1985. I learned that Wibb's teacher, Geoffrey Gilbert, was accepting masterclass students at his home in Deland, Florida, that fall. He was a legend: he had played flute in the Royal Philharmonic Orchestra in London, taught the soon-to-be famous James Galway, whom he referred to as "Jimmy." Geoffrey Gilbert was about seventy-four years old, and had retired in Florida.

I hadn't finished university yet, but I had a deep sense or intuition that I should apply now, without hesitation. I asked Wibb for a reference, and along with that, had to prepare an audio demo-tape. I sent both to Geoffrey, and about one month later I received a courteous and formal invitation to come down to Florida to study with him.

Years prior, both Wibb and Jimmy studied with Geoffrey at the same time, back in London. (I love Jimmy and Geoffrey's flute playing, but always preferred the colours in Wibb's tone.) Jimmy's mastery of the flute made him one of the world's greatest flutists of all time. He had popularized the flute for the masses, including popular pieces in his repertoire, and added traditional Irish music to his mix of classical, baroque and other music. He had many gold flutes, his principal home was in Switzerland, and he recorded over 100 CDs. What an honour for me to be studying with Geoffrey Gilbert, Wibb and Jimmy's teacher – the teacher of all flute teachers!

And, as it turned out, I was the only flute student in Geoffrey's masterclass class who had not completed a master's degree, let alone a bachelor's. I somehow just *knew* that it was the time to study with him, and fortunately, I got to! My intuition was on, and the stars seemed to align.

Every day, at 9:30 am, we international students would cycle up his driveway, getting ready for our morning flute masterclass with Geoffrey. Here he was, every single morning, diligently playing his scales and technical exercises. What an inspiration to hear him at seventy-four years of age, practising the studies we were about to do as a class thirty minutes later, under his guidance!

We would have our masterclass in the morning from ten o'clock to noon, and then have the afternoons to practise. Most of us would go to the beach, by bike, for a break, and then use the rest of the afternoon to practise. A lot of the flute students I met that year at Geoffrey's class went on to become principal flutists in international orchestras, as well as soloists of great renown.

Deep down, I knew there would never be a masterclass like this one again. After my six-month masterclass stint with Geoffrey Gilbert, I returned to Toronto.

I had learned so much at such a masterful level. It truly was an experience of a lifetime for me.

A few months later – on my twenty-third birthday – I received a couple of messages on my voicemail. The first recorded voice said, "Laura, I'm sorry, but Geoffrey Gilbert has died." The very next message was another voice saying, "Laura, I'm calling to tell you it's a boy!" A very dear friend had just given birth. These were the only two messages, back to back.

How could two opposing life moments exist back-to-back on my voicemail? Life and death, two distinct realities we all have to experience. But, how ironic: to receive both messages, one after the other. Life is full of unexplainable mysteries, that's for sure.

What this experience taught me was to seize the moment and live life now. *Carpe Diem*! I was both glad and thankful that I had taken a sabbatical between my second and third year of university to do this timely masterclass. I was at the right time at the right place. Had I waited to graduate with a bachelor's degree, or even longer for my master's, I would have missed out on the brilliance of Geoffrey Gilbert. I feel so blessed to be in touch with my intuition, which has led to so many synchronicities in my life.

Can you remember a time when you followed your intuition and it ended up the perfect time for your experience? What happened as a result of your following your intuition? What would have happened if you hadn't?

This reminds me of a set of questions we were asked in a Tony Robbins seminar:
- *What will happen if you do?*
- *What will happen if you don't?*
- *What won't happen if you do?*
- *What won't happen if you don't?*

11. Be an Exciting Performer, Not an Excited Performer

I loved my flute masterclass days. I was fortunate in being able to attend so many classes with world class flutists and master teachers. One such flutist was Jeanne Baxstresser, then the principal flutist of the Toronto Symphony, and later, the New York Philharmonic. She was elegantly poised, and played with technical facility, musicality and sheer beauty.

I used to be an avid note-taker and list-maker. Jeanne noticed I took copious notes at her masterclasses, and asked me if I would send them to her so that she could make a copy of them. I felt complimented. I loved keeping my notes neat and organized. There definitely must be an "inner German/Swiss" in me. After all, my Dad was a Berliner, and my mother's father was of Swiss descent. Attention to detail seems to come naturally with these nationalities.

One of the most poignant and memorable lessons I learned from Jeanne was the distinction between being an "excited" vs. "exciting" performer. What I interpreted from her preference was that we musicians should contain ourselves physically when performing on stage. That leaves room for the audience to feel the music, and not be so distracted by the external movements and emoting of the performer.

This is definitely more easily said than done. Emoting and moving has always been so much part of my playing – but what I ended up discovering is that excessive movement can not only distract the audience from the performance, but it can also reduce available energy for playing the flute.

I have found that focusing on being an "exciting" rather than "excited" performer has given more value to my audiences. They get to decide how they feel listening to me, rather than having my excessive movement affect their interpretation. I'm forever grateful to Jeanne Baxstresser for making this distinction. I hope that I've become an exciting flutist rather than an excited one.

When have you experienced wise advice that was hard to follow, but was worth the effort? How did you benefit? How did your results improve?

12. My Accidental Music Teacher

I've been so fortunate to have studied flute with some of the best flutists in the world. Thanks to Geoffrey Gilbert (James Galway's teacher), William Bennett and others, learning to play flute has been very inspiring. From private lessons to international masterclasses, I've been exposed to many flutists with great methods and unique personalities.

One day, I had a different kind of music lesson – one of my favourite lessons of all time. I was in my neighbourhood park and heard the most beautiful birdsong. I couldn't locate the bird at first, but thought it must be a cardinal. (I believe cardinals have some of the most beautiful birdsongs.) I kept hearing his call, but couldn't spot him. Finally, I saw him in plain sight, sitting on a tree branch overhead. What I then saw and heard was truly fascinating. I was in awe, taking in his cherry-red beauty and cheerful song.

I watched closely as this vibrant cardinal prepared to sing. It seemed like he had his own process, and it was in three deliberate steps. First, sit up straight with good posture. If he had had shoulders, he would have put them down and back. Next, he took a very big breath that was visible to me. His chest expanded noticeably. Finally, he sang out his melodious birdsong. Simple. Nothing more, nothing less. The image that came to mind as I listened was of an opera singer, preparing to sing and then belting out a famous opera aria.

I have often used his simple, three-step process when playing my flute, and I always remind myself:
- Sit up straight with good posture
- Take a deep breath while expanding my chest
- Sing out with all my heart through my flute

Birds are definitely nature's flutists!

What special teachers or mentors have left a positive effect on your life? Did you have any accidental teachers, like the bird, that offered you spontaneous wisdom? What made this experience so memorable for you?

13. Delicate Distinctions

Playing my flute can often be a "butterfly" experience for me. While playing tricky technical passages, I love imagining my fingers are the soft butterflies' delicate feet. I've found that when we think of butterflies, more often than not, we think of their graceful wings and fluttery beauty. But since visiting the magical Butterfly Conservatory, in Niagara Falls, Ontario, I actually got to experience their most delicate soft touch, their legs and feet. I've never felt something so magical as having a butterfly land on my shoulder.

Butterflies put me into such a state of awe and wonder. From their angelic wings to their soft-touch feet, it's all so otherworldly. I also love imagining playing my flute with tone-colours and melodies that feel as free and boundless as the colourful wings of butterflies in flight.

Visualization and embodiment are two techniques I often use when playing flute. If a passage is very fast and technical, I imagine the ease and lightness of butterflies and hummingbirds as I play. These tricks help me to embody their carefree and easeful essence. They make playing flute more imaginative and effortless!

Butterflies are transformative beings. So are we. The wings of the butterfly are what usually gets the most attention – but what about the lightness of their delicate legs, perched on our shoulders, and that unparalleled feeling of them flying off?

What gives you a sense of boundless ease in your life? What have you noticed makes your life more effortless? When and how have you applied this to your life?

14.   The Curious Invisible Letters Beside My Name

I'm always fascinated by the letters we see beside people's names, whether on business cards, websites, books, or in other places. In a way, they proclaim the intellectual or experiential prowess people want to display.

For me, letters beside a name aren't that important. What's more important to me are kindness, good intentions, abilities, talents and results. In fact, some people question the use of the word "doctor" when used for some healing professionals, such as naturopaths and chiropractors – while blindly accepting the authority that medical, dental and academic doctors have.

I went to the University of Toronto for one reason alone. I wanted to study flute with a teacher on the faculty – and it would have cost me more to take weekly private lessons with him than it did to enroll at university. So I went to U of T. I didn't get into the performance degree program the first year, so I applied a second time. At U of T, music performance programs are very competitive, and they only accept a few of each instrument per year. Fortunately, the next year I got in.

I couldn't stand the smell of the building, and would often get a nauseous feeling in the corridors. I probably linked the smell of the building with the fierce competitive spirit, which I found overwhelming. After all, I wasn't even interested in harmony, theory, musicology and all the written courses; I just wanted to play flute and become the best flute-player I could be.

I would often get the second flute position in the U of T Orchestra, and was rarely chosen as the first flute, who got all the prominent solos. At the time, I felt defeated and a bit of a failure as a flutist. Was I "less than"? Would I ever be chosen as first flute? My self-identity as a homely band nerd lived within me for years.

Anxiety was an issue for me, and I experienced a lot of it at the faculty of music – a palpable force of unease I felt being a student in a competitive musical environment. I joked with myself that I could easily have two titles (sets of letters) beside my name: OCD (obsessive compulsive disorder) and ADD (attention deficit disorder). It was unlikely that I would obtain the BMus (bachelor of music degree) title, since I was skipping my elective class, Italian film, and my degree depended upon passing all mandatory and elective courses.

I didn't really care. I just wanted to be a flutist. And that's what I did!

What is your relationship to titles and degrees? Do you attach importance to having professional titles? Has this changed over the course of your life? How?

15. Beta-Blocker Boredom

Playing flute has always inspired me, and sometimes others who hear me play. My final jury at the University of Toronto, in my fourth year, was a nerve-wracking experience.

I heard that many symphony musicians routinely take drugs called "beta-blockers" in order to avoid the interference of jittery nerves during their performances. I was interested in experimenting, since I wanted to ensure that my final jury at U of T would go as well as possible. I decided to give the beta-blocker a try.

I couldn't believe what happened! It was the most unusual feeling I've ever had playing my flute. I was both performing and witnessing my performance at the very same time: the performer was going through the motions and the witness to my performance was saying to me inside, "This is going by so slowly and I'm feeling so bored. I hope this will be over soon." What a strange on-stage inner dialogue! I've never had this experience before or ever again. Usually, I've been preoccupied with managing my jitters as I play the music, distracted by shallow breaths that often couldn't get me to the end of music phrases. Now, in this beta-blocker boredom, I was just wanting my flute jury to be over!

In concert settings, usually a good dose of adrenaline gives performers a little kick, and performances end up amazing because of this added energy. However, with the beta-blocker, I felt like my performance was lacklustre and uninspired: like I was just going through the motions.

Based on this one-time experience, I decided to never use a beta-blocker again. I want to live my life as it is, not blocked or restricted. Funny how the word "blocked" has many uses: "writer's block," "emotional block," "energetic block," among others. I've decided that I prefer words like "flow," "ease," and "motion."

My life has changed since the unique flute concert that day, when I first experienced a slower heart rate, induced by the beta-blocker. How? By deciding not to manipulate my energy with drugs, but rather to approach my life holistically. I've never used a beta-blocker since.

When have you done something with the hope of enhancing your life, or preventing something bad from happening, and the outcome was not at all what you expected? How has this experience shaped your future decisions?

16. Parachuting In: My Artistic Process

As a creative type, I have expressed myself as a professional flutist for most of my life. And I have really enjoyed the gift of producing CDs, creating a concert series called "An Elegant Affair," and other musical undertakings. I have never really been a process-oriented person – more of a visionary and innovative type. For a long time, I've felt that life could manifest as quickly as my thoughts and ideas.

When I was planning one of my first flute CDs, at age twenty-six – a French impressionist CD called *The French Connection* – I actually waited till a week before the recording to practise and prepare my repertoire. Most people would plan and prepare well in advance. For me, though, too much planning, preparation or practising has always made me feel restricted – a sort of "claustrophobia," lacking a sense of freedom and boundlessness.

I have often used the term, "parachuting in" to describe how I act when I have an idea or project. Rather than working away at it for weeks, months, years, I just swoop in like an eagle. It's been quick impulse and instinctive follow-through. Of course, most likely my subconscious mind has been chewing on ideas for years, so I'm poised and ready to execute my next creative idea when the impulse arises.

Recently, however, I have learned that process orientation is helpful, even though I'd resisted it all my life. In writing this book, *Sparkle*, I have worked on it progressively, adding stories every day. I've felt inspired – wanting to write, as opposed to being hesitant, which can result in writer's block. The sheer energy of being plugged in gave this project motivation and momentum. Little by little, the days have added up to getting the book done: one *Sparkle* story at a time!

When have you tweaked your habitual "modus operandi"? And are you now incorporating new ways of doing things that complement your old ways? Can you think of one example, and how you have benefited?

17. Recording *The French Connection* CD: More Edits than Music!

For *The French Connection* CD, I was invited to record with the renowned Canadian pianist John Arpin and an experienced engineer. John wanted to use his own piano, so we ended up recording it in his living room, with a mobile studio set-up.

Most of the pieces were tranquil in nature. (After all, it was a French impressionist CD.) The challenge was the scheduling of the recording, which was just a few days before Toronto's annual Air Show at the Canadian National Exhibition. What strange timing! There I was, in a peaceful state of mind, ready to record the French impressionist pieces – and almost every few minutes a loud airplane flew overhead on its way to the CNE. We would stop and start, over and over again. It was very distracting and frustrating. A truly unique recording process, that's for sure.

What was even more remarkable was the outcome: a tranquil CD. There were more edits than notes, to eliminate the sound of the jets, yet the disc turned out! People who bought *The French Connection* consistently commented on how peaceful and relaxing the CD was. Little did they know the challenges involved in recording it!

What I learned from this is that circumstances may be noisy outside, but we can find the calm in the middle of the storm, even if that means copious engineering edits, or edits in our own lives: editing out negative people, negative noise and negative information.

When have you experienced an "interruption" in your life, like the sound of airplanes, or something else, and adapted to the situation? How have you edited out distractions in your day-to-day?

18. My Gold CD, *Lullababy*

I met a wonderfully talented music producer named Keith in 1994. We had one thing in common: the same entertainment lawyer. But I learned over time that we had many things in common, and he became one of my very best friends. We share a sense of "anything is possible," an entrepreneurial and innovative approach to life, and a positive mental attitude. Keith is a music producer, drummer, author, ballroom dancer, and he has a double-black belt in karate. There are probably many other talents he has that I don't know about!

At the time, Keith was creating a series of themed CD greeting cards. They were a combination of greeting card with correspondingly themed music CDs for the special times of our lives: themes like wedding, birthday, Christmas and lullaby. He asked me if I had flute CD recordings to insert into the greeting cards, and I had all but the lullaby one.

Boldly, I asked him, "Keith, can you give me a week?" I was taught in sales that if you're asked if you can provide something, but you don't yet know how, it's best to say "yes" and then figure out the details. This was the strategy I used for the lullaby recording. What an opportunity to create a lullaby CD card!

I found a music book collection of lullabies and invited my dear friend and pianist John to record it with me. We got it recorded in under three hours one afternoon at my then-boyfriend's recording studio. The music was simple as were the keyboard samples I chose: very suitable toy-piano sounds. After all, the audience was newborns!

To this day, I can remember looking through the sound-booth window at my boyfriend, the engineer, and while playing thinking, "I love you so." There was a feeling of deep love in my flute tone. As I looked at my pianist, John, I thought, "You are so special to me, John." At the time, I didn't know much about energy and how it transmutes and permeates things. I was just interested in playing flute as well as I could.

I think the emotion must have come through the flute, since eventually the recording, called *Lullababy*, became a Canadian Certified Gold CD. People would tell me that there was something very special about this CD. I believe that the music was infused with the feelings of love and gratitude I had for my engineer-boyfriend, and for my pianist, John. It must have come through in the recording.

Another auspicious thing happened during the mixing process for this CD. Almost suitably, while listening to the playback, I actually fell asleep! I had added so much reverb to the flute to give it an echoey, dreamy sound, like the sound you'd imagine hearing if a flute was played in the bathtub.

Falling asleep to my flute lullabies must have been a good sign: if I dozed off listening to the disc, most likely babies would too! Hopefully, *Lullababy* would do what it was intended to. And it did, for literally thousands of babies worldwide. To this day, people tell me that *Lullababy* is their favourite CD of mine.

I will never forget the email I received from a mother who bought one of the original *Lullababy* cassette tapes, back in the late '90s. Her toddler called it "his music." When the tape ran out and stopped playing, her little boy would stand in her bedroom doorway, crying, and insisting on saying, "I want *my* music," as apparently no other music would help him get to sleep. His mom ordered the CD, since the cassette tape had been played so much, it wore out!

Mothers giving birth would also use *Lullababy* during labour, on repeat for over fifteen hours while in labour. And others used the CD multi-generationally. I actually met a father who introduced me to his daughter of eighteen, who had been listening to it since infancy! What an honour – and what a gift to share music with new souls coming into being all over the world!

Lullababy became my most successful CD, in terms of sales. What's ironic is, most babies would fall asleep, mothers told me, after the third song. This must have meant that it really worked. I joke about the fact that it is the most popular CD I recorded – but ironically is hardly ever listened to all the way through, since the baby is sound asleep so early in the CD.

Have you had an event in your life when you sprang into action, based on an opportunity, and it turned out beautifully for you? How has this shaped your life?

19. Appreciation Goes a Long Way (It Pays Royalties!)

Receiving a framed Gold CD for my *Lullababy* CD was a complete and utter surprise. I had no idea it would be such a hit among the newborns and toddlers!

I'm a great believer in showing gratitude and celebration. In this particular situation, royalty cheques were quarterly. I decided that each time we got a cheque, I would take my lawyer and producer friend out for a fancy lunch at a restaurant of their choice. This would be my way of thanking them for the initial introduction that led to such a financially rewarding and heart-warming success!

I would also buy bouquets of flowers and have them delivered to the front desk at the record company, to show appreciation to the entire company for their ongoing efforts. Somehow, knowing that the staff would all get to see the beautiful bouquets reassured me that they'd know how much I appreciated them.

Fortunately, the royalties continued pouring in for at least the next decade, and many newborn babies were put to sleep to our music. I think we must have had two kinds of fans: the babies themselves, and also the parents – who, as a result of our sleep-inducing music, were themselves able to get a better night's sleep, due to their babies' slumbers.

The connections that help us along our way to achieve our goals are so meaningful. Appreciating and acknowledging the people who help us generates more positive energy, and opens the door for more expansive manifestations. It's generative, and propels even more good to happen. When have you given thanks and shared the celebration of your success with others who helped you achieve it? What were the results of this? What did you discover about this process? How do you show gratitude to others?

20. Meditating While Recording *Above the Sound of Gravity* CD

We all experience meditative states, whether we know it or not. Times in the shower, daydreaming, just waking up or falling asleep, swimming, walking in nature and more, can all give us a state of meditation.

Then there are other times where we consciously decide to meditate. It may be at the end of a yoga class during *savasana*, during a mindfulness meditation class, a guided visualization recording, or simply "sitting" – the frequently used term for being still and focusing on our breath.

I've found that a lot of meditative states have occurred for me when I play my flute, swim or am in the shower. I've also loved listening to guided meditation CDs. Perhaps it was only a matter of time before I got the idea of making a meditation CD of my own.

This idea came to fruition a few months after I bought a bunch of tuned wind chimes. And after a chance meeting with my friend Michael – a multi-instrumentalist and sound-healer – we decided to make a CD together. We composed and recorded it on the spot, in our own state of meditation!

I'd never worked this way before. In the past, most of my recordings had an opposite approach: intense accuracy, sharply focused, plus awake and aware. So this idea of recording a CD in the very state we wanted the audience to be in was a novel experience for me.

We went into the studio, I with three of my flutes: my regular C concert flute, my alto flute and my handmade Native American Indian flute; he with his vibraphone, violin bow and the wind chimes. I used the alto flute most, along with the beautiful Native flute. Having met the flute maker in Colorado, this made playing his gorgeous instrument even more meaningful.

We arrived at the studio and set up. I looked over at Michael in his calm, already meditative state. Yet for me, it felt like nothing I'd ever experienced before: I was both curious and excited at the same time. I wondered, "How do I improvise peace?" I began by looking over at Michael. He embodied peace, and had been a meditator and very gifted sound-healer for years. (Michael also has Asperger's syndrome, a high-functioning version of autism.) I allowed his presence to melt into mine.

Then, I closed my eyes and in synch, we naturally began playing music we'd never heard before. It was spontaneous composing, unfolding organically, moment by moment – a musical meditation. I slowed myself right down, took very deep breaths and allowed my long notes to extend in time.

We were creating something on the spot, in a completely improvised manner, and in doing so, I was lulling myself into the very state I was recording in: I was both the performer and the one benefiting from the meditative nature of the performance. It was a sort of simultaneous feedback loop: inhaling calmly, playing a tranquil melody for the very first time, and while listening, actually being affected gently and positively. It was all very mysterious and organic in nature.

Michael played the vibraphone most of the time in two ways: with the felt-tipped hammers and with a violin bow, gently sliding over the bars. This created an otherworldly sound – a sound that I imagined would come from outer space.

This lulled me even more deeply into my meditative state. For one track, I actually spoke/sang into the mouthpiece of my alto flute, mimicking the sound of dolphins. I named this tune "Dolphin Dance," and people remarked on how similar it sounded to gleeful dolphins.

After the initial recording of flutes and vibraphone, I recorded the wind chimes. This was probably the most challenging part of the recording process for me. I am not a percussionist and playing chimes is a very delicate process. You have to approach the chimes with a keen sense of the speed and weight of your hand, while embellishing the flute and vibraphone melodies already recorded. (I have gained great respect for percussionists for this very reason.)

Later, once the CD was finished – beautifully recorded and mixed by my friend and amazing engineer, Dyniss – we began thinking of names for this unique CD. Of course, various names to describe relaxation came to mind, but felt flat and uninspired.

Then, after pondering names for over a week, I came up with *Above the Sound of Gravity*. This title was inspired by my thinking, "What if there were a special type of sound and it existed above gravity, what would it sound like?" I think this title really suits the CD, although some tracks, like "Dolphin Dance," take the listener under water, deep diving into a myriad of oceanic dreams.

It became a very successful CD. People use it for many healing modalities, such as meditation, yoga, massage, and more. We were approached by Hemi-Sync (standing for hemispheric synchronization), to have our music re-mastered with binaural beats in the *theta* brainwave, to help induce relaxation and even sleep.

They retitled this version of our CD, with binaural beats, *Dreamland*. A befitting title, for sure. They also remastered my *Lullababy* flute and piano CD, and called it *Lullaby*. It, too, has suitable binaural beats in the remaster to aid sleep.

What I learned from this process of improvisation is that when we simply "allow" the unfolding and organic process to arise from within – in this case, music compositions to bubble up – the result is a very authentic and pure sense of self. And life itself, I have found, can naturally and gently bubble up, if we allow it, rather than force. Not everything needs predetermining. With an intention for healing, the music can compose, perform and record itself, in a gentle state of allowing.

Have you experienced yourself or your life expressed in the form of improvisation? When you have allowed the unfolding of something in your life, what did you learn, or experience? Has it given you the confidence to allow more into your life in this organic way?

21. First Time, Right Time, Best Time, Perfect Time

Trust the moment, have an intention, focus on succeeding, and getting into the "zone" and flowing. These phrases are often used by pro coaches with their athletes. Trusting the moment, jumping into it with both feet and riding the waves, being in the zone, really can work. Surfers are experts at this.

I remember meeting the gifted Canadian guitarist-composer Richard Fortin for the very first time. We'd spoken on the phone when I responded to a posted request on the Royal Conservatory bulletin board. Richard was looking for a string quartet to play on his next CD. Since I was a gigging musician and had a list of string players, I gave him a call to help him out.

He had a lovely voice, French-Canadian accent, humble personality. We stayed in touch, and after about six months I decided to ask Richard if he would like to meet. There was a deadline coming up for FACTOR – which I call "the musician's bank," since it's an acronym for Foundation to Assist Canadian Talent on Records. Musicians send in demo recordings, which are judged by a jury. If they win, they receive a loan that is repayable based on sales.

Richard and I met at a downtown recording studio on Soho Street, in Toronto. He brought two original pieces – one which he had remarkably just finished writing on the way to the studio that day, while riding the streetcar. We greeted each other warmly. Then, we went into the sound booth and recorded both of his original pieces, never having met or played music together before. Our playing was in sync and musically connective, like we had played together for years.

Three months later, we received a letter from FACTOR, informing us that we had won the maximum funding for our original CD, written by Richard. We were surprised and overjoyed by this victory.

We went on to record the CD, entitled *Fantasma*, which is Spanish for spirit. What was incredible was the fact that our surnames lined up under the title, *Fantasma*, where the "fan" was above Fortin and "asma" was above Nashman. This seemed otherworldly, suiting the mysterious title of the CD itself.

Sometimes, the first time is really both the right time and the perfect time. It's like the command directors give improvising actors: "First thought, best thought." This is also a helpful idea for perfectionists. Instead of sitting and mulling over actions to take or words to write, if you're writing a book, you simply trust and do it. There's always time for editing and refinement afterwards.

Tracey Erin Smith, my Soulo theatre teacher, instilled this in her students' minds. When we did writing exercises in her classes, she would say, "first thought, best thought" often. Also, my author friend Michael Gelb encouraged speaking into a recording device, rather than typing, since editing could take place after you get the content down. Speaking words into a recorder is definitely a way of unleashing the stream of consciousness. I believe it is a very intuitive and natural way of "writing" a first draft.

Can you remember a time when you threw caution to the wind and just went for it with confidence and belief? Have you brought this feeling forward in your life to other things you can approach boldly and without hesitation? I believe that confidence and allowing the flow go hand in hand. The more we practise trusting this flow, the more confident we become.

22. The Show Must Go On

As a flutist, I had to perform – whether I was feeling well or not. And God forbid I should be suffering an asthma attack at the time! I remember playing flute at outdoor summer weddings in the height of hot humid August afternoons, and suddenly experiencing debilitating asthma attacks. These moments were so disconcerting, but the show had to go on. After all, it was someone's wedding! In extreme cases, I had to let the other chamber musicians continue as I caught my breath.

One day I experienced menstrual cramps while in a local mall in downtown Toronto, right across the street from my apartment. The pain was so excruciating that I literally had to lie down on the concourse floor in the mall. It was almost 9 am on a weekday morning and business-men and -women were hustling by in their navy suits on their way to the office. All at once, I felt a group of concerned "suits" staring down at me. The pain was excruciating – I could barely speak.

They took this as a cue to call an ambulance. The pain was unbearable, and I almost blacked out on the marble concourse floor. The irony was that I was within just twenty steps from the pharmacy, where I could have easily remedied my condition with over-the-counter pain relievers. Unfortunately, I was unable to speak: the pain prevented me from communicating this to concerned people gathering around me.

Only a few minutes later the paramedics arrived. They began asking me many questions. The volume and timbre of their voices was abrasive and was making me feel sicker by the second. I was nauseas and woozy. One of them even asked me if there was a chance I was pregnant. How ironic, since it was my period that was causing the acute pain!

Parched, I asked them for water, but they wouldn't let me have water or any pain medication till the doctor saw me. The ambulance drive to the hospital felt like one of the longest rides I have ever endured. Later, at the hospital emergency ward, I was left alone in the hallway on a stretcher with a thin orange blanket, waiting for a doctor to see me.

I'd had dysmenorrhea for many years, and I knew its pattern. First, excruciating abdominal pain, then the conch shell sound in my ears, and if it got worse, sometimes I would black out. Naproxen would help with the onset of pain. Just like the paramedics, the hospital staff also prohibited me from taking anything, including drinking water. I hid under the thin orange blanket, cradled myself and rocked, trying to alleviate the intense pain on my own.

As I expected, after thirty minutes in the hospital hall, my abdominal pain subsided. Usually, my dysmenorrhea only lasted a short time. Relieved, I got up, walked over to the nurse's station, orange blanket in hand, and asked them to inform the doctor that I was leaving. I had to play a corporate luncheon function on my flute at the Albany Club, a high-end business club in Toronto.

Leaving the hospital in a rush, I flagged down a cab, used the rear-view mirror to apply my lipstick, popped a mint into my mouth – and walked into the club like nothing had happened. I started playing my flute without a hint of hesitation.

I have never had to "fake it" at a performance like I did that afternoon! It felt like I had spent the hour before "backstage," in a very strange "green room," and I had just now arrived at my performance venue. Yes, the show must always go on!

As the saying goes, "the show must go on." Can you remember a time you had to push through when you didn't feel like it, or thought you couldn't? What did you learn about yourself, and who have you become because of your tenacity and courage?

23. Some Days, Everything Goes Wrong

One spring morning, I was invited to perform flute and be interviewed on a Toronto TV show. Not having a driver's license, I have always taken Toronto's subway (the TTC) to my appointments. This morning was no different.

Running late like usual, I hurried off the subway to grab a cab to the TV station. When I arrived, I was quickly ushered to the make-up room. There I sat in front of the mirror, gazing at the morning bags under my eyes that I hoped would be quickly remedied by some magical professional make-up artistry and concealer.

Just before I went on stage to be interviewed and then play flute, I froze in my tracks, and my heart was in my throat. Where was my flute? Oh my God! Did I leave it on the subway? I quickly called the TTC and described my flute. Thank God, they had found it under a seat at the very end of the subway line. Whew! And Yikes!

What was I going to do after the interview? I had a flute piece prepared to play after the next commercial break! Could someone deliver my flute to the TV station from the TTC office? I took a few quivery, shallow breaths and put on my "confidence" armour. I stood tall and smiled. Hoping to conceal my panic, I stepped onto the brightly lit television stage. I faked it – I was literally shaking in my boots.

I was invited by the host to sit on the high stool in the centre of the stage. The interviewing began, but still no flute in hand. When the commercial break came, a TV crew member rushed on stage, handed me my flute in its case, and I quickly put it together, getting ready to perform after the commercial break. Thank goodness the TTC people were quick in retrieving my flute from the subway, and a television employee was free to drive over to the TTC to pick it up for me!

When I was about to go on the air, playing my flute, there was a microphone positioned over my head, hanging from the ceiling so nothing would block the visuals, like a microphone stand would. Finally, and much relieved, I prepared to play my piece on the air – my little television spot. No sooner had I started, when suddenly the mic fell from the ceiling onto my lap! Could anything else possibly have gone wrong on that day?

I laughed and chalked it up to experience, knowing the show must go on – with or without my flute! Afterwards, I laughed.

When has your show had to go on, despite sudden, surprising and unexpected challenges? What did you do? How did you get through it?

24. Spicy Food, a Flutist's Foe

Being a musician is like being a "melodic athlete." We have similar attributes: tenacity, discipline, focus, concentration, determination, dedication and passion, to name a few.

One discovery I have made as a flutist is the respect and awareness we flutists must give our bodies. Our arms, wrists, fingers are needed along with diaphragm, lungs and spinal alignment. What I didn't think through thoroughly enough was my lips. Sure, I put lip balms on to keep them moist, but that was it.

One afternoon before a flute performance, I craved Chinese food. At the time, my favourite soup was vegetarian hot and sour soup. It was such an unusual combination: hot yet sour. An acquired taste, for sure. I gulped down my piping hot bowl of it, eyes watering like a waterfall, yet feeling satisfied and satiated.

What I didn't realize at the time was the effect the MSG was having on my lips. They were starting to go numb and were swelling up a bit. Yikes! When I went to play my flute, my embouchure (the precise formation of my lips) wasn't able to form properly, due to the surprising and not-too-subtle effects of the soup. When I went to make a sound, it was fluffy and unclear. The MSG had really done a number on my resultant flute tone! I hadn't realized just how important it was to keep my lips in working order!

From that day forward, I have avoided hot and spicy foods before flute concerts. A lesson well learned, since the flute sounds a lot better when it isn't spicy!

When have you been mortified by something – a surprising outcome you didn't expect or something you would never have expected? What precautions or protocols are you following to avoid these pitfalls happening again?

25. A (Long) Evening Gown Goes a Long Way

Mastering the "art of confidence" is a real craft, especially if you are shaking in your boots. Performing flute recitals, no matter how prepared I was, always shook me up internally. I reminded myself always to think of the audience's experience, not just my emotional state, fraught with stage-fright. This helped me to focus on giving to the audience, rather than just being focused on myself, distracted by my nervousness.

Another interesting performance challenge is the timing of the "jitters." They aren't always with you when you walk out on stage and greet your audience. In fact, sometimes they insidiously creep up a few minutes into the performance.

On one occasion, my knees really started shaking uncontrollably. As I was busy concentrating on performing the music at hand, while trying to give my audience a beautiful experience, I was mentally juggling and contending with my shaking knees.

In that frazzled moment, I decided that the best way of concealing my terror was to adopt a very erect posture, so that my body language *looked* confident. I put my shoulders back and imagined, like a ballet dancer, that there was a string from the ceiling pulling my head up from the centre. My knees continued to shake, but no one noticed. I was victorious over my emotions.

I hoped I'd fooled the audience: I wanted them to have a good experience and not be distracted by my nervous state. After the performance, I was congratulated backstage. It appeared that people enjoyed my music and didn't even notice my nerves. Thank God I was wearing a long gown, that flowed below my knees, hiding my jitters.

I will always remember that a long evening gown always helps – and so does great posture!

When have you had to fake it, in order to get through a challenge? What did you do? Have you used this strategy again? When?

26. A Flutist's Secret to Helping People Quit Smoking

Smoking and flute playing have many things in common. For one, both require very deep breaths. A second common quality is the "dreamy bubble" state of mind while playing flute or smoking a cigarette. You know, that far-off look in the eyes of smokers as they are indulging their habit. Flutists have that look too. For both, the exhale of air is a long, drawn out one, too.

So, knowing this, I have always suggested to smokers that they should simply quit smoking and take up the flute – since the only obvious difference between playing flute and smoking is that with the flute you inhale air and exhale music. Sadly though, with smoking, you inhale tar, nicotine and other toxic chemicals, and exhale smoke – and blow your money on cigarettes. And most dramatically, you may shorten your life span due to possible lung cancer.

My dear mother succumbed to lung cancer when she was only sixty-three. I wish that I could have saved her life. I now wish she had quit smoking and taken up the flute, instead.

When have you experienced a new learning that you wished you could have shared with a loved one? How have you used this knowledge? Have you been able to help others with your knowledge?

27.   Commitments: What About Committing Out?

In my early twenties, after almost completing my Bachelor of Music degree in flute performance (short one elective credit), I was offered a scholarship to the Orchestral Training Program at Toronto's Royal Conservatory of Music. What fun that was! We had guest conductors from all over the world and we played most of the standard orchestral repertoire, along with a lot of the major piano concerti, in one year alone. It felt like being a professional orchestral musician. We even received a small honorarium for our participation. Bonus!

After this special training, I did only a few orchestral auditions. One that I remember most was for Symphony Nova Scotia, in Halifax. As with most orchestral auditions, I was competing for one position with over 100 other well-qualified flutists. The orchestral excerpts that we all had to play were hand-picked for technique, breath control, musicality, and other important considerations. The jury was sitting behind a scrim: They couldn't actually see the candidates, to assure they would choose a winner without race or gender prejudice creeping into the process.

Like many auditionees, I often had stage-fright and jitters. I was all too familiar with shallow breathing, trembling fingers, and shaky knees. Being in this compromised physical and mental state made it difficult to perform at my best. It seemed like such a waste to prepare for orchestral auditions for several months, many hours a day, and then go to the audition and be so nervous that I would blow it.

On this particular occasion, in the five or six minutes that my audition lasted, I fumbled over a few technical passages, and ran out of air, due to nerves, during another passage. I blew it. It has always reminded me of watching Olympic figure-skating. All is going perfectly until a skater falls doing something challenging, like a triple axel. It always seems like such a huge shame. After this audition, I felt like a defeated skater.

When I left the audition room, I sought out another flutist who had completed her audition and I declared out loud to her, "I am committing *out* of an orchestral career." Then I shook her hand. In some way, this ritualized my decision. I felt good making a commitment in a different direction – a direction that was not an orchestral career. I'd never heard of this committing *out*, but it seemed intuitively right for me. This way, I wouldn't feel like a failure, never becoming an orchestral musician, since I chose to stop that trajectory in its tracks. I chose something else that would suit my personality better: entrepreneurship and being self-led.

Since that time, I've created my own live-music agency, Montage Music, and recorded over ten CDs – including a Gold CD called *Lullababy* with a gifted pianist and dear friend, John. I also put on a chamber-music series with John for many years at Toronto's Heliconian Hall called "An Elegant Affair," complete with a wine and *hors d'oeuvres* reception following.

It's such a relief to follow your instincts and have a life that suites *you*.

When did you decide to opt out of a certain life direction and choose one that suits you better? Did you "commit out"? How did you declare this to yourself and others?

Chapter Two

My Two Families

The concept of two families is a strange one for me.
Being adopted at five months was a true blessing for the life I have been privileged to live. At age three, I found out that my parents had chosen me, wanted me, and adopted me: Mom sadly couldn't have her own children, but lovingly welcomed me as her and Dad's little girl.
Yet I've always wondered who my biological mom is, and whether we might meet some day. Would I look like her, talk like her, have similar interests? Would we bond or would we simply be strangers with the same bloodline? These questions have preoccupied me for much of my life.
My adoptive parents always welcomed my searching for my birth parents, but I felt I might be betraying their love. Eventually, I decided to bite the bullet and go for it – to start the process, the unfolding of my birth story, my birth mom and blood relatives. My heart remained open while I felt distinctively mixed emotions. My two families: stories that endure with me forever.

28.   Adapting to Adoption

I've heard that a lot of adopted people share common qualities: they are fiercely independent and high achievers, yet can be insecure people-pleasers. I definitely have fallen into all these categories.

Feeling abandoned – whether on a subconscious or conscious level, or both – adopted kids experience a host of common emotions. I can say that I was very anxious and insecure, never feeling like I belonged anywhere and with anyone. It was no fault of my adoptive parents who showered me with love and care. In fact, this anxiety and insecurity is a common state, even if you aren't adopted.

I suppose, turning inward with music lessons, horseback riding lessons, going to art school, and being a top student gave my life an achievement focus or sense of personal determination. I also became a perfectionist, and along with this came self-criticism and reticence, a hand-in-hand pairing.

As an adult, I learned several sayings that really work: "Done is better than perfect." "First thought, best thought." And "Starting is better than stalling." I used to think I had to be in the "right" headspace to start things – and if I wasn't, I would wait. Often, I waited for that perfect moment to happen, and my tasks got bogged down in procrastination.

Now, I simply get an idea and go for it, remembering the quotations above. As an adult adoptee, I still do my best, and aim for perfection – even though perfectionism, *per se*, doesn't even exist. I am so grateful to all the mentors, teachers, human and animal, self-development gurus, therapists, family, friends and boyfriends I've had to help me along the way.

Adapting to adoption has been a search; a lost-and-found phenomenon.

How has your identity been formed by your birth and childhood years? Have abandonment, insecurity, overachievement and people-pleasing been a part of your identity? What other roles have you played? How do you think they formed? Who have you become as a result of your past and your day-to-day evolution?

29. Nancy Nashman, My Mom of All Moms

My adoptive mom – the only mom I've ever known – really cared. It was a special type of caring, uniquely Nancy's way. She showed her support in so many beautiful ways. I remember so fondly getting up on mornings when she was already off to work, and finding sweet and encouraging notes for me and my brother, Adam, on our kitchen placemats. They were positive, loving notes, sending us off to school with love from Mom. I collected them in a shoebox – and there must have been literally hundreds of them! My brother and I always looked forward to waking up to these special notes from Mom.

Another surprising thing Mom used to do was lay out brand-new outfits, complete with earrings and necklaces, on my bed, for me to discover when I came home from school. She had a great sense of style and accessorizing, and I loved those unexpected after-school surprises from Mom. Her thoughtfulness was unparalleled.

Mom also supported my life's passions and helped me so much. She drove me to riding lessons, bought me my very first flute and music book, and put it under the Christmas tree when I was just twelve. It was called *Montage, Flute Solos*. (Coincidentally, when I was twenty-five, I registered a music entertainment agency and called it "Montage Music." I wonder if my subconscious mind remembered thirteen years back and linked the two?)

Mom also supported my summer music camp and flute masterclass experiences, seeing to it that I went. These musical adventures took me to so many beautiful places, including Mt. Orford, Quebec; Shawnigan Lake, British

Columbia; Breckenridge, Colorado; Little Switzerland, North Carolina; and many more places. She was so proud of me and told me often that she was.

What would life have been like had my birth mother kept me when I was born and she was only eighteen? I think I would most likely have had a very different life. Yet I'm truly grateful that she made the right choice for me. After all – lucky for me – she didn't abort me, but rather gave me up for adoption. This way, I could have the fortunate life that she might not have been able to give me. I look at it this way: My birth mom gave me life itself, and my adoptive mom gave me the opportunity to express it fully.

A mother's love given so selflessly and so supportively is a treasure. Think of times your own mother, or a figure in your life, nurtured you and shared love with you. What do you remember most about this person's unique way of loving you? Who do you nurture and care for, whether you are a mother or not? How has your own life shaped your way of nurturing? How do you express it?

30. Birth Mom, Adoptive Mom, "Real" Mom?

All my life, as an adopted person, I've had people say to me, when referring to Nancy Nashman, my mom, "So is she your *real* mom?" I would cringe inside, wondering why "real" seems to imply biological to so many people.

In my case, my "real mom" *is* my adoptive mom: she was all a mother can be, except for carrying me and giving birth to me. I believe that giving birth to and raising a child are clearly two very different things. My adoptive mom, whom I have always referred to as my mom or "real mom," deserves this title – and the one who carried me nine months and gave me up, gets the title, "biological mom" or "birth mom." For me, it's as simple as that.

When I'm asked this question, I respond by educating people about the distinction between "actual," biological, birth mom, and *real*, as in the one who loved me, raised me, encouraged me and supported me all these years. So, this politically incorrect question can be answered with my own deliberately thought-out explanation.

Have you ever experienced awkward questions about you and your relation to others? What did you say? What distinctions have you made about this? How have you communicated clearly and directly to help dissolve any confusion?

31. Tom Nashman, My Dad and Personal Philosopher

Dad was truly an amazing man, full of spirit and elegance. I feel so fortunate to have been adopted by him and my mother, Nancy.

Dad was a Berlin Jew – and before World War II, both he and his brother were fortunate enough to escape to Dublin when he was very young. His mother was not as lucky, and sadly his father died by suicide, feeling so badly that he hadn't been at home to protect her when the Nazis came for her.

After several years in Ireland, my dad and his brother bravely came to Canada – a new country, offering new hope and opportunities. Dad had a bold wish: he wanted to become a ballroom dance teacher. At the time he was living in Montreal, and he would travel over an hour a day each way to study ballroom dancing at the famous Arthur Murray Dance Studio. He had a vision and a passion to learn how to dance, and he did it. At the age of twenty-five, Dad's dream was realized. He was joyously teaching ballroom dancing in Montreal. World War II was left behind, even though some anger and sadness lingered deeply in Dad.

Dad had such an elegance about him. He was over six feet, moved with ballroom-dancer grace and always dressed impeccably. I remember his silk ties, ascots and cufflinks – such attention to detail. He was a Taurus, and it's said Taurus people love beauty and style in all its forms. Dad's sartorial talents definitely proved that!

He would often quote a famous motivation speaker (I think it may have been one of his favorites, Zig Ziglar), saying, "You are what you think about most of the time." Dad would urge me to "Go for a walk, and get out of your stinkin' thinkin'!" whenever I was feeling a little stressed or blue. He was an advocate for going out and getting some air, and walking away worries and upsets. I think Europeans know and understand the value of clearing the mind with fresh air. Dad sure did.

Some of my favorite memories are of our long, philosophical, nature walks. Nothing soothed my soul as much as these heart-warming and nourishing times with Dad. Both of us loved birds, and were fascinated by their unique songs and colourful beauty. Often, we would stand in the ravine, faces pointed up to the sky, searching for the source of these beautiful melodies. From our favorites – cardinals, red-wing blackbirds, chickadees and more – Dad and I bonded over birds, philosophical conversations, and just a love for life, itself.

Now, after dear Dad has been gone for years, I still think of him on my nature walks, while I breathe in the fresh air and look up to find the source of the magical birdsongs. These treasured times with Dad live on with me forever.

Having a positive mental attitude and open outlook on life are gifts to be cherished. My dad showed me this often. Who lives on in your heart? What are some of the beautiful memories you cherish? Who has been a positive influence on you and your life? What gifts have you shared and passed on to others, to positively influence their lives?

32. Picking Up My Baby Brother at Sunrise in Ottawa

I was just three-and-a-half years old, and it was just 4:30 am. The sun was hinting at rising, as it peaked out over the horizon, offering a magical start to the day. And a special day it was destined to be. Mom said to me in the hush of dawn, "Laura, today we are going to Ottawa to pick up your brother." What a concept!

At the time, I already knew that I had been adopted, so the concept of adding another adopted child to our family did not seem unusual. It was the phrase "pick up my brother" that seemed strange to me. We arrived in Ottawa after a four-hour drive from Toronto, and picked up a sweet, curly blond-haired, seven-month-old boy, and named him Adam.

Life as an adopted girl with an adopted brother from two different families isn't an unusual phenomenon for us. Both Adam and I grew up to express our lives in the creative arts: Adam, a playwright, novelist and director; and I a flutist, visual artist, voice actor and entrepreneur.

I often wonder if the fact that we were adopted gave us an inherent sense of independence, and a proclivity toward the arts and self-expression. Does one's unique "voice" come out naturally when a single child is adopted into a forever home? Something to ponder.

What surreal experiences have you had that have changed your life forever? What did you discover from these events that have deeply impacted you and your perspective on life?

33. Nancy's Farm, Gift-Wrapped with a Yellow Bow-Tie

When I was just thirteen, Dad surprised Mom with the most unusual and generous birthday gift: a farm! Some of her youth was spent on a farm, and thanks to this wonderful birthday present, so was some of mine.

Many of my favourite summers were spent there. Our farm was just outside the town of Hastings, Ontario, in Northumberland County. The old white wooden farmhouse, with black shutters, had a long, narrow driveway leading up to it. We had sixty-five acres of rolling pastures – plus a big barn where we helped out with the hay; and a drive shed, equipped with a ping-pong table, where my brother and I often played. Birds, butterflies and crickets filled this pastoral setting. It was a real-life fairy tale.

How Dad surprised Mom with her present was astonishing: On her birthday, he drove a beautiful brown and white pick-up truck into our suburban driveway with a huge yellow oversized bow and ribbon around the front of it. Dad brought her out of the house to the driveway, and there it was! He asked Mom to hop in and eagerly drove her to her birthday gift.

Excited, Mom sat in a state of anticipation, not knowing where Dad was taking her. After one-and-a-half hours of highway driving, Dad pulled up a sideroad in the country, with beautiful rolling hills full of grazing cows and sheep. Dad turned the truck along the long, tree-lined laneway, and took Mom up to the nineteenth-century white wooden farmhouse. Happy birthday Nancy! What a touching way of showing Mom he loved her.

The farm was our summer family oasis: the air so fresh, the birds singing at the top of their lungs, and the fields, where I practised my flute with butterflies in the sunshine. This was "the farm," as we called it. It somehow took on an identity of happiness, freedom and adventure, along with deep tranquility. Roosters started our mornings, and evenings were filled with a hushed coziness.

One of my favourite memories was preparing for dinner: putting a big pot of water on to boil, while going to our garden, picking and husking fresh corn, and then immediately popping it into the boiling water. It was the best tasting corn I'd ever had, so sweet and delicious – just like the times up at "the farm."

Sadly, twelve years later we received a phone call at home, informing us that our farmhouse had burned down. Apparently, it was most likely a problem with the old electrical wiring. However, the cause of the fire remained a mystery. Mom was completely devastated. It was a family treasure, up in smoke and gone! We ended up selling the land. We all felt at a loss, like the death of a family member.

The very next year, Mom got her cancer diagnosis. I will always wonder if somehow the grief of losing her farm sped up the cancer cells in her body. She died seven months after the diagnosis. In just under two years, both Mom and the farm disappeared from our lives.

Some gifts are so special; their heartfelt sincerity and originality are beyond belief. Can you remember a time when you either gave a gift, whether material or non-material, that was such a surprise to the receiver? Consider the lasting effects of your thoughtfulness on their lives. Who has done something so unique and thoughtful for you? Why was it so special? What impact has it had on your life?

34. The Volkswagen Camper Summers

Mom was very special. She cared about us kids, my brother Adam and me, so much. From early morning love-notes and best wishes for our upcoming day at school, lovingly left on the kitchen table, to flute lessons, horseback riding lessons, I couldn't have asked for a more caring mom.

One particular memory that stands out strongly in my mind is our trip across Canada one summer, in our camper van, to British Columbia. Picking wild blueberries was one favourite memory. (There is something exceptional about the taste of wild blueberries!) I also loved stopping by little fruit and vegetable stands at family farms, and picking up fresh produce and meeting the families. These farmers were welcoming and hospitable to us.

The very next summer Mom drove my brother and me to Prince Edward Island and all the Maritime provinces. We loved traveling in our mustard-coloured Volkswagen van. We would travel for hundreds of miles every day, and have so many unique adventures! Mom had an adventuresome spirit, and Adam and I got to be part of these amazing and unforgettable cross-country summer travels. Unfortunately, Dad had to stay back in Toronto, earning a living – but we managed to have fun anyhow.

I still have flashes of these trips: picking wild blueberries along the side of the highway, seeing a bear cub in BC, and those perfectly tranquil nights under the twinkling stars, sleeping in the Volkswagen camper. The fresh air and raw sense of moment-to-moment, day-to-day adventure was a true gift in my childhood years. As an adult, I still love experiencing my life as an unfolding adventure!

I am forever grateful to my mom for taking us on our cross-country adventures those two summers in our Volkswagen camper! These unique vacations gave me a lifetime of great family memories!

We all have special childhood memories that stay with us forever. What memories do you have that have lived with you for years? If you have children, what adventures and memorable moments have you shared with them?

35. The Inspiring Creativity of My Awesome Brother, Adam

Café Naked was better than any cup of coffee I have ever tasted. My brother, Adam, an amazing playwright, theatre director and writer, conceived of this show, which revealed the many behaviors of café people. In *Café Naked*, he created an awesome, true-to-life satire on the café scene in Toronto – a sensational tongue-in-cheek masterpiece. The brilliant tagline for the show was "to be seen, being seen, in the scene."

Adam's play was staged on location at Future Bakery, one of Toronto's most celebrated cafés, in the Annex neighbourhood. It was launched at Toronto's Fringe Festival, and his play had line-ups around the corner, and sold-out performances, night and day. I saw *Café Naked* three times, and loved it every single time. There were so many things going on simultaneously on stage: never a dull moment, with many witty, hilarious moments.

In addition to Adam's play, "Café Naked", he has written a documentary on John Nash, the famous mathematician with schizophrenia, along with other plays and prose. His keen awareness about life and his deep perceptions inform his impressive writing. His productions have made it to Stratford, and other international stages. In Stockholm, he worked with the famous director Robert Lepage at Ingmar Bergman's Royal Dramatic Theatre.

I've always been so proud of my brother's accomplishments, and his unique ways of thinking, writing and directing. He's a true creative force – and also happens to be a very nice, down-to-earth, guy.

Are there any family members you are super proud of? What have you learned from them? What inspired this feeling in you? Have you told them yet?

36. Almost Goodbye: That Snowy Day in Dad's Red Convertible

It's strange how fragile life is: it's here one moment and taken away the next.

Spinning through four lanes of highway traffic in Dad's red Mercedes 190 SL, that snowy winter day, I desperately looked over at Dad and – thinking I was uttering my last words – tearfully said, "Goodbye, Dad. I love you." There we were, swirling uncontrollably on the icy four-lane highway of terror – so fast that I couldn't even see if there was any oncoming traffic. I shuddered and covered my eyes, terrified. I couldn't utter another word.

In moments like these, life seems to stand still for an instant – to be almost in slow motion, despite how fast it's racing by. My heart was up in my throat and I could barely breathe. I peeked through my fingers, disbelieving what was happening before my very eyes.

Together, Dad and I were in a spinning moment of time, dizzied by its unpredictability. Were we about to crash and die? I felt completely out of control. Everything was happening at lightning speed.

Suddenly, the very next moment, I felt a deep thud. We had just been hurled into the snowy shoulder of the highway – a fluffy, welcoming, five-foot snowdrift. With Dad's red Mercedes covered with snow but all in one piece, I couldn't believe my eyes. We had survived! I was barely twelve years old at the time, and in that moment, I felt, saw and experienced the very fine line between life and death.

Life is fragile, and the distance between life and death can be a split second. What are some ways you are mindful of the fragility of life? How do you give your life respect, without being overly cautious, fear-based, or trepidatious? Have you experienced a near-death moment? What stands out for you? What has it taught you?

37. Celebration of Life: Mom's Living Tea Party

Celebrating life can be a daily activity. It's a mindset; an attitude. I've played my flute at many "celebration of life" events, a way of honouring the deceased with a focus on the positive, avoiding the formalities that funerals bring.

When my mother was diagnosed with cancer and given approximately seven months to live, I decided to ask her if she would like to have a tea party with her favourite musicians performing her favourite music at my home, to celebrate her life while she was living.

My mom was overjoyed with this idea: to be celebrating her life at a tea party and concert planned by her. We all knew that this might be the final time people were gathered around my mom while she's living, so I made a meaningful afternoon of it.

I invited musicians who were also my dear friends, and we all played our hearts out for my dear mom. There she sat, in her wheelchair, a turban elegantly covering her head. She listened sensitively, then said something so heart-wrenching and heart-warming at the same time: "Laura, no one has ever done something so beautiful for me in my entire life." She had tears in her eyes and voice. I was touched and moved and relieved, hearing her say this.

I had played many chamber-music concerts to date, but nothing felt so deeply heart-inspired as that special living celebration of mom's life that day. Having all my special musician friends there to celebrate Mom with her favorite music really made my heart sing.

We may not have known how long dear Mom had to live, but what we did know was that she was being loved and celebrated right then and right there. I will never forget this special concert for Mom. She will always be in my heart.

Have you wondered about doing things out of the ordinary that reflect you and your uniqueness? Perhaps in advance? What things could you do now, rather than postponing?

38. The Politics of Dying

Some people say that everything in life is politics, not just the obvious political issues. I felt this most poignantly when my dear father of eighty-seven was nearing his final day. He was living at a long-term care home up in Midland, Ontario, and his power of attorney was his wife, my stepmom.

My brother and I would call the nurse's station often, to check in on our dad. Unfortunately, we got very generalized answers – phrases such as "He's having a good day today," or "No changes from yesterday." I wanted to know more, but there was often that awkward pause by the nurse on the other end of the phone line, hesitant and officious, saying, "I'm sorry but I don't see you or your brother's name on your dad's chart, just his wife." She had power of attorney, we didn't.

This deeply angered me. But instead of blasting the nurse, since she was doing her job, I simply replied by saying, "Aw, the politics of dying. You can't even find out how your dad is really doing."

I was really irked by how politics takes a front-row seat to something where heart, connection and inclusion are needed, in my opinion. It wasn't until I experienced my lack of access to information about my dad's day-to-day health, due to legal restrictions, that I realized how living and dying are riddled with politics.

I shrugged my shoulders, understanding that the nurse didn't want to lose her job over leaking out information only legally available to Dad's wife. I pondered quietly, "Job over justice?" (Legally, there was nothing I could do).

When have you experienced policies that overrode your heart's desires? Did you speak up? Have you been able to make peace with life's policies and politics?

39. Moving from Life to Death

It was May 3, 2016, a beautiful spring day, alive with nature's cacophony: birds singing, squirrels squawking, the gentle rumble of traffic passing by Dad's nursing home. The clear, crisp air belied that sickening, foreboding feeling of death felt so often in such a home. This time, the nauseous feeling was more personal. Soon, Death would come visiting my dad.

There was Dad, lying peacefully yet very ill – his familiar fingers cupped in my warm smaller ones. Knowing he was running out of time, I wanted to capture this memory before we ran out of time. I took out my camera and recorded this special embrace. Our hands, our life, life's fragility. Ours.

Dad's hands were long and elegant, just like him. The ballroom dancer and teacher, the chic and sophisticated dresser with a puff of tasteful silk design in his blazer pocket, the open-hearted, full-body listener – yes, this was my dad. Tom Nashman, the German Jew who as a child fled Berlin with his older brother to seek refuge in Dublin. My frightened dad, my courageous dad, my caring dad – always the best dad to me.

As I sat by his bed, I knew deep down that today was to be cherished and remembered. And when my stepmom and uncle went home after an afternoon of visiting Dad, they encouraged me to do the same, since we all could use a good night's rest. They said they would bring sandwiches tomorrow and we could have lunch with Dad by his bedside.

I had different ideas.

A week earlier, I had consulted with a clairvoyant/psychic, asking her about dad's wishes regarding that final moment. Apparently, he didn't want to be alone. He was mostly going in and out of consciousness, so I couldn't ask him directly. Yet I knew in this moment, after they left, I was definitely going to stay.

I found myself alone with Dad, knowing this was the day. Earlier in the week, I researched the signs to look for when someone is nearing death: the chilling "death rattle," the patchy mottling of the skin, the shallow, laboured, irregular breathing.

I sat with hawk-like eyes, carefully watching over Dad as I saw his life change to death – gently, gradually, yet with finality. His sea blue-green eyes that offered softness and true connection during our many meaningful father-daughter talks were now shut. His body was frail and skeletal, and the oxygen mask was making a strange sighing sound, eerily human. I watch Dad's chest rise and fall, but he was weak and only seemed half here.

My stepmother – who had been urgently called from the nurses' station on Dad's ward, returned to the hospital just in the nick of time. The two of us held Dad's hand from either side of his bed. All I could do was say, "Daddy, it's okay to go." "We all love you." "We'll be okay." I said this spontaneous mantra over and over, hoping to reach his semi-conscious state – wanting him to feel free to go, as his dying was inevitable.

All of a sudden, I couldn't see a rising or falling of Daddy's chest. There was a cool silence. I looked at my stepmother. We called the nurse into the room, and she arrived with that dreaded stethoscope. "Yes," she confirmed, "I'm very sorry, Tom's gone."

This must have been one of the most significant moments of my life. I've often pondered life as birth, death and the in-between. All parts make up life and all are important. Often, we don't consciously remember our own birth. It can dwell deeply in our unconscious minds – until, unexpectedly, we may recall moments after birth and in our very first days, weeks, months and years.

Eventually, we reach our final day, our final breaths – and then what? Up until the day of my dad's passing, I had been afraid of my own death and dying – but also scared of witnessing a loved one in the moment of passing from life to death. Somehow this vision terrified me. I didn't want to look at my parent lying there lifeless.

I walked away from the bed. A beautiful, full-bodied, African-Canadian nurse came to me for comfort, sobbing as she draped her head over my shoulder. "Tom was such a wonderful man." I agreed. He was the best father I could have ever asked for – and I was lucky to have been adopted by him!

Being present to a newborn's life or to a life passing out of this world are true honours. And being a "death doula," whether formally or informally, is a unique experience. Have you experienced a loved one's death? Were you present for the moment the last breath was taken? How did this affect you? How has this affected your outlook on death and dying?

40. Blood Relatives Came Late in My Life

"It's never too late" is a concept that rings true with me.

Like many adopted people, I've wondered about by birth family all my life. My adoptive parents who chose me, raised me, loved me, always said it was okay to pursue meeting my birth parents. They said they wouldn't be offended. And after a long search – to my relief – I finally met some of my blood relatives!

My search began on my thirtieth birthday. I went to the Ontario Ministry of Social Services to get what they call "non-identifying information." Here I was. It was finally happening.

To my sheer surprise, my birth mother's information was all neatly presented in just two single-spaced pages. I had waited all my life for *this*? I read over the two pages with the social worker in that small, private room. I couldn't hold back – tears ran down my face.

It was the very first time I found out anything about my birth parents. I learned that my birth mom was a Polish Jew, who had me when she was just eighteen. There wasn't much about my birth father – except for the implication that my birth mom didn't think I would have had a good upbringing with this fiery, hot-tempered, Israeli man, my birth dad.

At that time, I decided to cut short my search. I was partially satisfied knowing this little piece of family history, and at the same time, scared to proceed, for many reasons. There were a lot of "what ifs." What if I pursued meeting my birth mom and either she didn't want to meet me, or I couldn't find her in the end? What if deep down, my adoptive parents – although they said it was okay with them that I search for my birth parents – were hurt by my pursuit?

At the time, I gave up on my adoption story, and returned to my regular life. What I'd found had adequately quenched my curiosity, while protecting me from any unexpected heartache. Sadly, the very next year, my adoptive mom – the only mom I had ever called "Mom" – was diagnosed with cancer, and died, only a few months before my thirty-second birthday.

Later, in my early fifties, I revisited my birth-mom curiosity. I still felt hesitant, but my inner voice, my soul, wasn't done with my search yet. Since my dear adoptive mother had died thirty-one years ago, it felt okay to look for my birth mom once again. It didn't feel like a betrayal. So, I applied to the Registrar General of Ontario for my birth records. After six weeks, the long-awaited envelope arrived. My hands trembled as I eagerly and carefully opened it.

I learned my birth mother's name. I also found out what hospital I was born in, and where my teenaged mother lived when she was carrying me! Both were familiar places to me. I chose to join a support group, sponsored by the Adoption Council of Ontario, led by a very kind, down-to-earth and compassionate former social worker.

Everyone in the group represented a different family member in the adoption world. One man was a birth father, who when he was sixteen, decided with his pregnant girlfriend that they would put their daughter up for adoption. Now, years later, with a quiver in his voice and tears welling up in his eyes, he mentioned that he had reunited with his daughter on Facetime many times so far, but hadn't met her in person yet.

It was strange for me to see a father who gave up his child at birth. I thought most searches would be by people like me looking for their birth moms or birth moms looking for their adult children. I suppose the search and reunion process is important to all people in the adoption story, even dads.

The cast of characters at the meeting seemed like characters who could be in a *Seinfeld* episode. There was a former homeless woman, who had been a teenage drug addict when pregnant. She desperately wanted to meet her autistic twin boys. Another was an angry adoptee whose only connection to her birth mom was through a guarded aunt, who stopped taking her calls.

And here I was, wanting to learn the best navigation techniques to my own birth mother. Bev, the support group leader, gave us a gem of advice: "If you want to meet your birth mom and you know her maiden name, look *her* mother up in the obituaries, and if she's died, you'll find a lot of people in your family."

I did just that – and it worked! I hit the adoption jackpot. My grandmother, had indeed died, only a few years back. From her obituary, I learned the names of my extended birth family – my blood relatives.

Toward the end of 2019, I met my cousin and my aunt, but not my birth mom. She was on vacation with her two daughters – one named Michelle, the same name given to *me* by her at birth. Was she trying to erase me, the original Michelle, from her mind? Or was she trying to repair her conscience and have a replacement Michelle so she could forget the pain of carrying me and giving me up at birth? I may never know.

My cousin was very supportive and helpful, and offered to forward an email from me to my birth mom. I prepared the email very carefully, not wanting to upset or alarm my birth mom. I worded it in such a way that it preserved confidentiality and offered to keep this life-long secret between us.

A few weeks later, I was informed by my cousin that my birth mom, upon reading my email, replied to her, saying: "This is trash and I'm throwing it right into the trash." Case closed.

Was she denying my existence, or refusing to come forward with the truth? I didn't push the matter. I thanked my cousin, and got to know her daughter well. It was amazing seeing similar eyes and facial similarities, after all these years! In a way, meeting my cousins and one of my aunts sufficed. I was content. Also, since I had seen pictures of my birth mom and heard stories about her through my relatives, my curiosity was satisfied. For now, at least.

I no longer felt the strong urge to meet her – especially after hearing her dismissive reply to my forwarded email!

I decided since I had a very loving upbringing with my adoptive parents – whom I viewed as my "real parents" – why sully the waters of my emotional life with a mother who doesn't want to meet me? I've really enjoyed my times with my new relatives – especially my cousin's daughter who is lovely, gentle, kind and very talented. We are like sisters – the sister I never had!

What have you waited for, longed for, and taken action on that has taken longer than you hoped, but it was worth it? What have you pursued, and in the process found yourself no longer feeling the strong need to complete, or felt satisfied in a way you didn't expect? How has this changed your life and your thinking about strong urges and pursuits? What have you learned? Have you had any epiphanies?

41. Seeing the House I Lived in Before I Was Born

I was told at a very early age that I was adopted. I accepted this, since I understood that my mom – the mom who adopted me, and the only mom I have ever known – couldn't have children. I felt chosen, wanted, loved. What I didn't know was where I was born and were I had lived as a fetus, before my birth mother had to make the very difficult decision of giving me up for adoption.

For many years, I was on-again, off-again, about my own relationship with finding my birth mom, and knowing about my life before adoption. When I was in my fifties, I finally obtained my birth record from the Registrar General's office. With the information on the record, I was able to find the house in Toronto where my birth mom lived when she was carrying me. It was on a street just off Spadina Avenue, near Toronto's Chinatown. What's so coincidental is that one of my favourite Chinese restaurants is a stone's throw away from my house of origin, the place I lived *before* I was born, as my birth mom carried me.

What an unusual feeling, to stand in front of a house that once was my home, my temporary home, my place of hiding in my teenage birth mom's belly. Already, fifty-three years had gone by since I had been in that house. And, now for the very first time, outside my mother's womb, I was seeing it as a full-grown adult, well into menopause. I chose not to have children, but feel more complete, knowing where my birth mom grew up.

I haven't met my birth mom, but viewing the house she grew up in was another piece of my life's puzzle solved.

Have you experienced a discovery, years later, that filled in the blanks about your life? Did it change you in any way? What impact did it have on you?

42. My Precious Gem of a Cousin

She opened the door of her apartment and greeted me warmly. There she stood, a stunningly beautiful woman in her mid-thirties, long straight black hair, green eyes and perfect cheekbones. Smiling at each other, I impulsively video-recorded our first "hello" on my cellphone to remember and cherish this extraordinary moment.

I was in awe.

I could see myself in her eyes. There was a family similarity: she is my cousin, my blood relative. I was fifty-five when I first met her that day, and she was thirty-two. Her cherub-like round face and kindness brought a new feeling to me I'd never experienced before. This was my younger relative: hip, fun, a fashionable beauty – and a millennial.

We had so much to talk about, and soon discovered we had so many things in common. We both had a dog – in fact, she had two! We love to talk on the phone, and we both have very curious minds. A family similarity.

I said to her, joking, "Wouldn't it be fun if I could adopt you?" We had so much in common, it felt like we could talk for hours, and she was young enough to be my very own daughter! I thought about how ironic it was that in my search for my birth mom, I met such a sweet, kind soul of a friend, who happens to be my cousin!

I feel so at ease and happy when I'm with her. She's so comfortable in her own skin and is a wonderful listener and conversationalist. We talk for hours, joke, laugh, share pictures and videos of our dogs, and coo over them like they are newborn babies.

Perhaps my search for my birth mom led me down the road to meet my wonderful cousin, and that may have been God's plan in the first place: the destination I was led to on purpose.

What unexpected miracles have emerged in your life? What gifts have you offered others that could seem like miracles to them?

43. *Lullababy* CD, Dedicated to Nancy, My *Real* Mom

Completing my *Lullababy* CD involved more than just mixing the CD. It also meant having Solitudes (the record company) create the front-and-back-cover artwork, the insert jackets with the song titles, and print and press thousands of copies.

One very memorable day, I was playing my new CD, straight off the press, for my dear mom, Nancy. We were sitting together in the living room. It was a very special time for us, since she didn't have much longer to live and I wanted to share *Lullababy* with her. Sitting humbly, turban on, she listened to my new CD. I sat closely beside her with tears welling up in my eyes. I remember whispering to her, "Mom, this CD is dedicated to you."

I could see she was moved by this, seeing as she was my *real* Mom: the one who chose me, adopted me, supported me, nurtured me, and *now was leaving my life*.

Mom had given me my very first flute as a gift, under our Christmas tree. She drove me to hundreds of flute lessons and supported my flute camps and masterclasses.

Now, like a scene out of a movie, I remember that gentle afternoon, playing *Lullababy* for Mom for that very first time – for the mom who loved me so much, who soothed my life, and made it worthwhile in so many fulfilling ways.

Have you dedicated something to a beloved in your life? What was it? How did it affect you and the loved one you dedicated it to?

44. Every Visit with Him Was Bittersweet

I love my brother, Adam. A sensitive, talented, intelligent, original thinker, my brother is definitely one of a kind. As kids, we were like a lot of siblings – we fought a lot. When I'd practise scales in my room, next door to his bedroom, he would defiantly crank up the volume of his music: it could be Deep Purple, The Doors, or another rock band. Like many siblings, we irritated each other.

Later as adults, we have tried to be a better brother and sister to one another. Memories of our childhood still exist, but our wish for a closer relationship with each other prevails. As the years go by, we visit each other more often, acknowledge each other's birthdays, and call more frequently.

Sadly, my heart still hurts from the wounded past, and our sibling relationship that seems to be able to go only so far. Now that we are in our fifties, I am more aware of the fragility of life, my wish for complete resolution between us, and full participation in our family bond. Whenever we have a visit, I leave with mixed feelings. It's a sort of bittersweet feeling: a longing that never gets fully resolved. Yet our connection is increasing with each visit, along with the depth of our friendship and sharing.

Life has a way of surprising us – from sudden deaths or endings to transcendent connections. I really hope that my relationship to my dear brother Adam will be one of utter joy and transcendence. I must continue to make more of an effort to speak with or write to him to say how important he is and how I want to be closer.

Do you have anyone for whom you feel a bittersweet twinge whenever you have a visit? Have you decided what you may want to do to shift this? Have you begun this process? What have you discovered? Are you glad you did it?

Chapter Three

Ito, Kito and Tigger, My Furry Friends

Companion animals have a very special place in my heart. They are both family members and dear, furry friends whose language of love exists without the need for words. From cat-squints ("eye kisses") to deep canine stares, my pets have brought such fullness of love to my life. Not only has their love been so pure, generous and unconditional, the lessons I've learned from them have been invaluable.

I believe the need for expressing with words is hugely overrated. Pets communicate non-verbally, but with open hearts and loyalty. In their own way, without words, they say everything. My life has been deeply impacted by the love – like no other – of my dear companion animals. Without them, life just wouldn't be the same.

45.   My Ito Years

Ito, my fifteen-pound Pomeranian, came into my life when I was thirty-seven, and left my life when I turned fifty-three. It's funny: when he was a puppy, I couldn't imagine him growing up and getting bigger, older and finally dying. He seemed both invincible and eternal – and perhaps the combination of his sweet nature and his sage-like otherworldliness seemed divine.

Later in my life, when he was about twelve, I realized that he wouldn't be with me forever. He was experiencing some health challenges, but was managing very well, and always with that classic, never-ending Pomeranian smile. I was still in my late forties, and I mentally prepared myself for his eventual passing by "visiting" my future. I thought that by preparing for it, I would be able to cope a lot better when the final day came. I told myself that I would be over fifty, probably going through menopause and experiencing a lot of life changes, at the time when Ito, my dear best friend, would leave this world. I was blessed, and fortunately, he lived another four love-filled years.

The "Ito years" were my favourite sixteen years of life. I committed my life to Ito, knowing his life was short and finite – being a dog, with a much shorter lifespan than most humans. Knowing this, I took him everywhere with me, enjoyed doing photoshoots, creating two books – *Doggie Bliss with Ito*, and *Ito Knows, Reflections On life By a Wise Pomeranian* – and I even did an animal welfare photoshoot with him and a pet pig named Annie, with the headline "Why Love One, but Eat the Other?"

Ito would often sit on the couch, mouth open, with that classic Pomeranian smile, and his eyes would half close, looking like he was staring into the beyond. He had a very peaceful presence, almost sage-like. He also had a non-stop happiness. All was well with Ito. Just being in his presence filled me with love, acceptance, joy, adventure, forgiveness, bliss and more! And I loved watching others react to Ito: touched so profoundly by his unconditional and joyous ways.

Ito influenced my life immensely – through his kindness, his love, his forgiveness, his wisdom, his inclusiveness with strangers, his sense of joy and always being ready for the next adventure. I live without Ito now, but my heart is forever filled with rich memories of our life together.

After we have had a profound experience in our life, whether it be with a human, animal or otherwise, we are changed forever. In the case of my beloved Pomeranian, Ito, uncanny mystical things occurred that made me wonder about the spirit world and the physical world. Have you experienced mystical occurrences in your life that asked you to consider your existence, spirituality, and other big existential questions?

46.   How I Met Ito, My Soulmate

My dog Ito was with me 24/7. He understood me at a deep level. His powers of observation, perception, intuition and sheer innate wisdom made him my "Doggie Lama." I've never experienced a more powerful connection, a fusing of souls, as I did with Ito. And, ironically, because my apartment building had a rule that no dogs were allowed, I never expected to even own a dog.

But all that changed in early July, 2002, when I made a trip to Montreal to my summer rental apartment – on a day that turned out to be one of the best in my entire life. Looking back on that day, I can see there was a series of mystical and auspicious events that all led up to my meeting Ito. In retrospect, it really seems like the stars were aligned for us to be together.

The story begins in January 2002, when I placed an ad in Toronto's *Vitality Magazine*. A health-oriented magazine, it has an abundance of helpful information on a healthy lifestyle, along with opportunities to advertise. I bought a business-sized ad, promoting my coaching in Neuro Linguistic Programming (NLP), to help people get a successful start to the new year.

Only two people replied, both orthodox Jewish men: one was an accountant wanting more success; and the other was a New York orthodox rabbi, who had moved to Toronto, with eleven children. In fact, one of his girls came to pick me up from the subway that day and drove me to her home to give a consultation to her father. All the way to their home I felt an otherworldliness – here she was, one of eleven children! What could that be like? We chatted in the car all the way there.

Upon arriving, I was greeted by the rabbi: an effusive man, interested in palm reading, astrology, Kabbalah, and many other esoteric modalities. Today, he was interested in learning about NLP. After my session with him, I was driven back to the subway. My head was spinning, just trying to mentally digest this fascinating event. I felt suspended from reality, in a "spiritual zone" – and I believe this prepared me for what was about to happen next.

I took the subway downtown and went to my favourite fast-food restaurant: Toby's Good Eats. There, I ordered a veggie burger and fries, and read the *NOW* magazine, our Toronto local events newspaper, reviewing the apartments for rent in the ads at the back.

One ad seemed to jump right up at me, since it had the exact same phone number as a former boyfriend, Jon – but the prefix to the number was 514 (for Montreal), rather than 613 (for Cornwall, Ontario), where Jon was raised. The ad said, "Montreal Sublet for Rent, May to September 2002." Funny – I was already considering how nice it would be to travel somewhere within Canada and have a different summer experience.

From a payphone, I called the number and said, "I'll take it." This wasn't the first time I got a gut instinct to act on something sight unseen. The young woman on the other end of the phone said, "Don't you want to see the apartment first?" I said no, and offered to pay her in full. She was taken aback, but suggested we meet in Toronto's Little Italy neighbourhood the following weekend, when she'd be visiting her parents. (What was so ironic was the fact that I had considered renting a place in Little Italy earlier, before seeing the ad for the Montreal sublet.) We met, and I rented the apartment from her, paying in full.

Fast-forward to my monthly holidays, in my new summer pad in Montreal. The apartment was above a motorcyclist café and bar in the gay area of Montreal. The place didn't have air conditioning, and it smelled of oil and grease from the restaurant below. Finding myself missing my four cats back home in Toronto, I ventured off to a pet store nearby to pet their kittens. I was stopped in my tracks as I approached the storefront window. There sat what looked like a cream-coloured teddy bear. I did a double take. It was a live puppy!

I went in and asked the owner if I could hold him. What happened in the very next moment had never occurred before in my entire life. I felt a magnetic pull as I brought this sweet ball of fluff to my heart. It was uncanny. I tested the feeling by holding the puppy away from my heart, and felt an energetic pull away from me. I realized in that very moment that I needed to buy this adorable little puppy. (At the time, I didn't know anything about puppy mills – and in retrospect, I really hope that he didn't come from such an atrocious environment.)

As we left the pet store, we were greeted by many men, cooing over my puppy, saying, "Mon Dieu," (my God) in French. Some asked if it was real and if they could hold him. I decided to call him "Ito," because I'd just heard a jazz guitarist called Mr. Ito at the Montreal International Jazz Festival. When I saw the puppy in the cage in the pet shop window, I tried the name, "Mr. Ito" out on him. Somehow, the musical lilt spoke to this little pup, and he turned 180 degrees clockwise, clearly delighted by the sound. I repeated this and he spun around the opposite direction. Mr. Ito it was. Later, I just called him Ito.

Returning to Toronto by train, my puppy and I were only about an hour out of Montreal when the conductor officiously approached us, demanding we get off at the next stop: Cornwall, Ontario. No dogs were allowed on the train, except in proper pet carriers, in a special compartment away from the passengers. (It was an allergy issue. Apparently, Via Rail had been sued before over this.)

I simply got up, holding my sweet two-month-old pup, and confidently disembarked at Cornwall. After all, my former boyfriend used to live here, and all I had to do was dial his number. Coincidentally, it was the very number I had seen in the *NOW* magazine that day that I called for the Montreal apartment, but with a "613" rather than a "514" area code.

What a completion! This Montreal sublet came full circle. I had an unexpected but welcome overnight stay with Jon's parents in Cornwall – and was given an extra pet carrier to take Ito home in the very next morning!

I returned home to my apartment in Toronto, stealthily carrying my new puppy past the "No Dogs Allowed" sign – and enjoyed my next sixteen years in pure bliss with my accidental soulmate. By the way, I was never scolded for bringing a puppy into my menagerie of four cats. It all worked out!

Sometimes, when things seem to go wrong, we find ourselves on the path to an even more exciting adventure. And sometimes, when we break the rules, and no one gets hurt, we experience the best treasures life has to offer. Can you remember a time when a series of serendipitous events led to an unexpected but wonderful outcome?

47.   Ito Listened with His Heart

I will never forget the day I was in my bedroom watching an emotional movie on my bed, and my beloved Ito was sitting on the living room couch down the hall, three bedrooms away. The film was deeply moving, and although I wasn't crying, I was feeling very emotional, on the verge of tears. Suddenly, I heard the familiar ching-ching-ching of his collar as he ran down the hall, and up he jumped onto my bed to kiss me.

Ito listened with his heart. His tongue kissed me rapidly and affectionately under my eyes, almost like he was kissing away my tears. Remarkably, there were no real tears, just feelings of sadness. I was so amazed that my sweet little Pomeranian had sensed my sadness and had come to my emotional rescue.

This special love was coming from my sweet dog, Ito. I was amazed that it seemed like he knew what I was feeling and came to rescue me. I've never felt this way before – being met so soulfully. My heart burst wide open, knowing I was truly loved.

Ito was an unusually intuitive and perceptive creature. Never in my life has the expression, "I've got your back" applied as much as with my faithful, dear Ito. He was an exceptionally caring and loyal best friend – always there for me, no matter what. There will never be another Ito, and I will miss him always.

It's common for us to underestimate the sensitivity of animals, and even people for that matter. By being open to sensitivity and empathy to and from others, we can be our best version of ourselves. Think of a time you were given great listening, empathy and understanding. How did this make a difference for you at the time? Now think of ways you have been compassionate with others?

48.   My Perfect Therapy Dog, Ito

One of the greatest sages of my life was Ito. When he was just two, I approached the volunteer services director of the Toronto Grace Hospital to inquire about offering him as a dog for the pet therapy program. I was told at the time that Ito was much too young and buoyant, and to come back when he was five. And we did.

Therapeutic Paws of Canada was the licensed pet-therapy service that the Toronto Grace Hospital used. In order for a dog to become a licensed therapy dog, it had to jump through several hoops, metaphorically speaking!

What a funny process it was, watching Ito do the tests that would result in his having a pet therapy license. Pomeranians are very intelligent dogs: they notice everything, and although they're often referred to as "little teddy bears," these dogs are quick, deliberate, and quite sneaky at times. I used to call Ito my little "urban fox."

The therapy dog test was made up of challenges that dogs would find difficult. Ito was designated dog number four, which bought him some time to watch dogs one through three do the test exercises before he had to do them. I also think Ito had a sixth sense. He knew he was being tested, so he was on his best behaviour.

The rules were very strict: no barking, no growling, no snapping, no snarling, no biting of course, and no signs of aggression or your dog would be immediately disqualified.

The first test was walking up to a dinner plate piled with cookies. If your dog grabbed a cookie, "see you later." But Ito simply sniffed, and left the cookies alone. First test passed.

The tests got harder: one was a "pretend" patient wearing a trench-coat over her head, disguising her face, wobbling over toward the dog. She also carried a garbage bag full of empty tins, which she dropped noisily on the floor. With her head concealed and this sudden noise, many dogs could have responded aggressively, even if it were just growling. Ito passed this one, too (of course, after watching three other dogs do it first).

After many challenging tests, the final one took the cake! Two pretend patients in wheelchairs, coming toward Ito while almost colliding with each other. This didn't even phase him. At this point I was absolutely convinced that he knew he was being tested.

Ito passed! We were in – and since he was the therapy dog, I was just *his* companion at the end of the leash. Every Wednesday at two o'clock, patients looked forward to Ito, grinning like a cross between a fox and a teddy bear. For five years, we enjoyed this wonderful therapy dog experience together.

We visited many patients young and old. People would pull at him, tugging at his fur, and he wouldn't growl, get upset or show any signs of aggression.

Somehow, the scents and sounds the patients gave off signalled to Ito that this was a very special population he was tending to.

I'll never forget the day we had finished a visit with a nineteen-year-old girl on the third floor. She had suffered a serious brain injury and no longer talked. As a result, she spent most of her time sleeping. Her dedicated Portuguese parents were at her bedside every day, praying that their dear Cristina would improve.

That particular day, I placed Ito on her bed, as she slept. Ito sat quietly and respectfully, watching over her. Tenderly, he started licking her face. Suddenly, she awoke, wide-eyed with glee and squealed with joy! What a remarkable moment. I looked at her parents, amazed too, since she rarely opened her eyes. Most of the time she was unresponsive.

In hospitals, it's customary for caregivers to speak in terms of patients having "good" or "bad" days. It's a way of simplifying a patient's present state. This was definitely a good day for Cristina and for all of us who loved her. After this "victory" visit, Ito and I headed for the elevator. I sighed a breath of relief as I pressed the button for the lobby. We had a successful and fulfilling visit that day. It was time to go home.

But after getting off on the main floor, I felt Ito tug at his leash and gesture to me that he wanted to go back to visit more with Cristina. According to Ito, his visit with her wasn't over yet. He pulled on his leash and led the way to her room. I complied and we spent another ten minutes with Cristina, by her bedside. I was deeply moved by Ito's compassion and loving initiative to return to visit with her more.

Although we visited all of the floors in the hospital, the fifth floor was most meaningful to me. My dear mother had died on the fifth – the palliative floor – or, as I have often heard it called, "God's Waiting Room."

This special day we were on the fifth floor, visiting Edna, a sweet and frail ninety-four-year-old woman. Tucked into her bed, staying warm, only her arms and long graceful fingers extended outward to Ito. I gently lowered him onto her bed right beside her, and her face lit up instantly. She smiled and ran her fingers gently through his fur. He sat patiently, offering himself to her and the moment.

Ito started to gently kiss her face, tentatively at first, with very soft, gentle licks – until he bathed her in full, enthusiastic kisses. After a satisfying visit we left, saying we would be back next Wednesday. She waved as we said goodbye to her from her hospital room doorway. The very next week, I eagerly walked into her room with Ito for our routine pet therapy visit. Her bed was neatly made. No one was there. Edna had passed away.

What a beautiful experience we had for that finite time. Neither Ito, Edna nor I had known that that Wednesday would be our last visit together.

What special moments of connection have you experienced? What did you experience, celebrate, observe or remember most about it? Was it with an elder, teacher, child, or perhaps an animal?

49.   Uncommon Adventures: Ferry Rides with Ito

Life definitely offers many journeys, and many modes of transportation. One favourite trip I took regularly was the seven-minute ferry rides across Toronto's harbour to three landing-points on the Toronto Islands: Ward's Island, Centre Island and Hanlan's Point. They each had their own individual charm.

Ward's Island was my favourite: it's the one with many homes nestled in the narrow and quaint streets. Also, there's a long boardwalk, a beach and a café. Centre Island has a pier, a beach, and a children's amusement park and farm, offering kids an experience of country life and rural ways. Hanlan's Point is best known for its nude beach.

During the summer months, I took the ferry with Ito to the Toronto Islands at least two times a week. I always marveled at the fact that so many Torontonians love the islands, but complain that they haven't made it out there in years. It takes under ten minutes to get there by ferry or water-taxi, and it's always worth the trip. A visit to the laid-back Toronto Islands offers an immediate change of pace from the din and high-velocity rat race of urban Toronto.

These special ferry rides with Ito really made a difference in my life and my perspectives. The islands are popular with international tourists, and I had many conversations with open-hearted visitors to Toronto. Since so many of the people on the ferry were on holiday, they were friendly and happy to talk with me. This made them a well-positioned audience for that short ferry ride. Ito was usually the conversation opener. Tourists swooned over Ito's cuteness, and often asked if they could have their photo taken with him.

These encounters started my whole practise of "conversational activism" (a phrase I may have coined). Gently, and in a non-threatening way, I would inform people about veganism and animal welfare. I would ask questions, provide answers and talk with them about it. I even suggested to high-school students that they could hold Ito and have a picture taken with him if they shared information about animal welfare on their social media platforms.

I carried a stack of postcards I personally created with Annie the Pig, (a friend's six-month-old pet pig) and Ito, together eating vegetables, with the slogan, "Why Love One, But Eat the Other?" I asked the tourists to share the animal welfare sites listed on the postcard. I hope it made a difference for the animals.

A lot of animal-rights activists shame and blame people, rather than ask questions, inform, and be kind to humans, as well as animals. In order to create rapport and advocate for animal rights when we speak to people, I believe we need to have a conversation. The key, I believe, is to listen, speak, inform, and ask people to share the information. This can be done in a non-blaming way, and with kindness. This way, animals have more of a chance of benefiting than if we humans criticize each other, and the messenger gets shot. Kindness and compassion are always gentler ways of creating peaceful change. (One of my projects is to finish my book offering strategies for making the world a better place through "conversational activism." I'm thinking of calling it "Humane Being." It's still percolating.)

Who would know that an open-minded, upbeat group of tourists could be a receptive audience for animal justice, and for sharing it with their friends?

Have you taken a stand on a cause or issue, and done it in a way that is uniquely yours? Have you gone out on a limb for what you stand for in your core values? What actions did you take to make a difference? What happened? How have you and others benefited from your boldness and authenticity?

50.   Ito's Award-Winning Film at TUFF

Lights, camera, adventure! One particular Sunday in June 2010, I was at a vegan potluck dinner. Intuitively, I was led to ask a lovely Filipino woman if she knew a videographer. My "spider sense" was definitely on – and she did. It turned out to be her own brother, Dexter. Knowing I had a very short-term deadline, she immediately discouraged me from contacting him, saying he was super-busy.

The looming deadline was for submissions to TUFF, the Toronto Urban Film Festival. I wanted to create and submit a one-minute film – a silent "short" (no music, no dialogue), as they're called in the industry – called *Ito's Toronto*. If it made it to the prize level, it would be chosen to be broadcast on the TTC subway media-screens at various stations, while people awaited their trains. The challenge was that the deadline was just three days away, on Wednesday. When the woman heard this, she was even more discouraging. She knew just how busy her videographer brother was. Reluctantly but kindly, she gave me his number anyway.

I called him the next morning, and he asked if we could meet on Tuesday at noon. I agreed. He and I were on the very same page, both up for a spontaneous film adventure, in just one day! We ended up filming for just five hours, with Ito as the star, and people we met as supporting actors, in real life!

I must have asked at least fifty people if we could film them that day, all impromptu and improvised. I'll never forget the host of characters we met doing this moment-to-moment spontaneous filming. When I saw interesting characters, I approached them with a smile, asking if it would be okay to film them interacting with Ito. Most agreed, and were thrilled to be part of such a unique film project.

One such character was a bearded homeless man with a purpose. He would stand at the corner of Castle Frank Road and Bloor Street after getting his coffee at a nearby coffee shop, once he'd finished reading the morning paper. I thought since he had a cardboard sign, saying "Hungry, Homeless," it would be befitting to have compassionate Ito being fed by him. A sweet juxtaposition. He's homeless and has a heart to feed my dog, Ito. A touching scene in the one minute short, *Ito's Toronto*.

I arranged to meet him at noon, at his earnest insistence. He said I mustn't be late, as he emphasized that the panhandling is great at one o'clock at another street intersection and he had to meet his wife there then. I was dumfounded. I couldn't believe that I was being scheduled in for a twelve o'clock shoot by a homeless man! (I suppose bosses exist everywhere, and in all walks of life.) I brought him the agreed-upon fee, and he was featured in our one-minute "short."

Another moment I remember so well is the streetcar scene. Ito is featured, gleefully looking out the open window of a streetcar, smiling away in that classic Pomeranian way. (I was hidden inside the car, holding him up as he looked out, taking in all the Toronto sights. And for the passers-by, Ito must have been an amusing and welcome sight, himself!)

We submitted the film just in the nick of time – and a month later were informed that *Ito's Toronto* had received an award: "Most Ambitious Film by a Female Director." And I was excited to learn that the juror who had chosen our film to win this category was the famous Indo-Canadian director Deepa Mehta.

Sometimes, "the first time is the best time" and "the first thought best thought" is the best approach to writing, filming, directing and life itself.

With my winnings, I went to Grenada with Ito, to spend some more time filming him and our adventures abroad. It was certainly worth the effort to ask that woman at the potluck dinner if she knew a videographer: it brought me a "pot of luck."

Isn't it true that when we hop on our adventures at the speed of life, we get to experience life in real time – not planned time – without project management, perfectionism, and the often accompanying self-doubt? I've always loved how Ito interacted with strangers and life itself: it was one curious and joyous exchange after another. Can you remember a time you thoroughly trusted yourself to create or co-create on the spot? Improvise your life? And it turned out magically and magnificently for you?

51. Ito's Globe-Trotting Adventures

All my life, I have experienced certain degrees of anxiety. Yet I found that, for the very first time, my nerves were soothed by the presence of Ito. I called him my "calm Pom." Even my human therapist acknowledged that Ito was a very beneficial part of my life and well-being.

And because I love to travel, the idea of globe-trotting with my best friend Ito was compelling. I looked online for a special service-dog jacket, so it would identify him as able to fly with me in the cabin, rather than in the cargo area. I'd heard horror stories about pets arriving dead when they were stowed in cargo, so that was definitely not an option for my Ito.

I paid an online company for Ito's jacket, and with it, it was easy to fly with my best friend many times to many places. We flew to New York City at least twenty-five times. After all, New York is a city full of dogs and their owners! We also flew to Orlando, Florida; Denver, Colorado; and even the island of Grenada.

My therapist kindly wrote a letter, acknowledging my anxiety condition and citing the benefits of Ito in my life. This letter and the service jacket ended up saving me the additional pet fee for traveling with my dog.

One of my favorite trips with Ito was to Book Expo America, the largest international book conference, only second in size to The Frankfurt Book Fair. It was there that we met another Mr. Ito, a book publisher from Tokyo. What a coincidence. Unfortunately, our philosophical picture book, *Doggie Bliss with Ito*, didn't fit into his publishing themes. His books were business books; Ito's were about pure joy!

Grenada was another adventure that could have ended badly had the young videographer I traveled with not had family connections with the Grenadian government. I didn't have the exact forms needed to enter Grenada and Ito was going to be put into quarantine at least two weeks. With one phone call to the right government official, we were waved through the border and started our filming adventure.

Ito and I had many adventures abroad, thanks to our passion for travel, his service-dog jacket and that authenticating letter from my therapist.

Has there been a time have you benefited from a challenging condition you have? Did it contribute to an adventure in your life? What happened?

52.   Ito, My Model Friend

Our first day at photographer Stephanie's studio was memorable. A former Ford Model Agency photographer, Stephanie branched out to start her own business, shooting actors, models and other subjects. She emphasized to me that children and animals were the absolute hardest subjects to film or shoot. They can be easily distracted, squirmy, and in the case of dogs, always wandering off set and demanding more treats.

Well, this was not the case with dear Ito. Stephanie was thoroughly amazed at his ability to take direction – wearing different costumes and, as she put it, "being the best and easiest subject she had ever shot."

He seemed to love the camera along with all the treats he was rewarded with after each photo was taken. I would gesture him to hold a pose, and then when it was fine to move, he would enthusiastically go the treats and smile at me, with that classic Pomeranian smile.

My working relationship with Stephanie and Ito became a yearly joyous occasion. I would gather together props for the sets, costumes, treats and toys. We created two photo books featuring Ito: *Doggie Bliss with Ito*, and *Ito Knows, Reflections on Life by a Wise Pomeranian*. In *Ito Knows*, I added Ito-endorsed philosophical captions below each photo. Some of Ito's words of wisdom were:

- "Take time to smell everything."
- "You can never have too many friends."
- "Set your sights on inspired living."

Once, we even brought in a friend's six-month-old pet pig and shot a vegan-based animal welfare campaign. Ito and Annie the pig ate carrots and kale facing the camera. We made business cards and postcards with the slogan "Why Love One but Eat the Other?" I gave out stacks of these postcards and business cards to encourage compassion toward all animals, including farmed animals. It felt good having Ito as my "ambassador of compassion."

What a true adventure it was working with Ito as a model and partner in joy at these wonderful photoshoots! Now that he's gone, these two books provide a beautiful memory of these captivating and blissful days on set with Ito.

Capturing joy on camera is a special type of joy. The photographing, the photos and the memories. Have you ever wanted to play around with a special photographic "pet" project? Do you have any of your own photo collections that put a smile on your face?

53. Saving Ito's Life

I'm glad to say that most of us don't experience near-death experiences of our pets. They are traumatic and horrifying. Unfortunately, one such event happened in the life of my dear Ito.

I was volunteering at an animal rescue farm, and the other volunteers and I were invited into the kitchen to have homemade soup for lunch. I was told it was okay to bring Ito. There was a dog living at the rescue farm, but I was told my dog would be safe, as theirs was tied up outside in the garden.

After a long morning of volunteering in the barn, all twelve of us assembled at the kitchen table to have some lunch. Suddenly out of nowhere, a big German shepherd lunged at Ito. Someone must have untied him from the garden and let him into the kitchen, where we were eating.

Viciously, he clamped down on Ito's neck and shook him like a rabbit—treating him like wild prey. He was trying to kill my dog! I couldn't believe my eyes. Ito yelped at the top of his lungs – a pitch almost too high for humans to hear. I panicked, yelling at the owner, "Grab your dog!", as I rescued Ito from its clenched teeth – moments away from seeing my best friend killed. I climbed up onto the kitchen chair in my sock feet and then onto the kitchen table, holding Ito up to the ceiling, while the German shepherd bobbed on his hind legs toward Ito. The dog's owner grabbed his dog, and Ito was luckily well out of harm's way.

My poor Ito dodged a bullet, but acquired five stitches that day. Fortunately, he survived this trauma, and recovered fully. The imminent tragedy of watching my dog die horribly before my eyes didn't happen. Ito and I were spared this nightmare – and just in the nick of time!

Can you remember a time when a possible tragedy was right at your doorstep, and you experienced a blessing just in the nick of time?

54. CNE Midway Mischief with Ito

Some of my favourite moments have been both adventurous and a bit naughty. One such time was with Ito at the Canadian National Exhibition, the CNE. Families, kids and lovers were all welcome – but sadly, no dogs are allowed.

One summer day, late in August, I decided that I would sneak Ito in, carefully avoiding security guards. There's always been a bit of a mischievous gene in me, and my dog was happy to comply. We had many close calls, but finally when the coast was clear, we got in and had a ton of fun!

We had to remain on guard throughout our adventure. One way we avoided being found out was by asking a midway employee at one of the games booths if I could hide Ito among the stuffed toy animals that served as prizes. Since Ito was so well-trained, he sat there with the plush animals, not budging an inch while a security guard officiously walked by – not noticing one of the toys was real! Part of the fun was the joy of taking Ito's picture among the toys, and feeling like I was getting away with something.

Ito was my sidekick as we spent the day adventuring at the CNE. After all, midways are for fun and risk-taking, from rollercoasters to Ferris wheels, to real-life "toy" dogs on plush toy shelves.

Can you remember a time when you took a risk that was both thrilling and scary and a bit naughty perhaps? What did you do?

55. "Volley-Dog," and Fun Times with Toddlers

One of Ito's most amazing feats was playing "volley-dog": taking a soft beach ball in his mouth, tossing it up and volleying it with his nose or front paws. It was an amazing sight, seeing a dog volley like that. It made everyone who saw it smile.

Another playful habit Ito enjoyed was fetching sticks. Many dogs love to fetch, but Ito's fetching was done under very specific circumstances. Ito wasn't a big fan of children. In fact, he loved growling at them as we walked past them on sidewalks. He would even attempt to grab their pant-legs when they flew by on skateboards.

There was only one place where toddlers and kids were considered playmates and companions to Ito – at the beach! It was hilarious how Ito would round up the toddlers along the shoreline. He would see them making sandcastles, swimming and just having fun. Then, he would run along the shore, recruiting new friends between two and four years of age. The game was simple: Ito would bark at them to throw a stick into the water; when they complied, he would swim it back to them. Bark, throw, fetch and repeat – for literally hours.

Meanwhile, I would be thirty metres back on my towel, sunbathing, while keeping an eye on them. It was so much fun watching him. Ito would gallop along the shoreline, vocally and blissfully enrolling the kids for a game of fetch. Often, they would join Ito and swim with him, too.

I was astounded with his acceptance of toddlers and kids, only in this setting. I guess with some things in life, it's all about context. Having Ito taught me so much about the subtleties of life and living.

Have you ever discovered something you normally don't like is acceptable in specific circumstances only? How has this demonstrated your flexibility to you? How has it benefited you? Also, when have you been on the sidelines witnessing simple joy?

56. Ito, Part of the Feline Family

When I first brought Ito home from Montreal at the tender age of two months, he joined a loving household, complete with four unique cats: Mao, a Russian blue, gorgeous, with silvery fur and greenish golden eyes; Tigger, a Maine Coon with the personality of a dog; Lola, a sweet grey tabby; and Cleo, a calico. (Apparently, calico cats are almost always female, due to a genetic predisposition – that's what my vet told me.)

One of my cats' favourite perches was on my bedroom windowsill, above the sofa that served as a soft ladder to their perch. All four cats loved staring out the window at birds, at passers-by and daily outdoor activities. This particular day, Ito joined the gang. If it was a gang of dogs, he would have joined the "pack" – but they all happened to be cats, except for him.

On my way home, I would often look up from the street at my bedroom window, enjoying the sweet sight of my four cats. But on this particular day what I saw was unusually special: my dog was perched there with the cats, just like one of them!

I've often wondered if Ito took on some feline qualities. Since he was so observant, perhaps he decided to imitate the cats, or even act as if he were one himself. He didn't purr, but his "calm Pom" ways convinced me he was a very peaceful soul.

Have you experienced any of your companion animals being imitative of humans or other animals? How did they demonstrate this?

57. Ito's Lullaby

My dog Ito and I shared thousands of special moments. One daily ritual was practising my flute in the living-room while he took his afternoon nap. To help him sleep, I decided to write a lullaby specifically for him. It was a simple melody from my heart, and I loved playing it for him whenever I practised my flute.

What was so amusing was the fact that he would nod off at exactly the same spot in his lullaby every single time! I played *Ito's Lullaby* for him for many years. At the end of his life, when it was time to say goodbye, I played it for him at the vet's office in his "burrito": the little blanket vets put palliative pets in to keep them warm. (I thought it was fitting that Ito's final blanket was a "bur*rito*.")

It was so heart-wrenching to say goodbye to my best friend, my soulmate, that day. I couldn't watch him be euthanized, so I closed my eyes – and all I could do was play my flute for Ito. I chose to play *Ito's Lullaby* on my flute for the final time that day as he peacefully went off to have his final sleep.

Saying goodbye can be difficult, but sometimes it is easier than imagined. By sharing Ito's Lullaby, *a song I had played for him for years, it was comforting to both him and me, knowing it was a send-off gift from my heart. How may you soothe yourself when having to say goodbye, whether it is the end of a relationship or the passing of a loved one?*

58. The Dog Widow: Creating My Bereavement Bubble

After my dear Ito passed away, on May 29, 2018, I felt bereft. My soulmate had died and I was a "dog widow." I chose to go within. I took the time to connect with this experience deeply and personally. I would go to our favourite spots, like the boardwalk at the Toronto Islands, and remember our many joyous walks, along with many other fond memories. It was a sacred time for me to quietly celebrate and reflect upon the passing of my best friend.

Well-meaning friends were sending me condolences, cards, and offering me their open ears and hearts. It's hard to explain – but my dog Ito and I were so close that no human words of sympathy could meet the connection I had with him.

The most difficult part of accepting that Ito was no longer, was changing "Ito *is* …" to "Ito *was* …" I resisted changing the verb tense to "was" since I couldn't accept that he was entirely gone. He did leave his body, but his soul seemed to still be with me. I chose to put away his water dish, food bowl and dog bed, but it really felt like his spirit was still around me.

For this very reason, I wanted to cherish Ito in his new form, equally present, but not physical. I also didn't want to spoil this very potent spiritual time for me with strained sympathy conversations with well-intentioned friends.

So, I decided to start writing a book: *The Dog Widow*. I really did feel like a widow, since my soul partner of sixteen years had been my dog, Ito. We were together day and night, 24/7: from shared joys and adventures to sorrows like breakups with boyfriends. Our two hearts and souls seemed connected.

Someone witnessing our special connection might say that we had met in another lifetime. He also struck me and many others as unusually calm. More often than not, Ito seemed like he was in a state of utter bliss, both with his soft gaze or contented stare and his never-ending Pomeranian smile.

During my time of mourning for Ito, I also realized that I was creating a sort of invisible "bereavement bubble" for myself: a place for me to reminisce about Ito and our special times without any human distractions.

I worked on *The Dog Widow* for thirty days, and got about eighty pages written. It seemed strange to me that I didn't cry much, but instead was in a state of wonder, feeling as though I had been transported to an unusual state. Perhaps Ito, in his non-physical state, was able to continue bringing me bliss, calm and peace of mind. I like to think this was what was actually happening.

I haven't finished *The Dog Widow* yet, but I've changed the title to *The Pet Widow*, since I believe many owners of companion animals would benefit from this helpful guide for mourning the loss of their dear pet and best friend.

Writing the eighty pages while in my "bereavement bubble" served as a sort of healing and private time with Ito's passing. In a way, I was helping myself heal through journaling, along with compiling my tools for grieving in order to help others going through the same process of loss. It has taken me longer than I thought, and hopefully it will be finished one of these days.

Have you chosen solitude when processing the loss of a human or animal companion? How did this serve your healing process? What other approaches have you used in the grieving process? How are you now better equipped to grieve?

59. Kitty Kiss Goodnight

We've all heard that dogs and cats don't necessarily get along. But sometimes they do. In the case of my former affectionate Maine Coon cat, Tigger, and my beloved Ito, they were the exception.

What was interesting to me was Ito had some cat-like qualities: he observed a lot, and was quiet and placid. Similarly, Tigger had dog-like qualities: he would run to the door to greet me when I came home; he allowed me to take him for walks on a leash in the park; and was extremely vocal—a quality common with most Maine Coons. Tigger didn't bark, but caterwauled at times, in that classic Maine Coon, sing-song way.

Something else that Tigger and Ito shared was love. Whether it was sleeping side-by-side on the living room couch or coming to bed with me at night, their companionship was adorable.

Because both Tigger and Ito liked to sleep on the bed with me, I would give them both a kiss and say goodnight. I trained Tigger to lick Ito's ears goodnight, almost like giving him a goodnight kiss. I will never forget the look on Ito's face, patiently waiting for Tigger to finish kissing him – while at the same time, not completely trusting him, as cats are known for suddenly switching gears and swatting with their claws. Fortunately, the evening goodnight ritual never involved any swatting from Tigger, just kisses.

From seeing them lying together on the couch when I came home, to watching Tigger gently and tenderly kiss Ito's ears, I could see that different species could get along, like each other, and even love each other. What a beautiful sight, seeing a dog and cat as trusting, best friends.

Have you witnessed affection between two different species of animals? What were they? What did they do?

60. Picking Up My Dog Kito from Airport

It was a decision I made in just under a week. And now the day had finally arrived! I headed for Pearson Airport to meet my new dog – thanks to an international rescue and adoption service, Free Korean Dogs. He had travelled for thirty hours by air, in a dog kennel, from South Korea – and now my beautiful, white, confident, Spitz had arrived in Toronto.

I called him "Kito," my Korean Ito. (Ito, my beautiful cream-coloured Pomeranian had passed away three months previously, a few weeks after his sixteenth birthday.) I thought that it was a good name, since I might mistakenly call him Ito out of habit. Also, it seemed cute adding "K" for Korean to the name of my first dog, Ito, to make the name Kito!

I hadn't planned on getting a new dog, but synchronicity and serendipity brought this rescue dog to my awareness. My high-school friend Deena, who actively volunteers for this and many other animal welfare initiatives, brought him to my attention on the Canadian rescue website Free Korean Dogs. I learned some horrific news—over three million dogs are slaughtered a year in South Korea for dogmeat. Instantly, I wanted to be able to help, so I went through the adoption process and fortunately was accepted as his adopter. My rescue dog arrived in Canada the very next week.

At the Arrival gate of Toronto's Pearson International Airport, I waited with anticipation and excitement. I thought my dog might be anxious or exhausted when he arrived; but when I saw him in his carrier, he seemed to be neither. It seemed incredible. *He* seemed incredible! I looked at him as he came out the arrival gate with a Korean woman volunteer accompanying him. Here he was, after thirty hours of traveling. What a brave boy, flying halfway across the world! I squatted down and peered closely into his carrier.

I was blown away by what happened next: He kissed me! Did he have a sixth sense that I was to be his new, forever-home "mommy?" It seemed that somehow he knew I was his mom.

I felt so privileged to adopt him: After all, I was adopted, too – and here was my chance to be a mother to an abandoned dog. Deep down, I believe he was sent to me by Ito in Heaven. After all, I wouldn't have recognized Ito in him, if I hadn't had Ito *before* adopting Kito.

Kito is a beautiful white spitz, and looks like a Westminster Kennel Club show dog. And together, we promote rescuing dogs from the Korean dog-meat trade. When people stop me and ask what breed he is, I quickly chime in about his history, and the opportunities available for adopting, volunteering, and donating to this wonderful Canadian charity and dog rescue: Free Korean Dogs. While Ito was a therapy dog, I believe Kito is a real-life mascot for ending the dog-meat trade through education, participation, adoption, and donation.

When have miracles and serendipity played a role in your life? Can you remember some of your most auspicious moments? Why do they stand out for you?

61. Kito's PR, ESL And TLC

I've never taken too much note, or given much significance to letters beside peoples' names. I love people for who they are, not for their diplomas or accreditations. Yet it's funny how certain letters connected to one's name can carry so much meaning in the most unusual circumstances.

Kito, my dear rescue dog from South Korea, has many letters beside his name. As soon as his flight landed on Canadian soil and he was accepted into our country at Canada Customs, he effectively had his PR: his Permanent Residency. There would be no deportations, or jail-time leading up to expulsion. Canada became his forever home.

He left the hardships of his life back in Korea, where he was rescued from a snow drift, and could well have become one of the three million dogs captured or farmed every year for dog meat. Luckily for him, he got out of there alive, was rehabilitated through fostering and vet care, and arrived in Canada with his medical papers in order.

As a dog, his language is the international canine language: through exquisite hearing, a wagging tail, open-mouthed smile, licking (dog kisses), infrequent growling, yodeling, and other kinds of body language and vocalizing that dogs display. As a spitz, vocalizing is to be expected. Sometimes it sounds like he's training to be an opera singer. Other times, he sounds like a Swiss yodeler.

Kito also came to Canada with another mother tongue: Korean. I soon realized that he and I had opposite jobs. He had to learn English as his second language – ESL – and I had to learn Korean as mine. He responded instantly to the word "*anja*," which is the most important command in Korean for dogs: "sit down." He happily complied. He also recognized "hello" in Korean, "*annyeonghaseyo*," or "*annyeong*," for short. I found this so amusing, speaking another language to my dog. I guess dogs from other countries experience both culture shock and language shock – having to learn a new language!

The TLC element – the abbreviation for "tender loving care" – was something we exchanged and continue to exchange with one another. I suppose TLC could be letters beside both of our names!

I often wonder what Kito's Korean name was. If he were to hear a word that sounded like it, would his ears go up in alert recognition? I'm always on the lookout for words that he responds to that may be similar to his name while he lived his first three years in South Korea.

Have you experienced interesting language situations among people or animals in your life? How did you deal with these times? How does language impact the quality of your communication and your overall life?

Chapter Four

Loving the Animals

My life has been filled with animals – and I've learned that their sentience is remarkable. Some of my favourite moments have been playing flute for them. It's clear to me that they can feel music, just as much as they can feel pain. They are no different than us, except that they don't communicate the same way we do. Animals can say everything; they just don't use words. Their language is unique to them.

I've always loved horses: their majestic beauty combined with their sensitivity and spirit. I've learned so much from them. My dogs and cats have also been great teachers to me throughout my life. But sadly, not all animals are respected and loved like our companion animals. Farmed animals, especially the huge majority that are factory-farmed, are the animals whose voices are least heard. For this reason, I am vegan, and do my best to help them have a voice.

62. Horse Spirit and Horsepower Live Inside Me

Our lives have empowering moments and characters in them. For me, horses have informed my sense of self, my inner strength and courage. In a way, being on horseback and feeling the strength of their size, their majestic ways and their various gaits – from walk, trot, canter to gallop – is a way of merging with them. It's a union or fusion of two souls. I've also found that on horseback I feel a direct connection and transference of the horse's feelings and mindset. I have felt their strength, boldness, sensitivity, confidence, and boundlessness.

As a ten-year-old, I led trail rides through the forest. I'd see fallen tree trunks on the path ahead – nature's jumps – and we would jump over them on horseback each time. When we finally approached the log at a trot, I felt a sense of anticipation from the horse as he readied us for the make-shift forest jump.

Since I stopped riding at age twelve, and began playing the flute shortly after that, I realized there were similarities. Internally, preparing for a jump on horseback and preparing for an upcoming challenging technical passage on the flute felt similar. There was a sense of readiness and anticipation. Both flute playing and riding called upon two states simultaneously: "allowing" and "going for it" at the same time. That Zen-like state – not forcing, not driving, but just letting it happen – is fueled by internal belief and outward conviction.

I feel so fortunate to have spent so much time with horses. Their gentle yet powerful presence is so beautiful. Their intuition and extreme sensitivity have had a great impact on me and my approach to life. I can remember what it's like to be on horseback – and today I consciously choose to approach my moments with much more ease, flow and boldness

Have you had a person, animal or spiritual being inform you and guide your life? Were you surprised by this? What was your guide's greatest significance to you? How have you been affected, and how do you continue to use this inner guidance to express your authentic self?

63.   Horse Rump Rules: Testing the Boundaries

I learned so much from Skippy, the Appaloosa mare I rode when I was ten years old. She was a "green" horse, meaning she had never worn a bridle or saddle before, and ran freely in the fields. She was wild and untrained.

One day, I was given the opportunity to train Skippy. This was a challenge for me: although I'd been riding for two years already, I had never trained a horse before. I was only ten years old at the time but felt honoured to have been given this opportunity.

I approached my task intuitively and with sensitivity. I realized that being gentle was the best way to be, whether approaching a "green" horse in pasture, putting a saddle or bridle on for the very first time, or teaching her how to jump.

Skippy was a sweet soul, and I gradually trained her to trust me approaching her in the field. When she was ready, I put a bridle and saddle on her, mounted her, and finally rode her for the very first time. She got accustomed to me on her back and was no longer skittish, as most "green" horses are at first. We had a very special bond of trust and sense of adventure – a symbiotic connection.

She carried me safely and smoothly in all her gaits, from walking to trotting to cantering to galloping. We also did jumps up to four-and-a-half foot walls. Skippy even won first place in equestrian shows with me on her back. I was number eighty-eight when we won first place, and to this day, this number has been lucky for me. Some say that the number eight signifies fortune and infinity.

One day, I decided to take a risk – a big risk. I sat down cross-legged in Skippy's barn stall, right behind her rump and back legs. One equestrian rule is to never stand behind a horse's rear as it can get skittish and kick you. I definitely didn't want to get kicked or sustain a head concussion. Yet something inside me just wanted to test fate, and test Skippy. Very cautiously, Skippy made a 180-degree turn, in skillful slow motion. She carefully turned with her nose noisily sniffing as she looked down at me, being careful not to step on me.

This solidified what I already knew about Skippy; she was a sweet soul, and although I didn't own her, I considered her my soul-spirit horse.

She showed her love in so many ways, including the day a bunch of us were riding bareback over sand dunes at a fast gallop. As I slid off Skippy's shiny sleek back, she immediately stopped and waited for me stand up and to mount her again. Then we took off to catch up with the other horses. This feeling of a horse "having my back" was a unique and unforgettable experience.

Testing the rules can be fun, risky and even dangerous – especially with a 1200-pound horse, where injury could easily occur. However, sometimes a part of us wants to rebel against the norm, against safety. When we do this and things turn out well, we feel restored, have faith in our gut instincts, and risk-taking.

Have you ever tested something or someone in your life in order to gain a deeper trust and faith in something? What did you risk and what did you gain? Are you glad you did it?

64. Skippy and the Unruly Sleighride

One particular winter, at the stable in Pickering, Ontario, I was eleven years old and looking for fun. I decided to create a home-made sleigh out of an aluminum toboggan and binder twine, and tie it up to Skippy's saddle. I invited my friend Lori to test this makeshift sleigh by carefully getting onto the toboggan, while I got on the saddle to ride her. I was being both a rider and a sleigh master, reins in hand, ready to cue Skippy on.

Well, Skippy would have none of this! As soon as the toboggan started to slide along the snow, she would hear the high-pitched sound it made, and it would scare her. In her panic, she'd then attempt to run away from the sound coming out of the toboggan, but the toboggan continued to chase her. Lori went flying backwards, tumbling off the toboggan into the snow. Lighter without her weight, the toboggan screeched at a higher and higher pitch as Skippy ran faster and faster, attempting to get away from it. But she couldn't: it was attached to her and seemingly chasing her!

I felt so badly for creating this concoction of a sleigh, not having anticipated this happening. I could feel her terror, but there was nothing I could do but hold on tight, stay on her back, and pray that no cars came. Galloping at top speed over the snow and icy driveway, we finally came up to the familiar wire fence of her pasture.

First, she came to an abrupt stop and then, without missing a beat, Skippy leapt over the fence into the pasture she was all too familiar with. What I wasn't familiar with was flying out of the saddle, into the air, over the wire fence and into the snow! It all seemed to happen in a split second. Luckily, no one was hurt.

Have you ever experimented with an adventurous, yet potentially dangerous undertaking? What were the potential risks? What did you do? Are you glad you did it anyway?

65.   My Horse and I to the Rescue

Trail rides were one the greatest highlights of my childhood. I loved leading them when I was only eight years old. In exchange for riding lessons twice a week, we kids would muck out the stables on weekends and lead trail rides of eight-to-ten riders. Although we young trail-ride leaders rode English equestrian style, the tourist riders rode Western. This meant they had more support in their stirrups and a horn to grab onto at the front of their saddle. English required more leg and body support to remain firmly in the saddle.

It was funny learning the habits of the horses that we had to saddle before the rides. They knew the cinch was being tightened under their bellies in order for the Western-style saddle to stay on. But horses are very intelligent and don't want their cinches to be too tight. So, before we had a chance to put the saddle on their backs, they skillfully bloated out their bellies. Then, we attempted to fasten the synch under their bellies. They were still bloated. We would try to get them to allow another notch on the synch to be tightened, but they were stubborn.

Finally, all riders in their saddles, off we went in single file through nearby forests and trails. What a joyous way to spend Saturday and Sunday afternoons! There were songbirds galore, along with fresh apples ready to be picked from the trees as we rode past.

One day, a very funny thing happened on our trail ride. When we accelerated the horses' gait to a manageable trot, one of the riders fell to the ground, as their saddle gradually slid under the horse. Because the horse had bloated its belly earlier, the cinch was too loose, causing the saddle to slide under. After tightening the synch, the rider remounted and we continued on the trail ride.

What wasn't manageable was the time we crossed the newly paved country road and a horse had a sudden fall – right on top of the tourist-rider! The metal horseshoe had slipped on the cement and caused both the horse and rider to fall right on the road. In a state of panic, I mustered up the strength to do something immediately to help. This was a real emergency – and my horse was my transportation back to the farmhouse, where there was a phone. (Back then, there were no cellphones.)

Galloping back, I was an emergency service for the injured rider. Thank goodness, when the ambulance was called, she was taken to the local hospital at record speed. She had a concussion, but fortunately recovered. Over time, I also recovered from this traumatic experience – realizing that under pressure, we instinctively do what we have to do. This is one of my life's most unforgettable experiences!

Life presents us with moments of rescue—both being the rescuer and being the rescued. Think of a time you were rescued. How did you feel? Now, recall a time you were called upon to be the rescuer. How did this affect your life? How did it change you? Have you experienced an emergency when you were called upon as the "human ambulance"?

66. Balcony Birdsong with My Flute

It's a sound I loathe hearing: that unmistakable "thud" on my balcony window pane – that horrible sound of a small bird crashing into the window and falling onto the balcony floor. I've only heard it a few times, but each time, my stomach is in knots and churning.

On this particular occasion, I took out my Native American flute, hoping I could peacefully bring flute music to this little sparrow's flight to heaven. I was so overcome by my feeling of powerlessness. What more could I do than play for this sweet little creature? I closed my eyes, and trembling, took a deep breath, punctuated with quivers, and started to play. Tears ran down my face as I improvised a melody for this innocent bird's passing. The Native American flute seemed to play itself.

Then, after about five minutes, I opened my eyes, after finishing the phrase. I was astounded. As I went to look down, I noticed the bird was gone. Had my music healed him? Did he experience a healing slumber to the sound of my flute, wake up refreshed and revivified? I'll never know, but I like to think it did. I will always remember being the "human bird" – sharing a birdsong from my heart with this precious being that suddenly disappeared into thin air.

The unexpected continues to weave itself through our lives. The power of sincere intention can also cause unusual things to occur. What experiences have you encountered that caused you to do a "double take"?

67. Dogs as "Cocktails" at the End of Your Leash

I've always noticed that people with dogs say hello to each other's dogs first, before acknowledging the dog's owner. A typical meeting in the park is, "Oh, how's Buddy today?" "He's great. He's really loving his new ball. And how is Rosie?" "She's great. Almost two years old already – she still acts like a pup."

People don't ask about each other, and often the dog owners don't even know each other's names. I call it "the cocktail party in the park." The whole scene is very similar to parties where everyone is holding a drink. Our dogs are the cocktails at the end of our leashes. If only we could learn from our dogs and be more friendly, interested and curious. I'm not suggesting we do the dog bum-sniffing greeting, but perhaps a smile and "Hello, how are you?" could be a step in the friendly conversational direction!

Dogs love fun, games and open connection. We have a lot to learn from them. How many times do we hide from each other, putting focus on other things? How can dogs teach us about friendliness and approachability? Can you remember a time you opened up to a stranger and discovered you had so much in common? Did this encounter help you become more open, welcoming and confident?

68. Balcony Concerts for My Forest Friends

Practising flute is my ritual in the mornings. I like to do this in the living room, seated over a beautiful blue, coral and gold antique Persian rug. It feels like art, hung on the floor.

One morning after I had completed a flurry of major and minor scales, I suddenly heard a scratching sound coming from my balcony. I opened the wooden door and peered out of my screen down to see a curious little black squirrel, hands formed into little boxer fists at her chest. I brought her some nourishing sprouted multigrain bread. I broke it into little pieces and displayed it on my balcony where she patiently waited. I went back inside and continued my flute practising.

A few minutes later, I looked out the balcony door, and both she and the bread were gone. The very next morning, I heard the same sound. This time, the little black squirrel had brought one of her friends, a grey squirrel with mild alopecia. Somehow that made this squirrel even more endearing. Then, quietly, a female cardinal snuck onto the balcony under the railing and joined the two squirrels. It was nature's breakfast club.

I loved the fact that it was only one squirrel the first morning, and more animals the next. I imagined the black squirrel informing its friend, as the bird caught wind of the breakfast on the balcony.

I wonder if my flute was the "breakfast bell," and I was their Pied Piper?

Have you had precious moments with nature that made you feel very connected? What animals did you encounter? How did you feel?

69. Singing For the Cats and Dogs Behind Bars

I'm a morning-shower singer – at least, that's what I always thought. Then, one day when I was visiting the dogs and cats at the Toronto Humane Society, I found a new venue for my voice. It was quite unexpected.

If you've never been to the Toronto Humane Society, you won't know that as you enter the reception area, you hear echoes of distressed dogs, howling, crying, begging to be released from their kennels and be welcomed to their new forever homes. It is so heart-wrenching to hear them, since in any language a cry of distress and sadness is always interpreted the same way. In an attempt to comfort the dogs, classical music was played for them, but sadly much of it was buried under their forlorn and continuous cries.

I loved my trips to the humane society, to say hello to the animals, and to do my part in reassuring them that someone would come for them someday soon. I started singing simple little nursery rhyme-like songs for one of the dogs. To do this, I started by reading his name on the posting on the kennel. Seeing additional details – such as whether it was stray or surrendered, or how long it had lived there in its kennel – added to my intense sadness for him.

Then, a sudden inspiration came to me: a formula that could speak to them and reach their hearts, one dog at a time.

Knowing the phrase "good dog" is music to all dogs' ears, I simply squatted down in front of the kennel and looked into the timid, scared eyes of a dog named Taffy, and sang, "Taffy is a gooooddd dog."

The resigned loneliness I witness before starting to sing suddenly lifted – subtly, at first, and then in more pronounced ways. Taffy's ears fluttered, recognizing his name. Then there was a softening – a whole-body softening. He lay down, yawned, and put his chin diagonally across his front paws. I was astounded – and it worked when I tried it on the other dogs, too.

It seemed like my music therapy was really having an effect. I remembered the times I used to take my Pomeranian, Ito, to the Toronto Grace Hospital to offer pet therapy to the patients. Here, at the Humane Society, I was singing to the animals to offer *them* human music therapy! How ironic, yet reassuring to know that we can all experience healing from one another – human to animal or animal to human.

Next, I went up to the cat floor. They seemed to be more at peace, despite being in the shelter. Classical music wafted gently from the radio, and there seemed to be a palpable peacefulness on this floor. There was a lot of purring going on here. When I sang to a couple of the cats, some gave me "cat-eye kisses": those squinting eyes, that to me denote "I love you" in kitty language.

Music therapy works for dogs and cats, as well as humans. I wonder what it would be like for all animals? My documentary in-the-works, *Dinner Music* – in which I play my flute for rescued pigs, horses, cows, sheep, ducks, roosters and more, at sanctuaries for factory-farmed animals – has shown me that they, too, love flute music.

The amazing reactions I received when playing flute for farmed animals were varied but encouraging and heart-warming. The rooster cocked its head as I improvised a cheerful tune, and only after finishing my last note did he cock-a-doodle-doo, and I didn't even cue him! I sat on the straw in an outdoor pen with a six-hundred-pound pig who'd fallen off a truck heading for the slaughterhouse – and he was so calm and trusting that he yawned to the sound of my flute. Rescued horses sniffed my flute with their soft velvet noses, and sheep baaed while I played Bach's *Sheep May Safely Graze* for them.

Of course, Ito, my dear Pomeranian, loved my flute, and the piece I wrote especially for him to lull off to during naptime, was aptly called *Ito's Lullaby*.

I decided to continue visiting the Humane Society, singing to the dogs and cats, anxious or depressed, frightened or forlorn, from outside their kennels and cages. It seemed to consistently give them some relief from their isolation, and the cries of their companions. I believe they felt the tenderness in my voice, as I sang their names, delivering customized love, one kennel at a time.

My visits to the Toronto Humane Society were rewarding for me – and I hope they were for the animals living there temporarily, too. By playing in this shelter, and also for rescued farmed animals in sanctuaries, I discovered a lot about animals and music. Music has the power to heal, soothe and comfort whether you are a human or nonhuman animal.

When have you unexpectedly stumbled over a discovery that you may not otherwise have experienced? How did it affect you and others? Did it surprise you?

70. Inviting In the Animals

It was May 19, 2021, the morning of my fifty-seventh birthday. The day couldn't have been any more perfect: crystal clear blue sky, gentle warm breeze and sunshine like a late July afternoon. The temperature was ideal, like a San Diego "perfect every day" temperature of 24° C, with no humidity.

The day before I had been extra-productive, editing twenty of these *Sparkle* stories, so that I would feel great taking off the entire day on my birthday. I had made a wish though, the day before, that my birthday be filled with animals and nature. And it was!

After having a lovely visit on Philosopher's Walk at the University of Toronto, a friend and I went to another spot on the campus. Out of the blue, I heard her gasp and point. Across the street, huddled by the building off the boulevard, were a male and female Canada goose – along with four fluffy yellow and brown goslings. What a miracle! And what a sudden responsibility: to prevent them from running into oncoming traffic. There were gardeners in their noisy pickup trucks, filled with rakes, tools and maintenance stuff clanging by us over the speed limit, plus cars, bikes, motorcycles.

Indeed, my birthday wish came true. I got to experience nature that day. I hadn't expected it to come with such a responsibility: keeping animals out of harm's way.

Another ongoing prayer I've had is to be of service to the "voiceless" animals. Well, these geese definitely had voices, warning their goslings, that were still wet behind the ears, where to walk. Nevertheless, I knew I could be of service, directing and averting the traffic – literally for hours that day!

After four hours of following them, signalling to traffic to slow down, I was able to go home, not worrying so much about them. I later found out that these two birds have been on the U of T campus for over two years, and later on my birthday were seen with their goslings on a much quieter street, with little traffic.

What a beautiful answer to my birthday wish — with a safe and happy ending.

Just a few days later, on a walk in my neighbourhood, I suddenly heard a very high-pitched cry coming out of the shrubs on a nearby lawn. I asked my boyfriend if he heard anything, but he didn't. I think the pitch may have required "dog ears" to really discern what it was. Again and again, I heard this faint crying sound. It was disturbing not knowing what it was and how I could help.

A few minutes later, a neighbour came over and pointed to a lone hatchling, barely a day old, pink-skinned, no feathers or fluff, just a wide-open mouth to the sky, poised to receive worms from its mom. It was alone on the lawn; there was no nest to be found. There was no mother bird around. The crying got more and more insistent.

We hurried home and Googled wildlife sites to determine what we could do. We decided that the best place for it was where its mom could find it and feed it. It was a very hot day, so hopefully this would serve the hatchling in keeping warm without a nest or mother nearby. The next day, I cautiously walked up to see if the bird had died or been taken away. I didn't want to look, fearing the inevitable. Would I see a dead bird on the ground, or simply no bird? Would a cat or other predator have killed it? I took a deep breath and looked down at the lawn, and there that recognizable high pitch again! It had been hours! The mother must have found it. I was reassured, trusting nature.

Later that night, we walked by again and it was gone. Had it been eaten by a cat or perhaps taken by a well-meaning person to rehabilitate it? One of my life's unsolved mysteries.

And a few days after that, after sheltering ourselves under a maple tree from a morning sun shower, my boyfriend and I emerged, continuing down the sidewalk on our way home. Suddenly, out of nowhere, an unleashed dog bound past the two of us, approaching a street intersection. I quickly gestured "stop" with my flat outstretched hand to an approaching car, keeping the dog out of harm's way. Next, a barefoot twenty-something woman came running after the dog, panic-stricken, saying the dog had jumped out of the house, through a screen window on the third floor. It was a rescue dog, and it was bounding down the street at full speed. The woman took a quick momentary detour to my place to borrow my own dog's leash to use when she found her missing dog.

The search continued all day and night, with calls to missing animal services, the Humane Society and posts on Facebook. I was horrified with the thought of this dog being hit by a car, since all this was happening in downtown Toronto.

The next day, around noon, I got a phone call: it was the woman with the runaway dog! It had returned home, covered in mud and joy, demonstrated by his wagging tail. What a miracle! We humans could all finally exhale.

I'm still in awe of the fact that this dog was a rescue, and had only been in Canada three months, but was able to find his way home – which turned out to be over three miles away in the highly dense, traffic-filled, urban center. My faith in God increased that day, knowing deep down that there must be a higher power watching over and guiding our lives.

Inviting in animals has been a big part of my life and brings me closer to them, over and over again. I feel blessed to have this deep connection with them.

Is there something you consciously invite into your life? What has this allowed in? How has this helped you express your true nature?

71. Turkey-Talk on Christmas Day

Most people think of turkey as a traditional food served on Thanksgiving and Christmas. That's what I used to think too. However, this particular Christmas was very different. I was out in the small town of Dunville, Ontario, with my then-boyfriend, Chris, visiting his mom. The ten-pound turkey was in the oven cooking and wouldn't be ready for another five hours. We decided to pass the time by going on a beautiful country drive. It was a magnificent day, and in the holiday spirit, we belted out Christmas carols at the top of our lungs in the toasty warm car. We were in a Winter Wonderland: the snowflakes falling gracefully, like nature's doilies.

Driving a few miles down the road, we spotted at least twelve turkeys on a nearby farmer's driveway. Content, they seemed like one big bird family! We pulled up into the driveway, to get a better look at them. Excited to be up close to a bunch of living turkeys, I excitedly rolled down my window. Not timid at all, they looked up at me curiously as they gathered around our car. They strutted in the snow, cocking their heads at us. I looked deeply into their eyes and saw their beings, their souls. I had never been so close to turkeys – living ones, that is. Their sentience was palpable. We continued exchanging curious stares, back and forth.

A split second later, I felt moved to say to them, "Merry Christmas, and I promise to never eat you again!" Here I was talking to turkeys, rather than eating them – this was definitely a first on Christmas Day. A funny part of this experience is the way the turkeys have a tendency to interrupt, with their "gobbles." Each time I spoke, they would overlap my words with their "turkey talk".

I'll always remember this exceptionally special Christmas, when I made a vow to the turkeys, and got to celebrate Christmas with them – before dinner.

I kept my promise: I haven't eaten turkey since that day. Instead, I've cherished the fresh memory of the curious, living, turkeys gathering around our rolled down car window, sharing glad tidings with us on that Christmas Day, turkey-style.

Has there been a time you made a commitment and declared it out loud to another, and never turned back? How did you feel at the time? How has this decision impacted your life?

72. Side by Side, Highway Ride

It was particularly sunny, that late July afternoon. Not a cloud in the sky. I was in the car with one of my best friends and music colleagues, Canadian guitarist extraordinaire, Bill. We were in our black-tie outfits, driving to play cocktail music at a posh Toronto venue, the Liberty Grand. I knew that *hors d'oeuvres* would be served by uptight waiters and waitresses, with a cold, matter-of-fact elegance and officiousness. Animals (dead ones) disguised as precious little finger foods, like sliders and prosciutto, would be presented delicately on silver platters, with fine wine to accompany.

We were almost at the venue, when I rolled down my window and closed my eyes, elbow leaning on the ledge of the window, halfway down, inhaling the fresh breeze of this perfect summer day. I was really looking forward to performing flute-and-guitar jazz standards for the guests. I'm also a keen people-watcher, and love the variety of eye candy at such events.

When I opened my eyes, I couldn't believe what I saw. Horrified, I gasped for air. Here, eyes wide open, were pigs with wet, pink snouts, sniffing wildly in the highway lane right beside me. They were stuffed on a slaughter-truck, on their way to their final destination: the slaughterhouse. They were being driven to an inevitable, unimaginable horror – and there was no one to rescue them behind those thick slaughterhouse walls.

Panic filled the air – I could even smell and taste it. The pigs struggled, climbing over each other, desperately looking out the small holes of the truck. Becoming nauseous with this, I felt helpless, tears running down my chin uncontrollably. They poured down my neck, spilling recklessly onto my cocktail dress.

How could such a wonderful day be so terribly sad for both the pigs and me? I suddenly was one of them. I felt their pain, their collective victimhood. There was nothing I could physically do for them. We were stalled on the highway, in a traffic jam. The slaughter-truck crawled up beside our car. Now they were up close and central, they couldn't get away, and I couldn't help them or get out of this horror scene.

It was a parallel reality unlike anything I had ever experienced before. Trapped, choking and coughing with the asthma that comes over me when I'm really upset, I sat there, side-by-side on the highway: the pigs on the way to the slaughterhouse, me on my way to just another posh, well-paying, corporate gig.

As soon as the traffic started moving, I started breathing again, but the resonance of their panic and pleading followed me to my gig that day – and has followed me for years ever since.

My life has never been the same since that horrific moment. It's lived inside me. Despite this, I still am a person who likes to remain positive – to be part of the solution rather than the problem. I'm careful not to be a Pollyanna, pretending everything is fine, and turning the other way. I try my best to be with what is, and to change what shouldn't be. The best thing I can do for the animals is not participate in anything that involves animal cruelty, which means not eating meat. I believe meat, (from dead, often mistreated animals), is a product of unnecessary suffering, cruelty, and deep sorrow. For this reason, I like to inform people of the truth about this, since the advertising industry does a great job at covering up the truth. I want to be a voice for the voiceless: for the animals whose voices go unheard.

Although sometimes my words may land on deaf ears, and other times they may cause conflict, my hope is to be a messenger for the animals. The expression "Don't shoot the messenger" is always on my mind, since how we take a stand for the animals truly impacts the message being heard and responded to. If the messenger is shot, only the innocent animals end up suffering as a result.

I try my best to approach this matter with respect for the people I am speaking with so the animals can benefit most from the truth-telling.

When in your life have you experienced a paradox: two experiences side by side? What have you learned about paradox in life? When have you taken a stand for a cause that brings up a lot of conflict? How have you stayed true to being a voice for this cause, without the message itself being shot, due to being an unpopular messenger?

73. Standing Vigil Outside Hell

I will never forget that day with the Toronto Pig Save animal welfare group, led by Anita Krajnc.

I learned about this group during my days attending the Toronto Animal Rights vegan potluck dinner get-togethers. Sadly, I learned there was a pig slaughterhouse in downtown Toronto, on Walnut Street, near the corner of Niagara and King. The exact street address was 666 Wellington St – ironically, just a few blocks away from Toronto's Five Star Ritz Hotel. Just writing the number "666" and knowing the atrocities that went on there for almost one hundred years makes my stomach turn. I was told that, every day, 6,000 young pigs were delivered in slaughter-trucks to this inconspicuous location, with gates and walls disguising the disgrace occurring inside.

I stood vigil with these compassionate animal welfarists, holding a sign up for cars driving by, to inform them of what was happening behind the walls. Unable to hold back my downpour of tears, I heard the pigs squealing loudly as they were forced off the trucks, many being electrically prodded. I'd been told that it was legal to use electrical prods on them everywhere except on their faces and genitals. I couldn't believe this overt cruelty to animals could actually be legal.

So there I stood, along with a dedicated group of pig sympathizers, just before they were killed: put into crates, gassed, and lowered into boiling water so their skin could be loose enough to come off for leather products, like purses, jackets, shoes and boots. I was horrified to hear that some of the pigs weren't actually dead from the gassing, and landed in the scalding water still alive!

I was also aware that pigs are as intelligent – if not more intelligent – than dogs, love to play, and are very thoughtful and affectionate. They also have digestive tracts similar to humans, and we can use their blood for transfusions. It was so sad to learn they experience nausea and car-sickness like humans when they are being transported to their end on those overly stuffed slaughter-trucks.

Trying to hold back tears, I stood there, holding my sign, "Over 6,000 Pigs are Killed Here Daily." Some cars just drove on by, but others honked. This was their way of lending compassionate support to us at the vigil, and to the dear pigs being slaughtered.

This moment changed my life forever. I continued being vegetarian – later becoming vegan – and I learned that standing vigil outside a slaughterhouse is a very powerful experience. We humans can choose to turn the other way, shut our eyes, or avoid footage of the real experience of this living horror, but the pigs and other farmed animals can't. They are not given the choice to avoid this inhumane treatment and horrors.

I only did three vigils, but I still totally support Toronto Pig Save's efforts. It exposes humans to the cold hard truth.

When people speak of craving barbecued ribs, a picture of these sweet pigs flashes before my eyes, and I offer the picture out loud by saying, "these ribs once had hearts beating behind them, that were forced to stop," or with the bacon craze, I say, "Pigs are as intelligent as dogs; would you eat your dog?" or "There's a vegan bacon, made with coconut, and it tastes great, and is a cruelty-free bacon."

I will never forget holding a rescued baby pig at a farm sanctuary in my arms. He was no more than eight pounds and his little wet snout sniffed me all over. What was remarkable to me was that he smelled like cooked pork. I couldn't distinguish a difference between holding a warm, living piglet and the smell of dead pig, in a pulled pork sandwich. To this day, I can't bear the smell of cooked pig, since it reminds of that sweet little living piglet in my arms.

I also have very strong feelings about the pejorative ways people can use names for animals. For example, "She's such a pig – always pigging out – so fat," or "Your room is like a pigsty," or "You dirty pig!". In a similar way, people say, "You're such a chicken – such a weakling." When I heard that factory-farmed rotisserie chickens are pumped with so many growth hormones that they become too heavy to stand up, and often their imposed weight snaps their legs broken, I was appalled.

When I have chosen to make the inquiry into what is really happening, it has been easier to reframe past habits, cravings, and know what the cruelty-free choices are.

Some quotes that have really resonated with me deeply are:
- George Bernard Shaw: "I choose not to make a graveyard of my body with the rotting corpses of dead animals." And "Animals are my friends and I don't eat my friends."
- Leo Tolstoy: "One should not turn a blind eye to the facts that, by consuming meat, they demand the killing of a living being for the sake of luxury and taste." And "When you feel pain at the sight of the suffering of another being, do not give in to the initial urge to hide from the sight of suffering and flee from the victim, but, on the contrary, rush to the victim

and look for a way to help them." Also, "As long as there are slaughterhouses, there will be battlefields."

I've included more quotes in the Appendix to *Sparkle*.

Has there been a time in your life when you made a moral decision and stuck to it? What finally convinced you to do it and to remain steadfast? Did you experience criticism from friends and peers? How did you deal with this?

74. My Moment of Silence: Remembering the Cows

The most difficult part of my transitioning from being a vegetarian to being vegan was stopping dairy. I used to love pizza, ice-cream, yogurt, feta cheese, and especially coffee with cream. Somehow, soy milk or almond milk didn't seem to taste as good.

Just as Remembrance Day, on November 11, has a moment of silence, I've created my own personal moment of silence, tuning into the cruel reality of the dairy industry when I buy a coffee at a local café. I remember that calves are taken away from their mothers just hours, days or weeks after their birth, and both mom and baby wail and cry for each other for weeks to follow. Sadly, this fact often gets overlooked when people drink or eat dairy products. The dairy industry does a great job at concealing the truth, and personifies it with images of happy cows and warm, loving family-farm environments. The majority of dairy farms are in the factory-farm setting – not in pastoral fields with loving farmers.

I also realize that in order for a cow to give milk, she has to first have a calf. This biological fact is missing when dairy is promoted. As a result a dairy cow lives a life of ongoing grief, losing one baby after another, for years and years. She is exploited, hooked up to machines, stealing her baby's milk for years – until she is considered too old, and then she is killed for hamburgers at fast food chains. What a horrific, lamentable life for the dairy cows: mothers at heart.

The other hard fact is that newborn male calves often become veal. This is a very sad and cruel process: in order for their meat to be so tender, they need to be tied up in veal crates, unable to move. This is pure torture, in my opinion.

So, my moment of silence is for these blessed animals. And I tell myself – even though I crave cream for its taste – I must not to condone the cruelty that exists in the dairy industry. I decide to *save* instead of *crave*. Save, as in saving the animals when I am craving dairy. I picture giving the milk or cream back to the baby cow, when I get the craving for it. In a way, it's just a small gesture, but it reduces effort to zero in the reality of the situation.

This is my personal commitment to make an effort in these moments of wanting cream in my coffee. I will contribute to saving cows, even one spoonful of cream at a time. The effort it takes to bring my own non-dairy creamer with me reminds me of my dedication to their cause, and not to take their pain lightly.

When have you consciously given up something in your life for your own particular moralistic reasons? How has this affected your life for the better? What were the challenges?

75. Café No Lait

As an animal lover and welfarist, I'm noticing more and more how insidious the dairy industry is, and how many addictive foods and beverages contain dairy products. Pizzerias consume tons of cheese. And cafés and coffee shops do not promote a dairy-free culture. How often do we hear people ordering cappuccinos, café lattes and other coffees with milk or cream? The multi-billion-dollar fast-food business flourishes at the expense of humane consideration of cows and their babies.

Yet few people know that calves are removed from their moms within days or weeks of birth, and their baby-food, milk, is also taken from them. It is said that we humans are the only species who ingest the milk of another species. Also, milk is a baby-food, not to be consumed all our lives. And it's said that all humans are lactose intolerant; some just have more pervasive symptoms. Perhaps this lactose intolerance is due to the fact that we really shouldn't be drinking another species' baby-food.

One Sunday morning at the Toronto Antique Market, I began to collect cow-shaped creamer pitchers. They were all different colours and from all over the world. In an instant, an idea came to me: "Café No Lait." Somehow, these little creamer pitchers were acting as props for a concept I was creating on the spot: a vegan café called "Café No Lait." I haven't built the café yet, but perhaps the phrase "Café No Lait" can be a reminder to me and other coffee lovers that, at home or out at cafés, we can substitute dairy creamers with non-dairy, cruelty-free substitutes, such as almond, cashew, soy and oat milks.

One day, if this café comes into existence, I will display these antique cow pitchers on a shelf as a memento for the idea, and as a dedication to the cows' welfare.

Have you been inspired to do something unique by an object or thing? What was this symbol suggesting to you? What was your inspiration? How did it come into being?

76. Save, Don't Crave

Thanks to Anita Krajnc, who started Toronto Pig Save, there's been a worldwide movement to save factory-farmed animals, called the Save Movement. Because of this movement – and more awareness and compassion toward animals and the environment – people are making the transition to veganism, the cruelty-free choice.

Cravings are funny things. Somehow, they seem to be hard-wired, and we can blindly crave something that isn't good for us or the welfare of animals. Now, when I crave something, I take a deep breath and ask myself, is it cruelty-free? If it isn't, I quickly replace my *craving* a *food*, with the idea of *saving* an *animal*. Cravings for a certain habituated taste can easily prompt a moment of mindfulness, and then we can make a conscious, loving and cruelty-free choice.

This has helped me so much, and I suggest it to friends who are not vegetarians or vegans, but who have expressed a curiosity or interest in becoming one. The idea of transforming a *craving* for a food or beverage item to the idea of *saving* animals, in refraining from it, is a great reframe. (We can always choose new, better habits.)

It's really possible to do this with any meat or animal food-item. Instead of *craving* it and eating it, we can choose to do our part in *saving* it, by eating something plant-based, instead. Imagine the good you are doing for yourself, the animals and the environment. Over time, this becomes a new and healthy pattern, to make choices that are vegan and cruelty-free. Healthy habits are especially wonderful when we know we're making a compassionate difference for ourselves and other sentient beings.

When have you craved something, but in knowing that you have other choices, decided to choose something else? Have you used this technique with other things?

77. "Conversational Activism" and "Humane Being"

I'm an animal lover – all animals. When I discovered the pain and suffering factory-farmed animals go through in their whole lives: from birth, living in factory farms, often being transported in slaughter-trucks in painful circumstances, often going long hours without food or water, and then being slaughtered behind closed doors, I decided I didn't want to be part of this infliction of pain.

They say you vote with your wallet – and that's how I became a vegan. I've realized that what we choose to buy is based in our values and beliefs. If we want to make a positive impact, we can cultivate more compassion and a consciousness that includes all living beings and their humane treatment. Veganism addresses this approach to life.

Yet "vegan" has often been a vilified term. Vegans mean well – but when they are affected by the cruelty and inhumane treatment of animals, their empathy and compassion can lead to hostility toward non-vegans. Their passion about the cause of animal welfare can often arouse anger in others.

Despite the conflicts erupting between people on this subject, sadly, the animals continue to suffer, regardless. This is so tragic – and is often a case of "shooting the messenger", since non-vegans feel attacked by vegans, and attack back, by threatening apathy toward the animals. Unfortunately, the animals are the scapegoats of our human conflict.

I've learned that compassion for all animals, non-human and human, is a crucial and helpful attitude that can prevent the shooting of the messenger.

The message is valid. Animal welfare and anti-cruelty are vital. So, how do we say this, do this, and not create circumstances in which the messenger is shot and the message lands on deaf ears? How do we keep accusations out of the equation of animal welfare and compassion for all living beings?

I've thought about this a lot over the years, since I care about animals and don't want them mistreated, misunderstood for the sentient beings they are, or slaughtered. All of this is atrocious to me. I can't block it out, and often think about their plight.

One thing I've discovered about people is that they have a hard time dealing with shame and guilt. Humans will go out of their way to avoid these unpleasant emotions, even at the cost of animals and their welfare. In order for meat-eaters to continue eating animals, they need to block the horrors that occur in factory farming, or remain wilfully ignorant of them. And they can get defensive, thinking vegans are personally attacking them by providing vegan lifestyle options.

I've found that "plant-based diet" seems to be the less threatening term for the masses than "vegan." Somehow, the term "vegan" can really incite anger and animosity. I knew there must be another way to convey compassion without creating a conflict.

Years ago, I discovered that by just starting up a no-blame conversation about animal rights could be very helpful. It could help create a foundation for providing information and planting the seeds of transformation gently and respectfully.

Because I believe there's such a need for compassion when having these activism conversations, I created my own personal term for it: "conversational activism." I hoped this concept – rooted in compassion and persuasion – would serve the cause of helping the voiceless animals without offending humans.

I remember when I took Ito into Stephanie Beeley's professional photo studio, along with a friend's six-month-old pet pig named Annie. I brought vegetables, including kale and carrots, and had Ito and Annie face the camera, eating peacefully. I borrowed an already-existing headline I saw on animal welfare posters on the subway saying, "Why Love One But Eat the Other?", which we later printed on 1,000 postcards and business cards featuring Ito and Anne. I felt hopeful that we could make a difference.

It was so exciting and fulfilling to carry these cards with me everywhere. I would give them out whenever people asked me about Ito, or cooed over him, saying how cute he was. This was an easy way in with strangers – an entry point where I could easily share info about animal welfare and the surprisingly easy vegan lifestyle with them.

Conversational Activism is my title for a book that's still in the works. My goal is to offer ways vegans can speak with non-vegans in a non-confrontational, non-accusatory way, and where they can inform but not offend. And another idea I've come up with for a book-in-the-works is *Humane Being*, about being more humane with ourselves, along with all living beings.

What discoveries have you made about your values and how you talk with others about them? What conversational approaches have you used for the more touchy, potentially volatile, conflictive conversations? Have they served your causes?

Chapter Five

Joyous Journeys and Celebrity Sightings

Unexpected events and auspicious adventures have always been some of my favourite moments, and have made my life feel mystical. Some involve meeting celebrities randomly, while others are sheer serendipitous moments in life. When I tell people some of my stories, they are shocked and amazed that these events and coincidences happen so frequently to me.

I've lived like this all my life – and I often meet other people who seem to have moments like these themselves, apparently by sheer chance. I don't quite understand it all. Often, I feel as if I'm led by a higher power or force: God. It's a very powerful energy that seems to guide my life, and feels quite deliberate, yet intuitive.

78.   Traveling Sooner, Rather than Later (Or it May Be Too Late)
I've always loved travelling – inside and out. Reading books that open my perspective and outlook on life is one way I have travelled "inside." And I've also enjoyed "outer" journeys that took me to many lands.

When I received an ongoing "pot of gold at the end of the rainbow" with my royalties from my *Lullababy* CD, I decided that I would use a big chunk of this money to travel. I traveled to New York, California, Hawaii and Europe, including Holland, Ireland, Germany and Switzerland. Later, I went to Thailand twice.

My travels felt like a kind of *déjà vu*, taking me back to the time when I studied flute with master teacher Geoffrey Gilbert, in Florida. Even though I was in my early twenties at the time, I felt like I was experiencing a premature retirement lifestyle. Every other car that passed me on my bike was being driven by someone with a blue hair rinse. (In fact, at the time, Florida was the state with the most pedestrian and cyclist deaths caused by cars!) I would ask myself: "Am I twenty-two or am I seventy-two?" I felt like I'd skipped a bunch of years and transported myself to a ripe retirement age and lifestyle.

After getting back from Florida, I decided to continue satisfying my travel bug. I also had a voice inside my head asking me to ponder the possibility that I may not have the opportunity or means to travel as extensively in my (real) retirement years. I decided to travel more, when I was young – and I'm glad I did. At the time, I certainly did not know about the global pandemic that would shake everyone's world in 2020 and create the Big Pause.

Despite the traditional life plans we may make – like working for a set number of years and then celebrating freedom in many ways during retirement – life often makes decisions for us. With all the best-laid plans in the world, we may find our retirement years showing up very differently than we had imagined. In my case, I had a foresight early in life to celebrate and travel early, just in case I didn't get the opportunity to do it later.

By following my heart, and benefiting from my *Lullababy* royalties, I was able to travel and experience life in ways I wouldn't have dreamed possible. I am forever thankful for that day the Solitudes label signed *Lullababy*. I'm also thankful for being in the right place at the right time to meet Keith, the producer of the CD – and for believing miracles are possible.

When have you had a foresight that encouraged you to deliberately do something earlier than you would have, normally? What decisions have you made that have served you well, due to unexpected life outcomes? What decisions will you make, knowing life is precious?

79. Head in the Clouds from the Window Seat

I seem to get my best ideas looking out of an airplane window. The fluffy, billowy clouds invite a high-altitude stream of consciousness, with thoughts floating effortlessly into my mind. This creative and inspirational "download" is one of my favourite parts of flying. I always carry a pen and paper to capture my ideas and thoughts up in the air, thousands of feet above sea level.

On one particular flight, I was on my way to Denver, to the International New Age Trade Show conference. Suddenly, I was struck by a very strong impulse to go to Maui, Hawaii. I'd never been there before, yet I had a sudden urge to go. To this day, I don't know where this inspiration had come from, but I didn't question it.

Upon arriving at the conference, I saw a couple performing music at the welcome reception on stage in the convention hall. She was a beautiful, blond woman in a colourful, tropical sarong – the type of dress you would expect on a Polynesian island – and he was tall and wiry, with curly, black hair. Their music was beautiful: sensual and dreamy—like nothing I had ever heard before. I took note of it.

The very next morning in the convention hall, I saw the same couple standing at their booth, and as I got closer to it, I was dumbfounded, since I saw that it read, "Maui Records." Apparently, they lived in Hawaii and ran a beautifully spacious retreat centre. My heart was pounding in my chest and my arms had goosebumps as I went into "ready" gear. I approached the couple, first complimenting them on their beautiful music performance the night before. Right after that, I asked them if I could be of any assistance to them at their retreat centre on Maui.

Serendipitously, they were putting on a tantra retreat in just two weeks, and asked if I could help them transcribe the workshop onto a computer for a book they were planning to write. I was poised and ready. My answer was yes. I knew I could do what they needed. With a flutist's fast fingers, I could type at eighty to ninety words per minute. I was excited to know that I could be helpful to them and satisfy my urge to go to Hawaii. It all happened so quickly. I've heard that when we want something, believe it is possible and ask directly for it – while providing support to those we ask – that something can manifest very quickly. This was living proof of it.

I've always known that if we offer our gifts and can be of value to others, wonderful symbiosis can occur. It's happened time and time again in my life. Looking back to my flight to Denver the night before, it all made sense to me now. It tied together my sudden impulse to go to Hawaii when looking out the plane window, and hearing the couple perform music at the reception, to finding – or rather, creating – an opportunity to be of service.

In a way, it seemed like an "accidental recipe" or formula for manifestation. It's not a logical process, but something more intuitive:
- Feel the impulse or calling and don't question it.
- Be with the moment and simply observe.
- When the moment is revealed, connect the dots, and simply be ready to experience the outcome and offer value. Manifestation at work, full circle.

From this experience, and later ones, I've learned that opportunities can come to life for us when we are able to contribute or add value to someone else's life. Then, our wish comes true, too. It's a win/win for everyone involved.

The beautiful Maui couple were teaching a tantra course and needed someone to transcribe notes into the computer from the recorded tapes from the classes. Easy! And my impulsive Maui wish came true: serendipity in the flow.

Self-awareness, curiosity and openness to the invisible, can offer many gifts. By trusting and allowing our life to flow and take shape organically, we can invite and experience a mystical journey. When I've been open to my soul's nudges, life has opened up magically and beautifully. There was no straining or doubting, just unfolding effortlessly and with ease.

Has there been a time in your life when you were spiritually nudged to do something that didn't have a logical basis? Did it lead you in the direction of your convictions and dreams? What did you do? Did you go for it? What will you do next time you get a nudge?

80.   Feel Your Feet: My Bamboo Forest Journey

"Feel your Feet" has remained with me ever since that exotic walking meditation through the bamboo forest on Maui. Part of the tantra retreat I was on included a full-day journey. We started with a thirty-minute silent meditation through a towering bamboo forest, and walked all the way to a quiet, dream-like oasis – where a waterfall cascaded into a private natural pool. For me, this has been one of the best lessons in mindfulness and presence—walking in silence thirty minutes through a bamboo forest!

As a flutist, I've tried playing bamboo flutes, but hadn't ever walked silently in a Hawaiian bamboo forest, complete with swaying stalks that sounded like creaking wood. It was magically immersive. I felt like I was one of the bamboo plants myself!

At the beginning of our walk, we were gently silenced with a pointed index finger to my tantra teacher's mouth, awakening our five senses to this most delicious, otherworldly experience. Back home in Toronto, my experience with meditation was at the end of yoga class, where we lay stretched out on our backs for ten minutes in *savasana*, integrating the yoga postures and awareness. Either that, or a mindfulness meditation series, focusing on the traditional Jon Kabat Zinn body-scan, and other awareness exercises.

This bamboo experience was sensational and sensorial! By focusing on our feet, we were staying "grounded." At the same time, we were in motion, surrounded and immersed in a bamboo forest, drinking in the experience with all our senses. It was both peaceful and invigorating. I was awake, yet I felt like I was dreaming. What a mixture of sensations this walking meditation offered!

After arriving at the waterfall, we all disrobed and jumped into the pool, letting the waterfall cascade over us. What an arrival after walking silently through the forest. Some of us embraced each other while others simply remained solitary and self-contained.

Now, years after the bamboo forest experience, I still return to the sensation and awareness of feeling my feet as I walk, work, or play. I can still hear my tantra teacher's voice echoing in my ear: "Feel your feet." This awareness is the foundation for developing my sense of stillness, balance and centredness.

Can you recall a time when you discovered a unique way of finding balance and serenity? How has this approach impacted you?

81. When Thank-You Notes Led Me Back to Maui

It was a cold November night in Toronto, and I had just finished handwriting twenty-six thank-you cards to my corporate clients, hoping to get them in the mail in time for Christmas. Wanting to take a break from my work, I found myself searching "Maui" apartment rentals on Craigslist. I was curious to find out how much it would cost to rent an Airbnb room in paradise. To my amazement, I found out that it would be possible to rent a room in a residential home in Lahaina for only $120 night. This would include use of the kitchen, common spaces in the house and the garden, full of fragrant plumeria trees. Also, the beach town and ocean were just a ten-minute walk down the hill from the Airbnb. Was it for real? Or was I dreaming?

Curious to find out, I decided to pick up the phone and call Maui Vacations. A very cheerful voice, belonging to Melinda, answered. From the moment I heard her say, "Aloha, Maui Vacations, this is Melinda," I knew something good was about to happen. Her voice was warm, strong and welcoming. It was only 5:30 pm there, five hours behind Toronto time. I mentioned that my call might seem out of the ordinary and unusual. She listened with open ears and an open heart. I could feel it thousand of miles away. I told her that I'd had a sudden urge to return to Maui, and wondered if I could help her at her vacation property as a barter for staying there.

To my sheer shock and thrill, I found out that her mother was coming to Hawaii shortly, and that the two of them were traveling to Kauai for a five-day holiday. She offered me a work-barter exchange for my first five days: I would take reservations over the phone for her vacation property and for the following five days, I'd pay her daily rental rate.

Perfect! It felt right. The stars were lined up and I had co-created a miracle. I booked my flight the very next day, and flew to paradise just two weeks later. From meeting Pigpig, the pet wild boar on a leash on the beach, to the astounding award-winning Peter Lik Photo Gallery, to the handsome surfer dude bartender I kissed under a moonlit sky the night before I returned to Toronto, I had the time of my life.

Have you ever had a sudden impulse that's led you to one of your most life-changing experiences? How did it occur? Have you experienced anything like this since?

82. My Knight in Shining Armour, Maui-Style

My trip to Maui in 2000 was a result of a deep instinct and intuition. Maybe it was the Law of Attraction's magnetism: If you think about something you desire with deep conviction, experiencing the emotions of it already happening, the vibrational "frequency" attracts that which you desire right back to you. But if you doubt or question the "how," this can interfere with the straight and direct path that intention to manifestation needs.

The year 2000 also brought a difficult breakup for me, so getting away from Canada seemed like a good idea. What could be better than an unexpected trip to Maui, to work at a tantra retreat? The timing was perfect. I welcomed this diversion in paradise: a week-long course I got to participate in for free, in exchange for my services transcribing it into a book.

This particular training focused on "presence" exercises, including eye-gazing exercises, open-hearted speaking, along with listening and compassion in its many forms. Many of us were single, so the emphasis was more on the ancient spiritual aspects of tantra, rather than sexual.

One highlight of this trip was being invited to play flute at a traditional tantric wedding on the beach. I'd played literally hundreds of weddings back in Canada, but this wedding was unique. Our attire was sarongs and fragrant leis, made of tuberose and plumeria flowers, around our necks, and nothing else. I remember playing flute melodies with my bare feet in the water, along the breathtaking shoreline. It was beyond romantic – complete with a breathtaking Hawaiian sunset.

After only a few days of being on Maui, I met Dennis. He was a contractor/renovator, and recently divorced. And he was gorgeous: tanned, long black hair pulled back in a surfer ponytail. Masculine, with a chiselled jaw, he looked like the Marlborough Man.

Dennis took me for dinner at an intimate and quaint bistro, looking over the splashing ocean. But all I can remember is the number of geckos, scurrying and climbing up the walls as we ate. Distracting and quite disarming for me, I tried my best to maintain eye-contact with Dennis even though the lizards were climbing the walls, non stop. Dennis was used to them, but I wasn't!

After dinner, he enticed me with a moonlight swim under the stars. There was a perfect full moon, and it was simply heavenly – the magic of Maui. This was really some date, like nothing I'd experienced before. The night was balmy, and the floral, perfumed air under the stars made this date a fantasy that had come to life. We swam in the nude in the warm, salty ocean. After being satiated with sensuality, he drove me home, saying he'd come by to pick me up the next day. I felt like I was in a dream. I hadn't experienced a date quite like this before.

The next day, as he promised, Dennis arrived at our student lodging – on a white horse. Was I dreaming or was this life on Maui? Could he have been my "knight in shining armour"? He lifted me up, helping me onto his horse, then straddled the horse himself, grabbing the reins and sitting in front of me. With my heart fluttering and my arms wrapped tightly around his waist, we joyously rode off down the lush, tropical country lane.

Since the retreat centre was actually on the rainy side of the island, this made the vegetation very rich with colour. In fact, I was told that Maui has over 144 weather systems or climates alone: warm, balmy sunny weather in one area, and only a few kilometres away, a thunderstorm. I found this utterly fascinating.

Another thing I was told was that Maui could either draw you in or spit you out very quickly, so beware of its strong energy. Many people have noticed this, and a large number of people have come to Maui for the purpose of personal healing, whether it be relationships or other losses. Others come to Maui and fall in love. While some couples arrive in love, the power of Maui's energy, some say, can break up the relationship, if that is what is meant to be. A truly electrifying experience on all counts!

My time with Dennis continued to be very magical every time we met. He told me he'd come by and get me the very next morning at 3:30 am so we could go up

Haleakala, the living volcano, at sunrise. What an adventure! I'd been up mountains in Colorado, but never volcanos in Hawaii!

The very next morning, I heard my bedroom door squeak open – and there was Dennis, sprinkling flower petals on my bedroom floor leading up to the bed, and then on my bed and pillow. He lowered himself onto me and sensually kissed me good morning. Nothing more, nothing less. No sex. Then off we trekked up the volcano, me, flute in hand, ready to serenade the morning at sunrise.

Dennis and I spent a week together at his beautiful property, complete with fruit trees, native to Hawaii. He fed me fresh strawberry papaya and passionfruit from his garden for breakfast, along with other sumptuous fresh treats. I'd never tasted such freshly picked, tasty tropical fruit!

On my parting day, Dennis put a Hawaiian lei around my neck at the airport, as we stood in line near the departure gate. The beautiful, combined fragrance of plumeria and tuberose wafted up as he kissed me goodbye. Deep down, I knew it was the last time I would ever see him. Some experiences are short and sweet. This was one of them.

It was a perfect week-long moment in time, to be cherished forever.

Fairy tales can come true. And believing they are possible is the first step. What unimaginable moments have come to life in your world? How do you think about your "fairy tale" events? Have you experienced events that seemed surreal and dreamlike to you? Has your life taken on a new significance, knowing "fairy tale moments" can exist?

83. Pigs Fly, But Do They Walk on the Beach?

In January 2013, after receiving a morning email from Toronto Pig Save – a compassionate vegan group headed up by animal welfarist Anita Krajnc – I cried, feeling what's often referred to as "survivor's guilt." Why am I able to fly to paradise and go for a morning walk along a beautiful white sandy beach on the island of Maui, while back in Canada – as well as many other places – pigs and other animals are being stuffed onto slaughter-trucks, getting nausea and hypothermia on their way to slaughter?

Yet there I was, in Maui. I felt tears running down my face as I tried to focus on the tide coming in and going out – watching the idyllic, simple scene of paddle-boaters getting their morning exercise and sunshine. I looked down, scanning for heart-shaped coral and picked them up quickly as the tide came in, offering the ocean's love symbols. I became mesmerized by the foamy ocean waters delivering more and more coral hearts.

Suddenly, my eyes wide open in shock and surprise, I found a very special and auspicious piece of coral, and held it in my palm. It had two distinctive holes in it, and was literally like the snout of a pig! I asked another early morning beach walker what she saw when she looked at the coral. Without hesitating, she shrugged, "A pig's snout." It was confirmed. This piece of coral was an auspicious symbol for sure, matching my thoughts and feelings and mostly tears.

The next thing I saw was even more unbelievable. As I continued to walk along the shore, I looked up and coming toward me was a handsome man with a companion. It wasn't a dog. As he got closer to me, I suddenly realized that it was a pig! Who's walking a pig along a beach in the early morning?

This was all too strange and mystical. I have heard of alignment of thoughts and feelings. I have also heard about the law of attraction. But this moment was truly remarkable – not only was I emotionally tuning into the slaughterhouse pigs, freezing up in Canada, and being delivered a coral to acknowledge the connection, but I was also approached by a companion pig, not more than two minutes later!

I asked the tanned man walking his pet pig if I could walk her. He hesitated, but then handed me the binder twine leash and mentioned that "Pigpig" was quite attached to him. I happily took the leash and walked along the beach with him and his curious animal companion. It felt like walking a dog, but in a very paradisiacal place, with a very unusual being.

The man started wading gently into the clear ocean and I felt Pigpig tugging on the leash, following him. I waded in with her and handed over her leash to her daddy. She was definitely attached to the man who saved her from the jaws of the pit bulls. I later learned that she was a wild boar whose destiny was a Luau feast. (Sadly, the Hawaiians use pit bulls like hunting dogs, and have their sharp jaws clamp down on the wild boars, holding them so they can be shot for luaus.)

I will never forget this fairy-tale that came to life that day on the beach in Lahaina. Was this a prompt, a sign for me to "be there" for pigs? To bring to people's attention their sentience, their plight and more?

Since then, I've played my flute for pigs at the farm sanctuary "Happily Ever Esther." I continue to connect with all farmed animals, hoping to be a voice for them. I also play for many other rescued farm animals, and am amazed with their reactions to my flute and their sheer sentience.

Do you remember any life events that felt like waking dreams? What do you believe about events in your life that seem surreal?

84. Discovering Treasures at the Maui "Sally Ann"
I like to think that I'm content with simple pleasures. Don't get me wrong, as a total Taurus, who loves to express all my senses with a sense of deliciousness, I do love beauty and the nice things in life. However, I also love the thrill of the find, and a sense of surprise and discovery. This proclivity was easily satisfied in Lahaina, the main tourist town of Maui, Hawaii – at the Salvation Army Thrift Shop!

At the time, I was staying at an Airbnb just a five-minute walk from the beach. On my daily morning walks to the beach, I would stop in at the "Sally Ann" just to see if there were any hidden treasures. There was always something that caught my eye. I knew that every day the thrill of the find always awaited me.

Tourists, who had filled their suitcases with too many boxes of chocolate-covered macadamia nuts and other souvenirs, would often drop off great straw hats and beach cover-ups, among other surprises, and the nearby pineapple farms would donate whole fresh pineapples. What a delicious treat. I loved cutting up the pineapple and walking along the beach, savouring the sweet, fresh chunks of fruit.

No matter where you are, there are always hidden treasures. For me, it was also in Lahaina, where the thrill of the find was everywhere, even at the Sally Ann! My boyfriend later joked about it, saying that I travelled over nine hours to go vintage shopping at the Sally Ann. But it was worth it every single time!

When have you discovered treasures in the least expected places? Why were these experiences so special for you?

85. Moonlit Maui and the Barefoot Bartender
I've always loved flirting with life, not just people. It's like tickling my own spirit, to do things that slightly scare me but don't hurt myself or others. It brings life to my life, itself. I think that taking bold risks is part of my DNA.

Well, this particular evening, it was my final night on Maui, and a bunch of girls and I decided to go to the neighbourhood bar for a farewell drink. The gorgeous, tanned bartender had a flirtatious smile and made the best mojitos I'd ever had. He also happened to be a mushroom farmer who smoked a lot of pot. In a way this combination made him seem even sexier. He ran his own edible mushroom business too.

I watched him mix, pour and deliver drinks with expert bartender finesse. I couldn't help myself. I wanted my last night on Maui to be truly memorable so I leaned forward across the bar and said to this handsome bartender – at least twelve years my junior – "When you finish tonight, would you like to go for a walk on the beach under the stars?" I told him it was my final night on Maui.

He leaned forward and said, "I love your directness. You get what you want when you ask directly." Needless to say, we did go for a passionate, long midnight walk under the moon and stars to complete my trip to Hawaii with a beautiful dream, experienced in my own waking life.

I'll never forget that asking directly for what we want is more likely to give us what we want, so long as we are willing to take the risk.

When have you taken a risk and were happy you did? Has this experience led you to taking more risks and being more adventurous?

86. Living the *Aloha* Spirit

My times on Maui have been truly magical. There is something about the welcoming, open-hearted, *"aloha* spirit" that really speaks to me. It's hard to describe it in words, but if I could, it would be pure love, unconditional love, and positive vibes. It feels to me like the *aloha* spirit is our natural state of being: to love and be loved. Simply put, that's it. We don't have to live in Hawaii to express the *aloha* spirit. We can do it everywhere we go. It's a state of being.

I must say that I experienced the *"aloha* spirit" everywhere I went on Maui. People walking toward you on the sidewalk actually look you right in the eyes with warmth and compassion and say, *"aloha."* What a refreshing greeting.

Aloha is an essence of being: peace, compassion and mutual understanding of respect. In Hawaiian, *"alo"* means presence, front face; and *"ha"* means breath. So *aloha* is the presence of (divine) breath – and the word can be used to mean hello, goodbye, love, and many other things. *Aloha* also means living in harmony with the people and land around you, with mercy, sympathy, grace and kindness.

I try to bring the *aloha* spirit to my life, even though I live on what Hawaiians call "the Mainland" (North America). I try to offer my heart, my ears, my compassion as best I can. It can be a challenge sometimes, but somewhere, deep down, I still feel and carry and express the *aloha* spirit.

Different cultures can bring unique experiences into our lives that we may not have otherwise experienced. Have you had an experience away from home, or your accustomed way of being that brought you insight, peace or a new perspective on life? What was remarkable about it for you?

87. Returning the Heart-Shaped Coral to Maui

I loved my trips to Maui. So magical: that moonlit walk along the beach with the handsome bartender, that night before my flight home; meeting Pigpig, the rescued wild boar; walking along the beach every morning; plus all the other delicious moments Maui offers. I remember being awestruck by the beauty of Australian award-winning photographer Peter Lik's photography at his gallery on the main drag in Lahaina, the upscale tourist town where people from the "mainland" (North America) would often fly in for the weekend to purchase art. Even Sir Anthony Hopkins had his art displayed in a Lahaina gallery, along with Andy Warhol and other famous people.

There was a casual ease here – a beach-town sensibility combined with a hushed and discreet affluence. You could walk down Church St in Lahaina with a fresh fruit smoothie and go into a gallery, (smoothie left at the entrance), and purchase a piece of art for hundreds of thousands in your Hawaiian shirt, shorts and sandals! The casual nature of the town combined with fine art was unique to me. The only other time I experienced this casual easefulness was in Santa Fe, where art gallery owners would greet you with, "Are you collecting this weekend?" There was a discreet assumption that you were in for the weekend to buy and collect art. I was just there to enjoy the art.

Back to Hawaii: Bliss and beauty abound on Maui – and so does the range of lifestyle and holiday options. I've heard so many people say, "My big dream is to go to Hawaii, but it's so expensive." This perceived limitation of money has prevented so many from experiencing Hawaii on their terms.

I, on the other hand – always looking for possibilities and unexpected opportunities – stayed for $120 US at a bed-and-breakfast just ten minutes from the ocean. Maui was a possibility for me to enjoy at the price point I could afford. We can all enjoy Maui if we stay open to miracles!

One thing I did (but knew deep down I shouldn't have) was collect coral – heart-shaped, in particular – from the ocean, and bring it back to Canada with me. It seemed so magical: the tide would come in and flush out beautiful pieces of coral, almost like it was personally delivering it to me on a "sandy beach platter."

But I'd heard that in the Hawaiian tradition it's bad luck to collect coral and take it out of the ocean, and even take it home. I did, and some strange things did happen to me during this period that I wonder may have been attributed to my Hawaiian coral collection. I took the possibility seriously.

On my next visit to Hawaii, about five years later, I dumped it back into the ocean. This trip I had a very different experience from before. Pigpig was dead. She had been hunted down by some native Hawaiians who roast wild boars for their luaus. The restaurant where I'd met the handsome bartender was boarded up, and when I asked people if they had seen him, I was told he had moved an hour away to Paia. Everything had changed. It was a dark experience of Maui this time, enshrouded by horrific events.

One night, I was suddenly awakened to the sound of a girl pleading with a guy in a car outside my window to not hit her. I thought I was dreaming, but it was very real, right outside my Airbnb window. I felt scared – terrified, in fact. Right at this moment, Maui lost its magic for me.

I've noticed that life events are never the same. In fact, if you chase down a memory to bring it back to life, it never turns out quite the same. I do believe, however, that we can visualize and manifest our dreams. But can we replicate a moment in time? I believe no experience can be duplicated.

Have you had a peak experience, that when you tried to repeat it, was the opposite? How do you look at this phenomenon? Life never being repeatable exactly?

88. How Spa-la-la Met Baden-Baden

Some places in our lives leave indelible prints in our minds and hearts. For me, the German spa-town of Baden-Baden was such a place. When I visited in 1997, I fell in love with the town, and the pure self-care it provided. After all, it was a town full of mineral-water spas: deliciously decadent, while at the same time a normal German custom, not reserved for luxury, necessarily.

Fortunately, John (my pianist-music partner) and I were invited to do a concert in Baden-Baden. That gave us a professional reason to be there – and to luxuriate in the water-therapy when our work was done. What a treat!

Literally translated, Baden-Baden means "bath-bath." What was so beautiful was the variety of mineral baths, all with different temperatures, some with waterfalls to stand under, others with whirlpools, sauna and steam baths, and were always clothing optional. Most people enjoyed the freedom of their birthday suits – and I was one of them. Not only were the mineral baths so therapeutic and healing, but their smell was deliriously divine.

I didn't know at the time that I would some day have my own recording company called Spa-la-la. But five years after my unforgettable Baden-Baden experience, a friend of mine suggested the name "Spa-la-la" as an appropriate name for my new business. With Spa-la-la, I have offered flute and mixed instrumental CDs, voice-over meditations for relaxation, sleep, and stress management, "Spa-on-the-Canvas" paintings and various communication trainings.

In many ways, Spa-la-la was inspired by the sense of freedom and boundlessness my experience in Baden-Baden gave me.

What special moments have contributed to making you a happier person, and guided you to doing specific things with your life, due to these experiences?

89. "An Elephant Never Forgets" Led to an Experience I'll Never Forget

Visiting my guitarist-boyfriend in Bangkok in 2006 was the beginning of an adventure I hadn't anticipated. My boyfriend had been invited to perform music in the five-star Mandarin Oriental Hotel's posh dining room every night with a female jazz singer. It was January and the holiday parties I played in Toronto were over. January was here and I had a whole month with no work. So, off I went to visit my boyfriend – and unbeknownst to me at the time, meet some gentle giants who seemed to love the flute!

Bangkok was only a thirty-minute flight away from Chiang Mai, a city in northern Thailand and home to a beautiful sanctuary called Elephant Nature Park. Here, elephants live their lives out in this safe, forever home of grassy land, never to perform tricks again, be ridden, or abused. I was so excited to visit the elephants, so I took the short flight to Chiang Mai.

As we drove into this breathtaking elephant sanctuary, with its green rolling hills, and adult and baby elephants galore, a petite Thai woman greeted us. I immediately learned that it was she who ran this remarkable sanctuary. She must have stood four foot ten, with long, straight black hair down to her waist, and had a confident, commanding, yet sweet Thai voice.

Elephants are very intelligent – and as the saying goes, "an elephant never forgets," whether it is something bad or something good. It's also said that elephants are the fourth most intelligent mammals, after humans, chimpanzees and dolphins. I really question whether we humans should take first place, since we can be so inhumane, cruel, and often lack both IQ and EQ.

At the sanctuary, I learned some very interesting facts: that elephants eat grass sixteen hours a day, and sleep eight hours a night standing up. They are gentle giants – vegans. Who would imagine that such an immense being only consumes grass? I was overjoyed knowing this. It also helped me to see their deep gentleness even further! As George Bernard Shaw says, "I choose not to make a graveyard of my body with the rotting corpses of dead animals." Neither do elephants, such magnificent creatures.

Sadly, I also learned about the *mahut* training, which essentially was a "breaking of the spirit," usually used on baby elephants: they are isolated in a cage, beaten and not fed until their spirits are broken. This produces a sense of ongoing fear and obedience toward humans. With the elephants in this state, people would exploit them in the name of tourism. I believe no elephant really enjoys painting with its trunk, carrying tourists on its back or performing. They do it to avoid further beating and abuse.

I had taken my flute to Thailand, and packed it on my trip to Chiang Mai. Playing music for elephants would be a first for me! I prepared to play flute in the open field for a beautiful, seventy-two-year-old female elephant! She was missing an eye, due to past abuse. It was so sad to imagine someone doing something to this gentle and magnificent creature. There I stood in the open field, about ten feet in front of her as she grazed peacefully. I felt tiny in comparison to her, since she stood about seven feet tall.

I was eager to play for her and see what reaction I would get. I started playing a cheerful, upbeat Mozart piece in a higher register. Suddenly, the petite Thai sanctuary guide cautioned me: "Don't play high notes. The elephants don't like this. Play lower notes, or she may charge you." My heart leapt up into my throat and I couldn't breathe for a second. The reality hit me: I could be in a very compromising position, standing in front of a potentially perturbed elephant! I could be trampled, if I'm not careful.

I paused, took a deep breath, gathered myself and asked her, with a trembling voice, "What do you do if an elephant charges you?" She calmy and deliberately answered, "Run in the direction toward the elephant, and run past her. Since it takes her so long to turn around and chase you, this is better than running away from her. They can run very fast."

It all made logical sense, since these huge mammals would definitely take some time to do a 180-degree turn – but it seemed like a counter-intuitive move if you were actually confronted with this situation. Who would immediately think of running toward a charging elephant? I wouldn't, that's for sure!

I remained calm, and brought my flute playing down two octaves to the "elephant register" (as I now call it). I started to hear a slight low rumbling sound coming from the elephant. I quietly and respectfully backed away from her, flute in hand, and gently walked away with the Thai guide, knowing I was safe with her, she being an elephant behaviour veteran and elephant welfarist. She knew them inside out, and they trusted her, from her voice tone to her actions.

When I returned to Canada from Thailand in 2007, I started to put on "themed" elephant fundraisers. The first was a miracle in collaboration, intention and creativity. I rented the Church on Berkeley, a heritage building in downtown Toronto. Reaching out to my musician friends, two of whom were sound-healers, and together we put on an amazing concert and gathering. About 150 people showed up after hearing the "buzz" through three different community leaders on social media.

At one point in the evening, I invited all of the audience to lie down on their backs as six digeridoo players weaved around them, playing low tones, resembling the rumbling sounds of elephants. It was my intention through sound and imagination, to invite the elephants into the event.

Next, we did a jazz fundraiser at a hydroponic sprout farm in Toronto. It was a fitting location, since elephants eat so much grass. It was fun to have jazz music fill the fragrant indoor sprout farm, and to envision the elephants with us, dining on their favourite greens.

And the third fundraiser was presented in a beautiful Toronto yoga studio. Here again, a sound-healer friend set up his many instruments, and I accompanied him in an improvised manner on my flute. There were tealights lining the room, and the flickering light added to the delicate, prayerful atmosphere.

These three events were my way of helping the plight of the elephants in Thailand. I have never forgotten them, years later and so many thousands of kilometers away. As the saying goes, "An elephant never forgets" and I say, "So let's never forget the plight of the elephants." Elephants have forever lived in my heart.

When has your life taken on a deeper, more global meaning – and what impact did this have? How have specific events in your life given you a different perspective? How has this shaped you?

90.   "Follow Your Nose," All the Way to Switzerland

One thing I love to do is "follow my nose." I heard it for the very first time from my then-boyfriend Jon, in 1995, who encouraged me to be curious, explore and be adventuresome. He was a traveler, diver, songwriter/musician who lived by this philosophy himself.

"Follow your nose" really seemed to suit this perspective. I loved the way I felt around Jon – a sense of moment to moment living. A fullness and fulfillment I hadn't yet fully discovered until I spent time with Jon. I was always a spontaneous and intuitive person, but the idea of "following my nose" became a new way of *really* living.

Especially, when I'm traveling, I am often reminded of this way of being and experiencing life. I got to do this very thing when I was in southern Germany, in a very small town, called Lörrach, where a famous flute-maker lived. After visiting his home and trying out a host of beautiful flute head-joints, I ventured off to the closest Swiss town, Basel, right at the Swiss-German border. Silly me – I forgot my passport at the German hotel, and had to ask the cab driver to return me there when I was refused entry into Switzerland. Fortunately, it was only a ten-minute cab ride!

I rode the tram (which is like a North-American streetcar), looking out the window, and deciding when to get out and walk, by simply following my nose. When the tram reached a nearby square, I got off and started wandering around the street, window-shopping.

In Switzerland at the time, almost all women seemed to wear silk scarves casually and elegantly with their jeans and navy blazers. I guess it was a Swiss fashion thing. As I strolled down the narrow cobblestone street, I saw beautiful scarves in one store window and decided to go inside. I was on a mission to fit in here and dress like a Swiss woman. So I purchased a beautiful, handcrafted yellow, blue and white silk neck scarf. Satisfied with my purchase, as I was about to leave the store, I spotted a second floor and felt compelled to venture upstairs. Again, I was following my nose.

It was here that I laid my eyes on a human masterpiece. His name was Martin Interweiss, and he was a sales associate in this Swiss boutique. I'd never seen such a beautiful human specimen in my life before! He offered to assist me with navy blue blazers, and I tried on an elegantly tailored, form-fitting one. As he stood behind me with his large, smooth hands on my shoulders, assisting me with the blazer fitting, I felt a waterfall of perspiration cascade instantly down both sides of my body, landing on my waist. I was so embarrassed, and hoped he hadn't noticed my involuntary response to his sheer beauty. My perspiration had a mind of its own!

The blue blazer was a size too big, but he offered order me one in a smaller size from the Paris location. I passed on this generous offer – and he asked for my number instead. We spent a week together, touring around his hometown of Basel. He drove fast like most Swiss and Germans, and I'll never forget the tunnel – the longest tunnel in Switzerland – that took twenty minutes to drive through. (Being claustrophobic didn't make me a good match for this tunnel adventure.)

Martin had distinctively Swiss ways. He often used the word "perfect." (The Swiss are impeccable and perfectionistic, so "perfect" is a suitable word.) I would ask him questions, and he would answer with his simple and predictable response, "perfect." Sometimes he would even invent words to describe things. One word he invented was a way of describing me, and I took it as a compliment. He said I was expressive and emotional, and, as he put it, "feelful." I will never forget his beautiful expression. (Although this word doesn't exist in any English dictionary, there's a real German translation for it: "gefühlvoll," meaning "full of feeling.")

I returned to Canada, like stepping out of a European fairy-tale, forever changed by my experience in Switzerland. About one month later, as my birthday approached, a big box was delivered to my address. There were Swiss postage stamps all over it. I knew that it must be from Martin. I eagerly opened it, and inside was that beautiful navy-blue blazer, ordered from Paris, and sent to me in Toronto. What a memorable birthday! I'd never experienced such a surprise by air mail before or after that time. I wore the blazer often, cherishing our memories together.

Sadly, only a few years later, I received a call from Switzerland, from Martin's best friend. The quiver in his voice spoke of a tragedy I was about to hear about over the phone. Martin had died as a result of a serious mountain-climbing adventure gone wrong. He was only thirty. Time stood still. In this moment, I reminded myself about how fragile life can be. "Feelful Martin" remains in my heart forever.

Have you had a remarkable and memorable experience on your travels that has stuck with you for years? Did you stumble upon it? What did you experience? How has it affected your life?

91. No Guard Rails, No Licence

I never did get around to applying for my driver's licence. When I was eighteen, I went to driving school for just one week, but quit after watching dangerous, spine-tingling videos about hydroplaning. My fear of driving increased when I considered the carelessness of many drivers, and I opted out of pursuing my driver's license. Instead, I chose public transit as my usual mode of transportation, and when I needed a drive somewhere out of city limits, I either took a taxi or carpooled.

Back in the early '90s, I was dating a special guy in California near Santa Cruz. I spent so much time visiting him that I actually had a business card printed with both my Toronto and his California addresses on it! I felt "cool" having a California address on Seascape Ridge – and I wasn't even a bona-fide Californian citizen.

We would often take drives up to "the city," as he and many Bay-Area Californians call San Francisco. It took just over an hour on Pacific Coast Highway. I loved calling it "the PCH," like the rest of the Californians. My friend Russell trusted me driving his new Audi, even though I told him I didn't have a license.

What a thrill this was! There were no guard rails, and the corners were sudden and sharp. But, at the same time, I asked myself, "Do I have a death wish?" I'll never know, since I was so absorbed in the adrenalin rush. I was amazed by the exquisite, picturesque drive – perhaps best known for the narrow and graceful Bixby Creek Bridge that's often featured in car commercials.

One day, on our way to the city, we were making a quick and sharp turn around the corner on Pacific Coast Highway, and suddenly we saw a huge transport truck barrelling around the corner, towards us! I gasped and prayed for the best. What a close call! In a matter of seconds, the Pacific Ocean almost became our destination.

Why did I choose to take such a huge risk, endangering my life and Russell's, too? Was I being a reckless thrill-seeker? To this day, I don't know. All I *do* know is I had fun – and was graciously spared death.

Do you have a thrill-seeker gene in you? Has there been a time in your life when you have you taken a risk, that was both exhilarating but dangerous? Have you done it again? What have you learned from it?

92. Tram Scam in Amsterdam

I was warned by well-meaning friends to be very careful on the trams in Amsterdam. There was a lot of pickpocketing, and tourists were often the main targets for this. I appreciated my friends' concern, but got on the plane anyway, anticipating a phenomenal adventure ahead of me.

It was my very first trip to Amsterdam. Having heard so much about it, I was thrilled to be able to visit this cool city, although briefly. I was there on a stop-over to Dublin, Ireland, where I would meet a close friend and have a three-week holiday, visiting the lush green Irish coast by car for the very first time.

Deciding to be a typical tourist, I visited one of the classic Amsterdam "coffee shops" – which really weren't just coffee shops, but places where you could order from the marijuana menu: different types, from all over the world. If you didn't like to smoke it, another option was tea that gave you a sort of "body buzz," very different from smoking cannabis.

Since I abhorred the smell of marijuana, and because I'd had a dizzying experience with it a few years back, I decided to opt for the tea. It seemed a much tamer option. I sat on a bar stool, sipping my special tea, for the very first time. It surprised me by giving me a smooth but intense body buzz! Nothing I'd ever quite experienced before.

They say you can get the munchies with marijuana, and I sure did. It was dinner time, so I got on a tram and found a nice little Italian restaurant nearby. Alone, I ordered a delicious pasta meal and indulged in people-watching in my gently drugged state. After all, it was Amsterdam, and being stoned with a body buzz is acceptable there.

What wasn't acceptable to the restaurant owner was my inability to pay the bill. I rummaged around in my tote bag, but my wallet and passport were missing. There was a panic brewing deep down inside me, but I was too shocked and stoned for it to rise to the surface. I explained to the restaurant manager that my wallet had been stolen – and he boldly slammed the front door of the restaurant and locked it! I guess he didn't want me to escape without paying! "I'm calling the police!" he yelled, in a very accusatory tone. Instead of being insulted by his remark, I replied, "Please do. Someone has stolen my wallet and passport."

What seemed like an hour later, and after being made to feel like an utter criminal, I was taken away in a Dutch police car to the closest police station. I felt a mix of emotions: shamed, scared, but also very relieved that I was going to be helped by the Amsterdam police.

When I got to the station, I was greeted by a six-foot six, blond-haired, blue-eyed "movie-star gorgeous" Dutch police officer. He escorted me to his private office, gestured me to have a seat, then, slickly put his feet up on his desk, ankles intertwined, and matter-of-factly offered me a cigarette. "You smoke?" asked, with a cigarette bobbing in his mouth. "I will today," I sheepishly muttered. I don't think I've ever seen a sexier moment in a movie. Next, he uttered one word, "Coffee?" with his alluring Dutch accent. I humbly accepted, secretly in awe of what was unfolding in this real-life movie!

My Dutch police crush arrived back, a coffee in each hand from the coffee dispenser. The coffee was strong, intense and better than any coffee I'd ever had in Canada, including coffee from Italian cafes!

He filled out a report for my lost wallet and passport, and everything was resolved in due time. (It's funny, but I don't even remember the details – perhaps the marijuana tea lasted longer than I thought.) All my valuables were returned to me, and off I went to continue my adventures – without another visit to an Amsterdam "coffee shop."

It all worked out in the end. Three days in Amsterdam. Being high on marijuana tea led me to scrumptious pasta and an unforgettable trip to the police station.

Can you remember a time when things seemed to go wrong, but suddenly the silver lining appeared, and you wouldn't trade this scene in your life for anything?

93. When My Hug Was Shrugged in the Red-Light District

There is no place quite like Amsterdam. It's definitely one of my favourite cities, and I love the people. They're so confident and direct, and have a bold sense of humour that is unique.

One day, with the curiosity of most tourists visiting Amsterdam, I was walking through the city's infamous Red-Light District. It was like a carnival of dressed-up, vamped-up, women behind glass in their separate cubicles. Many had interesting sets and lighting, and their own seductive outfits would stop crowds.

As I walked through the district, I felt compassion for them, feeling sorry for women who have to sell their bodies for survival. I hesitated for a moment, but shortly after, I knocked on the glass window of one of the sex workers. Her cubicle was lit up in a smoldering light, red in colour, and she sat on a stool, dressed minimally. Her wild auburn hair caught the light as she kindly and curiously opened the door to her workplace. Not knowing if I should do what I planned next, I openly asked her if she would like a hug. She looked at me. I stared back openly, feeling my face blush. Had I done the right thing?

She paused and softly replied with that unmistakable Dutch accent, "Honey, I'm happily married and my husband is aware of my vocation. This is a legal service in Amsterdam, and we're all licensed. We are treated respectfully by our patrons, and police patrol the area 24/7." Again, in under five minutes, a hot flash came over me – not the menopausal type, since I was too young. It was a hot flash of embarrassment. She smiled at me affectionately and politely reached forward to swing her glass door shut. I looked at her one last time and sheepishly waved goodbye as I hurried out of the Red-Light District, having experienced enough for one day.

The awkward experience that day taught me something very important: I learned that different cultures have different customs and outlooks on many things – including prostitution. I came from Canada with a Canadian outlook. But I was still glad, in the end, that I had offered her a hug, like a good Canadian.

Has there been a time in your life when you have reached out to offer love to someone and learned they weren't suffering? What happened? Would you do it again?

94. Safe Landing In San Francisco

I was flying into the San Francisco airport and had a window seat. Usually, I prefer aisle seats, because I feel a little bit claustrophobic. But on this particular flight, I ended up by the window, since all aisle seats were taken.

Fortunately, I was seated beside a married couple, and we talked throughout the flight. I've found that it's often a hit-or-miss situation with airline dialogues. Sometimes you may not be in the mood to talk, yet your neighbour is a garrulous one. While other times, you prefer talking to pass the time, and your neighbour is reading a book or asleep for the entire flight. We've all been there.

On this occasion, I was lucky since the couple was fascinating, and our extended conversation lasted almost the entire flight, over four hours. It helped the time pass by.

All was smooth sailing, or rather, smooth flying – until my private, terrifying, moment. I was cloud-gazing out the window, when all of a sudden, I saw another plane's lights flashing right behind the wing of the plane we were on.

My seat was located over the right wing of the 747. I gasped and tried to breathe deeply. My panic was quiet and internal. No one else knew what I'd just seen: It actually looked like the plane behind us was about to crash into our plane. I felt as if I was the only witness, and had a "sneak preview" out my window. I've always disliked window seats – but this time, I was so sorry to be stuck in one!

What was I to do? Should I share the information with my flight neighbours and the flight attendants, or just keep this imminent tragedy to myself? Soon, it would all be over anyway, I thought. In the flash of a moment, I made an executive decision: I decided to keep this information to myself – and keep mass panic at bay. Soon, we'd all know about the plane behind us, since probably the pilot would make an announcement. I continued to bite my tongue and suffer in silence.

Miraculously, before I could even panic out loud, I saw the plane pass us. How was this reality possible? I was dumbfounded. Apparently, there's more than one runway at the San Francisco airport. What a relief! I'm so glad I didn't alarm my flight neighbours or the flight attendants. It all seemed to work itself out in the end.

Sometimes, I've found that it's best to sit back and observe situations in life, rather than panic or share too early. On a deeper level, we humans often fear things we imagine, but often, these things never end up materializing. In this particular situation, I was certain there would be an imminent plane crash. But that didn't happen.

At the initial time of observation and making my own premature conclusion, I didn't have enough information. I ask myself now, how many times have I panicked or braced for the worst, when those outcomes never came to fruition? It's taught me about catastrophizing and fearing the worst.

A lot of times, our anticipatory anxiety is stronger than what we're fearing. And what we fear may never come into being!

Have you ever had a scary experience that never fully came to fruition? What happened? What have you discovered about yourself? How do you deal with scary experiences now? Has your outlook changed?

95. My Accidental Twelve-Step in Santa Cruz

In the early 1990s I was in California, dating a man who lived near Santa Cruz, California. My years along the Northern California Coast were so rich with memories: salt-water air, healthy eating, birdsongs I'd never heard before, and some surfer mentality mixed in. After all, Santa Cruz has a Surfer Museum and there's some great surf there. Not a surfer myself, but one to always appreciate the exquisite statuesque form, I loved our trips to the nearby ocean. I even remember my boyfriend at the time lived on a street called Seascape Ridge.

Like a lot of West-Coasters, he was very in touch with his feelings, and also happened to be in recovery. He was a recovering alcoholic and found great peace and serenity in the weekly AA meetings. Like a lot of twelve steppers, he'd often advocate for the positive impact that regular twelve-step meetings had on his life. His life was living proof of it. He also happened to think that twelve-step programs could benefit everyone. There was Al Anon, Coda (for codependents), OA (for overeaters) and more! As a recovering alcoholic, my boyfriend spoke recovery talk often (too often, for my liking.) He even encouraged me to go to a meeting. Even though I had no substance or alcohol abuse issues, he thought it would be helpful to me, too!

One evening, I agreed to sample a meeting. He said it wouldn't matter what meeting I went to since they all followed the same format and were completely anonymous. I obliged, internally feeling a bit reluctant, but outwardly being positive and optimistic.

He drove me to downtown Santa Cruz and dropped me off at the weekly Thursday-night meeting. I felt a little uncomfortable going in, not being familiar with twelve-step programs and all. Shyly, I stood at the entrance, waiting a moment before going into the building. Standing in front of me was a tough-looking, tattoo-clad, weathered man in a leather jacket. In front of him was a bleach blond-haired woman in faded skinny jeans, with a gravelly voice, along with a bunch of beach-type Californians. This was not a glamourous lot. I felt so out of place, and wanted to leave before I even entered the building, but I mustered up the courage and went inside anyway.

After I sat down, one anonymous attendee quietly whispered to me, "Have you been to a meeting before?" I really wasn't sure what this meeting was. I soon discovered that I was at a NA meeting, Narcotics Anonymous. How shocking! I tried to stay cool and look unfettered. Then we did introductions: the usual. Each person announces their first name and follows with "and I'm an alcoholic," or in this case, "and I'm a drug addict."

When it came to my turn, I felt very strange. I hesitated, and then said, "My name is Laura, and I'm a drug addict." I didn't know what else to say. It was a lie, but seemed like the right thing to say there. (Funny how contexts in life determine what we say and do.) In a choir-like unison, the anonymous attendees all welcomed me with "Hi, Laura," as the twelve-step protocol dictates.

What an interesting, accidental experience! But I was still glad when the meeting was over. I felt very grateful to not have a substance-abuse issue. As the meeting concluded, I said goodbye as I left, knowing I would never see any of them again.

Have you ever visited a world by chance, in which you didn't belong? What learnings did you stumble upon? Was it worth it?

96. An Unexpected Opening at Letterman's Stage Door

I've always loved visiting New York. My friend, who won the green-card lottery and moved from Canada to live in New York, often let me stay for free at her place, a few blocks from Broadway and 55th Street.

It's exciting walking along Broadway with all the lights, shows and daily festivities. I truly believe that New York radiates with a sense of positive vibes and energy, since so many people love the city. T-shirts, mugs, and tourist paraphernalia all proudly boast, "I Love New York" on them – and when enough people feel this way, the city scintillates with a happy, upbeat energy: a daily celebratory vibe-like it's New Year's every day of the week.

One day on my way back home to my friend's New York apartment, I was walking down a side street, and saw a group of photographers positioned strategically by the stage door of the David Letterman show. Daily, sometime between four o'clock and 4:30, a limo would drive up and the celebrity guest would exit the car for that day's show. Even though the show is called "The Late Show", it is pre-taped at 5 pm each day.

There was always an air of excitement in anticipation of the arrival of the star. It could be an actor, a sports celebrity, a politician, and others. There was a hush in the air before the limo pulled up to the stage door. As soon as the star exited the car, the fans would cheer enthusiastically, and some would even get photos and autographs, if they could make it past the bodyguards and tight security.

Always up for an adventure, I decided it would be fun to hire a videographer to follow Ito (my little blond Pomeranian) and me throughout New York for three days, visiting the tourist attractions and just being New Yorkers. I figured one of the photographers would know a videographer for hire. So, I asked one of the paparazzi if he or a friend could help me with my little "pet project." He quickly texted his videographer friend, and within a minute, the videographer confirmed that he could do it.

What a thrill! My pet project was on.

For the next three days, I adventured in the Big Apple with Ito and the generous videographer. I mean generous since he agreed to help, while being super-busy with other film projects, generous since he gave me a flat rate that was very reasonable for three days, and generous since it was an endeavour that lit me up, but may not have been his cup of tea. He was a pro and it was just another paid gig for him, *but it was a dream come true for me.*

We made a short film called *Ito in New York*. It was a pure passion project. From Ito riding in a bicycle-pulled cart to being on a New York City Policeman's horse in Central Park, to sitting in a barbershop chair in the upscale Columbus Circle Shopping Centre, we had the time of our lives! Ito and I definitely painted the city red!

I've always loved David Letterman and, in a way, he had an indirect part in the making of my film. Because of this special stage-door experience, I got to use one of the paparazzi's videography services!

Can you recall a time when you have experienced pure joy, adventure and spontaneity in your life and just went with it? Who were you with? What happened? What was the best part of the experience?

97. My Story on a New York Corner: Meeting Tony Bennett

New York is full of surprises. In fact, isn't there an expression that says, "There's a story on every corner?" Well, this story is a personal one, and was on a New York corner, too.

I was walking down Fifth Avenue, enjoying the fresh, crisp spring air. The pulse of the city was intoxicating. I felt a sense of wonder just being in New York. You don't have to be doing anything in particular in New York – just being there can uplift you and give you a buzz.

I was simply standing on the corner of Central Park South and Fifth Avenue, and casually looked around as I waited for the light to change to green. Right there beside me, in broad daylight, was one of my all-time favourite jazz singers: Tony Bennett! He was waiting to cross the street, too.

I was amazed. Feeling a bit shy, but mostly excited, I introduced myself, telling him how much I loved his music. He was incredibly gracious and very handsome. Out of his lips came the words, "Where are you from, Sweetheart?" with that charming signature Tony Bennett voice of his. I blushed a bit, since he was such a hero of mine. We crossed the street together, he wished me a great time in New York with his velvety voice, and we parted ways with a smile.

I walked down Fifth Avenue, past all the fancy designer boutiques, window shopping, carrying a secret grin all day long, from my chance meeting with Tony Better, a person I so admired. Nothing mattered but that moment – a perfect moment on a sunny spring day in New York.

Since that day, whenever I've listened to Tony Bennett CDs, I always remember that chance meeting, and feel a sense of joy and wonder.

Have you ever casually bumped into someone you've admired when you least expected it? What did you say? What did you do?

98. Ray of Light and Wisdom from Ray Bradbury

I was in Los Angeles for a conference. and unbeknownst to me, I stumbled into the wrong conference room: a writer's workshop with the legendary science-fiction author, Ray Bradbury. He must have been about eighty-five years old at the time, and he was in a wheelchair.

He had short, thick, stubby fingers, and he spoke with remarkable simplicity and bold honesty. He said, "If you want to be a writer, you have to write every day." I looked at his thick digital instruments, those fingers of his, somewhat in awe, knowing that they had helped him write many bestsellers for over half a century. He still used a typewriter, which seemed to suit this elderly literary genius.

I also remember his saying that we even practise writing by doing our daily emails. This made sense to me. I suppose we all practise our writing by simply composing or replying to emails. That's a form of writing practice, for sure!

As he wheeled out of the room following his talk, I felt a deep sense of nostalgia. I couldn't believe what had just happened: I'd just met one of the science-fiction greats of all time! The combination of his dedication to writing daily, his straight-shooter advice and his wheelchair made him both charming and endearing.

I can say that Ray Bradbury was one of the humblest men I've ever met. There's something so admirable about a talented genius who offers his fans pure, simple advice that works. And I feel so touched and privileged having had the chance to meet such a legend.

Can you remember a time you met a wise elder, who impressed you so much? What stood out for you? How has your life been positively influenced by this chance meeting?

99. Standing Up to Jerry Seinfeld

I never knew that if you find yourself with a bunch of costumed performers, life can open up doors for you in spades!

A friend of mine was one of a group of tarot-card readers, hired by an event planner for a very high-end gala dinner at Toronto's Metro Convention Centre. It cost approximately $1,000 per person to attend this well-heeled charity event, all for a worthy cause. This included a full meal, dessert and a celebrity for after-dinner entertainment. There must have been over 1,000 people at this prestigious soirée.

What I found even more fascinating was being invited by my tarot-card reading friend to discreetly accompany him and the other readers to the dining area. They were hired to provide card readings at the tables between courses for the wealthy, philanthropic guests. The tarot readers huddled on the sidelines, waiting for the waiters to clear the dishes between courses. Hushed conversation, magical costumes and a sense of anticipation filled the air, as I waited with them.

The only difference was I wasn't one of the readers.

I was the opportunist, invited to wait to hear the keynote speaker (for free, so long as I wasn't caught), who would be on stage after dinner. I was willing to endure the long waiting period: after all, the entertainment was stellar.

It was the legendary Jerry Seinfeld – the king of stand-up comedy. I'd been his fan for over thirty years, watching every possible episode of the TV series *Seinfeld*, at least three times or more. Never having seen him do his stand-up routine live, I was in for a big treat.

Yet, at the same time, I felt self-conscious and out of place. I quietly eyed my escape route, knowing that I might have to leave before the show ended. I surveyed the area for elevators – hopefully a service elevator, so that I could be less conspicuous.

As he finished his hour-long comedy routine, followed by numerous standing ovations, I quickly dashed over to the service elevator, as discreetly as I could. It was tucked away about 100 meters from the dinner reception. There was no time to waste. I pressed the button immediately, hoping to get on before anyone saw me make my timely escape. From the corner of my left eye, I saw two men off in the distance coming my way. It seemed like they might be approaching the service elevator, too. I froze in my tracks, distracted by my racing heart.

As they got closer, I saw an elegant orange silk tie that I recognized from earlier. I couldn't believe my eyes: It was Jerry Seinfeld and his manager, also making their own discreet getaway, before the crowd approached them. The service elevator seemed to be the best escape vehicle for all of us. Yet it took so long to arrive – seconds crawled along like hours. I was really beginning to perspire now.

I smiled bashfully and uttered a compliment to Jerry, "You were amazing." He quietly thanked me and avoided any further eye contact. He actually seemed shy! When the elevator finally came, his manager officiously asked me to please step aside, and take the next elevator. Embarrassed and feeling "caught," I stepped aside. Of course, the next elevator came immediately, and no one saw me come or go.

I will never quite know why I was asked to take the next one. Did I look dangerous? Or did I just look like I didn't fit in with the well-heeled crowd? An hour-long stand-up by Jerry Seinfeld was worth the embarrassment I experienced in unexpectedly meeting him at the service elevator!

Have you ever experienced an awkward brush with fame? What did you do? Who did you tell first? What part of this event is most memorable for you?

100. Liza and Me: Meeting My "Twin," Twice

All my life I've been told that I look so much like the actress Liza Minnelli, and that I even have a similar personality. She has sported a short, dark-haired, spiky and fun haircut most of her life – and so have I. I've loved Broadway musicals, and have sung in a few in public school. So has she, but on the Broadway stage: *Cabaret*, and more. Her mom, Judy Garland, even had a dog named Toto in the movie *The Wizard of Oz* – and I had my dog, Ito, in my real-life "movie"!

Well, one typical day in Toronto at my office for Montage Music, I was wearing a short black t-shirt, along with black tights, and my hair was spikey. I didn't have to get "dolled up" just yet, since my cocktail music gig was five hours away. Most of the time, black-tie cocktail dress code was a must for our cocktail reception engagements.

This particular gig was at Toronto's Sutton Place Hotel – an elegant, upscale hotel in downtown Toronto. When I arrived, I surveyed the marble-floored lobby: lavish, floral-scented, with bouquets scattered around, and politely officious front-desk clerks. From the corner of my eye, I spotted someone that seemed to be my *Doppelgänger*! I couldn't believe what was before my eyes. It was *the* Liza Minelli getting onto the elevator, dressed in a black t-shirt and black tights! – embracing a "Toto" dog (like the terrier in *The Wizard of Oz*). I really had to do a double-take. Yes, it definitely was Liza Minelli, and yes, people were right: we definitely looked alike.

The next time I brushed up with her was in New York City, on one of those amazing Thursday-night art gallery reception tours. From six to eight o'clock, many galleries would open their doors for receptions, complete with wine and nibbles, welcoming in tourists, New Yorkers and potential art buyers.

It was a cold, rainy, windy night, and I had my ever-present Pomeranian pal, Ito, with me in an airline-approved carrier. I figured, so long as he is approved on planes, carrying him into a gallery like this should be fine, too – and it was!

The unfortunate thing was I got to the art gallery tour at 7:45, and there were only fifteen minutes left. At the first gallery I entered, they were completely out of wine. That was a deal-breaker for me. What's a gallery reception without a glass of wine in your hand? We scuttled off to the next gallery and ran in from the rain. This one was more welcoming and offered white and red wine on trays as we entered. I grabbed a red; Ito was offered a fresh bowl of water.

As I shook off my umbrella and stepped in, I heard a woman's voice behind me. It was strangely recognizable, which I found uncanny. I turned around, and there she was again, for the second chance meeting in my life: Liza Minelli. What a serendipitous meeting with my look-alike!

It all felt so natural yet surreal, at the same time. I introduced myself, and shared with her that all my life people told me I resembled her, so much so that I could be her sister, (actually, her daughter, but thought I would play it safe with Liza's showbiz and female sensibilities). She took a good look at me, and said, "Oh, yeah, I can see it – our hair is identical." She smiled warmly and then she introduced me to her then-boyfriend. I felt honoured: Liza Minelli speaking with me and introducing me to her date. Wow!

I politely walked away to one of the salons to see the art. As soon as I entered the room, my knees started shaking uncontrollably! I had a delayed reaction: I was starstruck by Liza. I've only one other time had such a moment: when I ended up on a river boat in Thailand outside the Mandarin Oriental Hotel with Sasha Baron Cohen and his then-fiancée, Isla Fisher. Coincidentally, Sasha's movie, "Borat", had just come out, and I had purchased a pirated copy at one of Bangkok's night markets just the day before. I was flirting with the idea of asking him to autograph it, but thought that might be too cocky, taking adventure a little *too* far.

Have you ever been starstruck by a movie star or any type of celebrity? What happened and how did you respond? Were you surprised by anything about them? Were you alone or was someone with you who witnessed it?

101. A Kodak Moment with Susan Sarandon

The Toronto International Film Festival has always provided me with a way of traveling the world without leaving home. I mean this in two ways: You attend films by international filmmakers, offering you a glimpse into their world, both geographically and philosophically; and you also get to meet people in person, in line-ups, following the screening and during the after parties.

One particular screening, I will always remember. That's because it was the night I accidentally dropped a Kodak Instamatic camera on Susan Sarandon's foot – on the top of her foot, with all the tiny little sensitive bones.

The strap on my camera had suddenly broken and that's why it landed accidentally on her shoe. She was a star in the TIFF screening we had just seen, and I saw her come out of that special section of the theatre where the film cast and crew were seated. Turning red with shame and embarrassment, I apologized sheepishly.

Susan was so gracious, but hopping up and down on one foot, in pain. In that moment I realized that we are all human, whether we are stars, celebrities or not. A camera on the foot is painful to anyone – what was remarkable to me was how kind and forgiving she was. Some stars may have wielded their celebrity status, shaming the person causing this accident. I felt blessed and impressed!

Have you had a brush with fame or celebrity? Was it awkward, painful or otherwise? What did you discover about yourself and that particular person that you may not have known before you had that encounter?

102. Alec Baldwin, Renée Fleming, Lang Lang: My Escape from the After Party

There are some moments in life when you're in the wrong place, but at the right time. Well, such an occasion happened in my own life when I was attending a special fundraiser in New York City's Carnegie Hall. Alec Baldwin was the host of the evening – and a spectacular evening it was! I had bought a rush ticket in the lobby of Carnegie Hall that morning, where I had to wait in line two hours before the box-office opened. It was definitely worth it. The acclaimed American opera singer Renée Fleming sang, along with the Chinese master pianist Lang Lang. In fact, it was Lang Lang's thirty-fifth birthday that day. And of course, it was a sold-out show: standing ovations galore.

Knowing that Alec Baldwin was married to a yoga teacher, Hilaria, who was both a vegan and animal welfarist, I decided to deliver a package backstage for him. It contained photos of my beloved Pomeranian, Ito, with Annie the pig, taken at a photo-shoot I organized. The photo was modelled on a Toronto-based subway-poster campaign: "Why Love One but Eat the Other?" I directed a photo-shoot where six-month old Annie was positioned beside Ito, eating carrots and kale.

After the concert was over, I went backstage again to see if Alec had picked up my package. Unfortunately, I was told that everything left with security had to be inspected, and only after that process would it be sent over to Alec. I thanked the security guard, and just as I turned to leave, there was a tall, elegant, fashionista, probably in her early eighties. She asked me if I was going to the after-party just around the corner, near Columbus Circle, in a posh condo overlooking Central Park. I said I hadn't been invited, but she swept me under her wing and asked me to come as her guest. Being a direct, straight-shooting New Yorker, she boldly told me that the beret in my hair had to go, along with my cap. She had been involved in the fashion industry when she was younger, so her advice was sound. I was completely embarrassed, still not sure it was a good idea to attend a posh party I hadn't originally been invited to.

Together, we left the crowded Carnegie Hall, as the lively audience spilled out in droves, and we crossed the street. Next, we entered the upscale, tony, condo building on 66th street.

Now, New York condos have their own distinctive breed of doormen. They are polite characters, but also very observant and protective of their tenants. I was concerned that the clothes I was wearing would be a clear sign that I didn't belong with the other guests. But, fortunately, I was ushered in without hesitation.

Trying to conceal my overt embarrassment, I discreetly got onto the elevator with my eighty-year-old new friend, some elegant guests and – of all people – Lang Lang, the star pianist, himself. I wished him a happy birthday, and told him how much I enjoyed his performance only a few minutes ago at Carnegie Hall.

When we reached the party floor, the elevator opened – and suddenly we were in a huge ballroom, full of many Asian socialites, wearing Chanel, Prada, Gucci, and the like. I saw the glamourous Renée Fleming and Alec Baldwin with his wife, Hilaria, visibly more than eight months pregnant. I made a dash for the ladies' room to fix my hair and touch up my lipstick.

Consumed with feeling awkward and out of place, since I was there with white jean bell-bottoms with thin stripes! I was the only one not wearing formal designer attire. I emerged from the ladies' room and got up the courage to head over to speak with Alec Baldwin. He was polite but curt, and had an arrogant air about him, like I'd expected. He excused himself saying they had to get home since Hilaria was pregnant and nearing her due date.

I felt sheepish, and left the party alone. What an experience, being in the wrong place at the wrong time!

Have you ever found yourself in a social situation where you felt completely out of place, yet fascinated at the same time? Where were you and what did you do?

103. Interrupted by the Queen

We've all had people put us "on hold" on the phone, since life has its unexpected interruptions. These moments are to be expected. However, I've experienced one interruption in my life that was so unusual, I love telling it.

For many years, I put together bands and chamber music groups to perform music at both corporate and social functions. I also performed in these ensembles as the flutist. This particular evening, we were invited to perform at the dinner reception of a large Shriner Conference at Toronto's Fairmont Royal York Hotel. It's well known that this is where the Royal Family members stay when visiting Toronto.

The lavish dinner had concluded, and we were putting away our instruments on stage in the grand Imperial Ballroom. The wife of the Head Shriner graciously approached us to thank us for our music performance. Unexpectedly, someone tapped her on the shoulder. She apologized for the interruption and politely excused herself, saying she had to greet the queen – Queen Elizabeth!

This is the first and only time that the Queen interrupted a conversation between a client and myself. It *was* excusable.

I quickly put my flute away in its case and discreetly hurried out of the ballroom to a crowded Royal York lobby, roped off with elegant, maroon coloured velvet rope. Surveying the lobby, there were hundreds of people on both the upper and lower levels. Suddenly I was immersed in a jungle of royal fans. I strategically planted myself behind the rope in a position I hoped would be a great vantage point to see Queen Elizabeth and Prince Philip.

I stood, waiting patiently, along with the crowd of over 400 people, for well over two hours, when they suddenly walked into the lobby. I positioned my cell phone camera up to my face – and to my amazement, they stopped right in front of me. I snapped the photo with the precision of a Swiss watch. This was the only place in the lobby they stopped and it lasted only a brief two seconds. Then, together with their security, they proceeded to the elevator and vanished.

I caught the moment: Queen Elizabeth and Prince Philip right in front of me! What a great "dessert" to follow a fancy reception at the Queen's preferred hotel. How lucky was I to be the only person she stopped in front of!

Have you ever had an abrupt interruption that turned out to being quite uncanny, unusual and unexpected? What happened? What did you do?

104. When I Met Harry at Harry's

It's funny where you will meet celebrities. I seem to have met so many of them – mostly at predictable places like fancy hotel receptions I was hired to play music at, the Toronto International Film Festival, plus many other tony venues.

This celebrity meeting was different. There I was with my jazz guitarist colleague in a high-end menswear store in Toronto, called Harry Rosen's, playing background instrumental music, to create musical ambiance. I looked up and saw a very handsome man approaching us. I did a double take. To my utter amazement, it was Harry Belafonte – at Harry Rosen's store! We were playing one of his songs, and Harry came right up to us, instantly becoming our musical coach, guiding us through his interpretation of *Jamaica Farewell*, one of his famous songs. What a remarkable moment: being in the presence of such a star, playing *his* music for *him*!

I made an effort to play with even more lilt and enthusiasm to honour Harry. He acknowledged our efforts as he walked past us, continuing his visit at Harry Rosen's.

As the British say, "He was quite the dish," and definitely looked dashing that day as he shopped for some more debonair clothes. I suppose that celebrities need to replenish their wardrobes, too!

Have you ever had a chance meeting with a celebrity? Where was it? What did you say, do? How did it feel? Did they seem like ordinary people when you met them up close?

Chapter Six

Adventuring Life

For me, life has always been an adventure, traveling through it, filled with first-time experiences, people-watching, chance meetings, and profound connections. All have been richly valuable experiences to me. And I've noticed a recurring theme in my adventures: encounters with unique individuals, deeply steeped in life's wisdom, curiosity and play. I've learned a lot from all of these people. I admire their ease at being themselves, full-heartedly and authentically.

I've also discovered things about myself, writing this memoir, Sparkle, along with creating handmade "sparkle" cards, that offer daily personalized inspirations to live by. Every single day is an adventure and a miracle to me. This journey called "life" is full of self-discoveries and unexpected surprises.

105.   Covid-19 Global Pandemic, 2020

The world was on a great pause, with lockdowns, isolation and social distancing. Borders were closed, and extreme measures were taken to deal with this unprecedented time.

At first, I was uncertain about my moves forward from day to day. But soon, I felt a delicious quietude, a spontaneous, uninvited solitude that I welcomed into my life. I slowed down, slept more, took up practising my flute three-to-five hours a day, as I used to as an eager student in my teens. I also began to paint canvases again. I was living life in real time. It became delicious, colourful, sometimes quietly emotional and other times, explosively turbulent within. The past, a memory; the future – uncertain, yet unfolding day by day, moment by moment.

Connecting with loved ones and friends took on a much greater significance, and I often arranged for coffee chats over the phone. This was deeply satisfying and connective. Personal journaling became a daily activity, and I got settled into a new way of life; a slower, more peaceful, self-reflective, inward way. The simple things took on profound meaning and value: walking my beloved dog, eating meals with my boyfriend, catching up with people I hadn't talked to in years, and calling my elderly friends regularly. We all learned a new way of keeping each other company: Covid-19 required this of us.

One of the best parts of the pandemic was Tracey Erin Smith's online Soulo Theatre classes every Friday, and her online Soulo courses. In 2012, I took her course in person, but during the Covid pandemic, I was fortunate enough to be able to do three complete online Soulo intensive courses, and performed them on Zoom for approximately 100 people each time. They were seven minutes in length, and were transformative stories told in the first-person and in the present tense, so the audience felt right there in real time. (A lot of the stories followed the "Hero's Journey" model, created by Joseph Campbell.)

It was a profound experience doing theatre on Zoom during the pandemic. At first, I was afraid to do something so personal on a digital device, but soon I got used to it. I've never been much for technology – and I found doing theatre on Zoom was definitely a growth curve for me during the pandemic!

I also enjoyed an amazing daily inspirational Facebook Live event with a spirited *and* spiritual, actor/comedienne/author, Frannie Sheridan. Her sheer joy, playfulness, humour and love added so much to this otherwise very quiet and inward period during lockdowns.

Writing this book was an endeavour I have relished and enjoyed, since my introspective headspace is so well suited to journaling and writing. Naturally being an extrovert, introversion is something I learned. I can say that going within has been a pandemic perk for me. I learned more about myself and ways of expressing myself, both as a natural extrovert and introvert in training. The term "extroverted introvert" comes to mind.

Have you experienced a time in your life when time stood still and you were called into reflecting upon what is really important to you?

106. Memoir Writing: My Life in a Book

Until I decided to write this memoir, I didn't know that I had so many life events I could talk and comment about. In a way, my memoir is made up of unforgettable moments – both positive and negative – and writing about them helps to bring the lessons I've learned up to the surface.

I started writing this book, *Sparkle*, about six months into the 2020 Covid-19 global pandemic. Thanks to the Soulo classes I took with Tracey Erin Smith, I felt very inspired to write. I enjoyed her teaching expertise and this really helped fuel my writing.

I also had so much time on my hands, since over seventy-five of my flute concerts were cancelled due to the pandemic restrictions. In a way, the timing was perfect. Ripe with ideas and steeped in contemplation and inner reflection, I felt my fertile soil was ready to bear fruit.

My flutist fingers, capable of moving quickly over the keys during technical passages, took on a new role: typing rapidly while I "downloaded" my past, almost in a stream of consciousness. I approached each story with fascination and enthusiasm as it unfolded. My fingers danced on the keyboard effortlessly, feeling like I was playing a different kind of flute: one without melody, but a deep well of feelings percolating and bubbling up from the deep well of my soul.

Writing this book couldn't have come at a better time, since somehow feeling gratitude for my life, and seeing it written on paper, helped me get through some of the more isolated times. By focusing on the positive and transformative moments in my life, rather than on what was missing, I felt renewed and motivated – even though the pandemic wasn't showing any signs of subsiding any time soon.

I ask myself, "Am I an optimist or a pessimist?" I think I'm an optimist, since I like to focus on the solutions more than the problems. I'm not saying I'm a Pollyanna, but rather one who has made a habit of looking for the silver lining. In my case, perhaps in retrospect, I was able to look back at my life so far and see a collection of "sparkly" moments, which informed the title *Sparkle*. One level, in recalling these personal life-stories, I hoped to help readers plug in their own sparks that may have become "unplugged" in by the pandemic.

I also can see that my life has grown into a collection of values, worldviews and behaviours that I live by. In a sense, reviewing all these past events helps make my future more potent and valued. My future is full of memoir entries waiting to happen! It's my hope yours is, too.

Your life is full of great stuff. Your life experiences, challenges you've overcome and lessons learned are a very important part of you. They are very personal to you. What do you feel moved to do next? What calls your soul into meaningful action? Perhaps you may be perfectly poised to write a book, memoir or collection of poems or essays. You and your life matter!

107. Sparkle Cards: My Most Popular Gift

Everyone is special and unique – and my "sparkle cards" celebrate this truth.

One day, I decided to buy some sparkly coloured paper at the crafts store, cut the sheets into little cards, and write short inspirational messages on the back of them. These sparkle cards were like Chinese fortune-cookies – but rather than being fortunes, they were acknowledgements or validations of the recipients' special qualities and gifts.

They were written in the first-person, as affirmations: "I am loveable," "I am creative", "I am capable", "I am strong", "I am talented" and so on. I loved customizing the messages for each recipient.

My friends were so overjoyed, and looked forward to opening their heart-shaped box full of sparkle cards every day. A few said that they were the most special and personalized gift they had every received. How humbling. What a hit my sparkle cards were. I'm so happy with the positive and encouraging effects they've had on the people I love.

The gift for me was knowing that the people receiving them felt good and appreciated. This was my way of showing them I cared and that they matter: a little reminder of their special talents and qualities.

Later, I decided to write my memoir, but found I was writing short stories about memorable moments in my life. For this reason, I named my memoir *Sparkle*, acknowledging the many moments in my life that are little gems for me to remember, and to learn from.

Have you ever made your own homemade gifts or given someone a gift that turned out to be a gift for you, too, by the very nature of how great it made both of you feel? What was the gift?

108. Starting My Very First Business in Bed

The title may sound misleading; it wasn't a job in the sex trade. Rather, it was a business I created to utilize my professional flute training. As I approached graduating from the University of Toronto's Faculty of Music in flute performance, I wanted to have a job to go to. I decided to create it myself! Just two months before graduation, I registered my own business called, "Montage Music," not exactly knowing what I would do, but imagining it to be something related to my flute playing.

As it turns out, just before graduating I came down with an awful flu that lasted about ten days. Thanks to my "entrepreneurial gene," I created my business from bed! I decided to book concerts with my then-boyfriend, who was a singer and keyboardist. I booked fourteen concerts at retirement residences and long-term care homes in less than a week – all from the comfort of my own bed!

What a joy it was to launch my music business, and to bring such happiness to the faces of the elderly with my flute, and my boyfriend on keyboards. He also sang a little – but I will never forget a very bold senior citizen saying to my partner, "Son, please do not attempt to vocalize."

With Montage Music, I also booked weddings, corporate events and celebrations of life, along with a concert series at Toronto's Heliconian Hall called "An Elegant Affair." We loved doing this, and we cultivated a fan-club of an audience. Many of our fans said they loved our events because they also had a social component, with a wine and *hors d'oeuvres* reception following each concert.

I've been running Montage Music for over thirty years, enjoying making music with a host of talented musicians. The great thing about playing music is the wonderful friends you make!

Have you ever started a business of your own? What were the conditions of beginning? What was special, unusual and memorable? How did you put your personal stamp on it?

109. Office Impulse

In the late '80s, I was living at the married students' residence of the University of Toronto. (I wasn't married, *per se*, but was coupled.) One day, I saw a sign in the window across the street from my apartment, in an old townhouse restored as an office building. I'd always wanted a place to go other than my apartment to do my work: a clear separation between work and home. It would be great to have my own office.

So, I crossed the street, went upstairs to the second floor and deliberately took the "for rent" sign off the window, without any hesitation. Then, I asked a tenant in the building where the property manager was. After I met him, I paid first and last month's rent, and there I was with my own office. It felt wonderful having a designated place to meet clients and do my work.

A few years later, a 24-hour café called Seven West, opened next door. I loved being able to just go next door and take a break, have a coffee, and visit with the café staff. What a time! Sometimes in life, you just need to grab a "for rent" sign and take up residence in the site of your inspiration. I had that office for over ten years, and loved my time there.

When have you made a spontaneous decision by acting on it immediately? How did you benefit from taking action so deliberately?

110. The Café that Cured My Heartache

After a particularly difficult romantic breakup, I knew I needed to get out of the house first thing in the morning. I'd been in the habit of staring at the ceiling, under my comforting duvets, ruminating sadly over the end of my relationship.

I discovered an amazing café nearby, only a ten-minute walk from home, called Broadview Espresso. It had a charming air about it, and was owned and run by a very open-hearted, young man from Victoria, BC. The ambience was palpable: open, welcoming and familiar. I used to refer to it as "the pub that sells coffee." Of course, it wasn't a pub – but with its welcoming and familiar atmosphere, it sure felt like one to its regulars. And I was one of them.

You couldn't be lonely having your morning coffee at Broadview Espresso. Everyone said hi to you, and there was such a cordial, neighbourly spirit. I will be forever grateful to Mike, the owner, and his team of employees who always welcomed guests with kindness, hospitality and open-heartedness.

I went there every day for over two years, and this sense of community healed my broken heart – one cup of coffee at a time.

I will always think of Broadview Espresso as the café that sells coffee and warms hearts.

When have you experienced healing in an unexpected or unusual place? What about this unique healing experience stays with you years later?

111. My Tooth-Fairy

For me, the Tooth-Fairy didn't just exist in my childhood, leaving me money under my pillow. My tooth-fairy was my amazing Finnish-Canadian dentist, Eva, whose soothing and whispery tone always calmed my nerves in her dental chair.

I remember a particularly difficult breakup. It was a rollercoaster, topsy-turvy relationship with extreme highs and plummeting lows. I knew being out of the relationship was healthier for me – free of drama – but I found myself relentlessly sad and lonely.

I couldn't be alone at home without extreme depression and anxiety. Coincidentally, around that same time, I needed to get dental work done: chronically grinding my teeth at night must have contributed to the need for a lot of my appointments.

One week, I had three dental appointments booked. I actually found myself curiously looking forward to going to my dentist. I joked to myself that my life must have been pretty bad at the time for me to find solace in my dental visits!

After examining the reasons why I looked so much forward to my appointments it was clear to me. The compassion, care and kindness my dentist and staff treated me with fed my soul. I craved attention and gentleness after such a severe breakup.

My dentist, Eva, my "Tooth Fairy" was very kind and soft-spoken. I always appreciated her forewarnings about the needle in the cheek before my cavity fillings or crowns. Her voice in my ear was a whisper of compassion that I've never quite experienced in a dentist since.

It still amazes me that frequent trips to my dentist not only repaired my teeth, but also helped to heal my broken heart. What an unexpected healer: my Tooth Fairy.

Have you ever been surprised by something that normally wouldn't have been a positive experience, but under special conditions and timing, were exactly what the doctor, or dentist ordered?

112. Mindless to Mindful in a Popcorn Kernel

I was sitting comfortably in the dark movie theatre. The commercials were over, and the feature film was about to come on. There I sat, mindlessly eating my popcorn, when suddenly – crunch! Yikes, I'd just broken my tooth on an un-popped kernel. I probed with my tongue, and felt the severed and sharp molar. As the film began, I pondered what to do. I couldn't really concentrate on the plot of the movie, since my broken tooth became my focus

Of course, I knew I'd have to go to a dentist. But I'd become fearful of dentists. I was afraid of them to a phobic level, due to a recent, unfortunate drilling incident. I'd asked him to stop, since I felt that horrible twinge of my exposed nerve. But he continued to drill. It felt like an unbearable length of time, like any dental pain, but it probably only lasted for a few seconds. I remember frantically gesturing for him to stop, but he continued and drilled briefly into a nerve. This was the dental-phobia defining moment – the source of all my future avoidance of dentists.

I told a close friend of mine about my popcorn incident and she referred me to her dentist, guaranteeing he was kind and gentle. My new dentist told me I was sitting on a ticking time-bomb. What a scary thought. He went on to suggest that I might need a root canal, but he'd need to further investigate. The words "root canal" horrified me – so needless to say, I avoided any further appointments with him or any other dentist, for that matter!

For the next eleven years, (That is, over 96,000 hours of my life!), I diligently chewed my food on the other side of my mouth for all meals: That means over 8,000 meals, if you are counting three meals a day, seven days a week.

This became an unorthodox exercise in mindfulness. I would often probe the broken molar with the tip of my tongue, chew on the other side, and even get seeds and small bits of food caught in the broken tooth. But I still avoided going to the dentist.

I often marveled at the fact that I had tolerated this broken tooth for over a decade, since the alternative scared me too much. I wanted to avoid the dentist at all costs – and I was definitely playing a "finicky" price daily.

Finally, in 2020, after dental offices reopened following a Covid lockdown, I decided to muster up the courage to go to my regular dentist, (the one who drilled too long into the nerve) and bite the bullet. I thought he was the better alternative to a potential emergency dentist, if I waited too long and there was another lockdown. I just didn't know – but I did know that being in a state of less certainty, with dental offices potentially closing down again, was even more of a risk.

So there I sat in the dreaded dentist's chair, having mustered up the courage after over a decade pondering, waiting, avoiding and massively procrastinating. To my utter amazement, the appointment I had been avoiding, lasted only forty minutes. And when he started to do the restoration, he discovered he wouldn't need to do a root canal after all. I had obsessed over a possible root canal – and I was so relieved I didn't have to have one. I couldn't believe it. Eleven years of worrying and avoiding the dentist. Then, finally doing it, and merely forty minutes later, finding relief. I don't think I have ever put something off for this long!

In the end, the only additional appointment I needed was to get a crown put on, and that appointment lasted two hours. After eleven years of procrastinating and waiting for the perfect time to have my broken tooth repaired, it ended up getting done in just under three hours and two appointments. What a host of lessons: a lesson in ease instead of procrastination; a lesson in knowing that anticipatory anxiety usually makes things worse in our imagination than in real life; and a lesson in putting up with the discomfort of a broken tooth, in order to avoid what I feared: an imaginary excruciatingly painful dental appointment.

Yet procrastination has its virtues: It taught me to have a "mindful mouth," deliberately chewing on one side for over a decade. I now refer to this long process as my "mindful dental" years. I call it this because every meal I had to exercise extreme sensitivity and mindfulness in how I chewed, what side of the mouth. I developed great focus and concentration with the inside of my mouth and chewing. However, in the future, I think I'd like to practise mindfulness in a more traditional setting – not in my mouth!

Life lessons are learned in all types of circumstances. Being mindful and self-aware are important aspects of living life consciously. When have you learned lessons in unique or unconventional ways? How have they benefited your life? When have you practised mindfulness in less conventional settings?

113. My Angel: Writing a Thank-You Note to the CRA

It's funny how the Canada Revenue Agency (the Canadian equivalent of the IRS) can evoke emotions of fear, anxiety and distress in many of us. For years, the CRA seemed like a big, scary monster to me. I used to leave my CRA envelopes shut for weeks, sometimes even months, fearing what I might discover when I opened them. It was never anything I couldn't deal with, and the anticipatory fear was always more amplified than the issue at hand.

Fortunately, I've been able to reframe the CRA, by imagining CRA agents as human beings, earning a living like the rest of us, doing their best every day and being individuals – not being this big and threatening "CRA Monster." This really helped to alleviate my anxiety around taxes, the CRA and unpleasant surprises.

One year, I received a notice from the CRA that stated I owed money, around $2,300. I was shocked, since I'd done my taxes thoroughly for the year, and had sent them in by the deadline.

Despite my diligence getting my taxes in on time, I was still afraid of dealing with the CRA about this matter. Somehow, just receiving a letter in the mail from the CRA is enough to rattle me. But finally, I managed to get up the courage to call. I took a deep breath, sipped from my glass of water and prepared myself for questioning.

To my surprise, a woman answered the phone – and her soft, gentle and kind voice put me at ease immediately. Her name was "Angel." I couldn't believe this was her name. She had a curiously kind, empathetic voice.

Ironically, as I've trained companies in the area of clear and empathetic telephone technique, I noticed such a warm and non-threatening customer service from Angel, that was both clear and caring. I commented on her wonderful telephone technique. I told her that I'd been nervous about calling the CRA, but was relieved by her warmth and human touch.

Angel told me that she had just come off a three-week customer service training at the CRA. It made complete sense to me. In that moment, I realized that Angel was a real person just like me: she just happened to be working for the CRA. I decided, in that moment, to treat her like an individual, not like the big, bad and scary monster I imagined the CRA to be.

As we began talking, I mentioned that I had experienced the death of my mother a few years back, due to cancer. She was sympathetic and then opened up to me, sharing that she had had a recent cancer diagnosis. How synchronistic! She was not only a human being with real life challenges, but someone who almost instantly trusted me, a complete stranger, with her personal health condition.

I shared some remedies and diet suggestions that I hoped Angel would find helpful. And throughout the conversation, I felt the most unusual sense of connection and compassion.

By the time we arrived at the end of the call, after she rechecked my file, she discovered that the CRA was at fault. I didn't owe the government $2,300 in overlooked taxes, but rather, the CRA had made a mistake in their calculations – and owed *me* $3,000!

What a surreal experience with Angel of the CRA that day: the day I'd been avoiding, that turned out to be a true gift for both of us! I asked Angel if I could have her boss's name and department, along with full mailing address, so that I could send a special thank you note, bragging about my wonderful customer service call with Angel.

To this day, I still have to shake my head when I think that I wrote a thank-you note to the CRA!

Can you remember a time in your life when you found yourself in a situation you had feared for so long, but when finally confronting it, you experienced a "gift" you couldn't ever have imagined?

114. Bad Behavior at a Backstreet Boys Concert

I tell this story with some hesitancy, since I'm not proud of my behavior, on this occasion. However, it was mischievous and fun – and I'm here to tell you just how much fun it was!

I used to be a fan of the Backstreet Boys – because I liked pop singers at the time, and I especially liked this band's unique energy. When they came to Toronto back in the '90s, I didn't get to hear them – but years later, I decided to go to their show in a big stadium, called the Rogers Centre, when they returned. I was all grown up by then, but my teeny-bopper days still lived within me. Secretly embarrassed but eager to see and hear them, I bought myself a single ticket. It was a $100 ticket on the floor level, but not that close to the stage.

Even though everyone had appointed seats, this didn't matter at all, since the crowd was dancing and standing on their seats, screaming at the top of their lungs. And there I was, in my mid-thirties, acting like a teenager, standing on *my* seat, screaming along with the thirteen-year-old fans next to me. Privately, I felt ridiculous, and was embarrassed to be joining in with the teens. But, deep down, I was having a riot, transported back to my youth.

The stage was at least a hundred feet away. Wanting to see them up close, I decided to leave my seat and meander through the crowd to get up to the stage. On my way there, I would stop and dance, so that no security would think I was out of place or would discover that I was gradually and sneakily moving up to the front to gaze at them on stage, up close.

All of a sudden, I saw another stage emerge near me. (It looked like the stem of the letter T.) And at this point, the Boys appeared on the second stage, ready to perform. The girls screamed and cheered and made their way to that stage.

I realized that this was the perfect moment for me to go right to the original stage, at the front, unnoticed. But one security guard, trained to spot people like me, grabbed my arm and sternly shouted, "Go back to your seat." I responded with a fiery confidence, saying, "Get your hands off me or I'll accuse you of assault."

My words pierced him, and his authority atrophied at once. He immediately let go and I went to the front, to the original stage. My plan was working. I must have been a fox in another lifetime.

By then the Backstreet Boys were back there performing, and I'd successfully made it to the front row, self-satisfied, and feeling a little guilty, looking the pop stars right in the eye! I made a face at one of the more narcissistic ones as he looked at me, causing him a knee jerk reaction-and he looked away. I felt like a royal shit-disturber.

Looking back, I realize it was an immature act, yet I enjoyed the ride. My Backstreet Boys experience took me back to the mischievous ways of my youth that still live inside me.

When have you done something so bold, you were both proud and ashamed at the same time? Why did you do it? Did you tell anyone or keep it your little secret?

115. Acting Like an Actor (It's Not for Me)

As a flutist from a very early age, and an entrepreneur, I've always called the shots in my life. I love the thrill of creating something out of nothing: experiencing it first in my mind's eye, and then manifesting it in the world. I've always been best suited to designing the fabric of my life with a combination of anticipatory joy and intention, along with a wild imagination.

For many years, though, many of my friends encouraged me to take up acting. I had actually won the grade 11 dramatic arts award, and many people thought I would be an actor when I grew up. I took scene-study, improv, voice training and some other classes, and fortunately was accepted by a reputable Toronto agent as her client.

As it goes in the acting world, I was sent out to auditions, and quietly sat in the reception area with other auditionees, trying to contain my jitters, while waiting for my name to be called. The atmosphere in the room had an almost-palpable nervousness. I waited my turn to audition, but every second that went by seemed like hours.

After several auditions, I finally landed a part as a Jewish woman in a series. I was amazed. It was slated to shoot in two weeks. Thrilled to have my very first booking, I reconsidered acting as a real career. A few days later, my agent called to inform me that my character was being written out of the script. Figures! My very first booked job, and my part was made redundant, as the British say.

That was it for me: my moment as an almost-actor. Perhaps having an acting career was not for me or my nature, since I love leading my own life, and not having to fit in with roles others want me to be. I realized that the whole auditioning process can be quite daunting and somewhat dismal, since actors never really know exactly what the director has in mind for their characters. So it's a bit of a crap-shoot.

I politely declined any further representation and returned to my ongoing career as flutist, music producer and entrepreneur. I felt so much better being me and returning to fully designing my life – on my terms!

Sadly, I believe that actors can become very self-conscious and insecure due to the nature of auditioning. It goes with the territory, since you're there to be your best, and even if you do an amazing audition, you still may not look the part.

Life is our grand stage – to be all the authentic characters we inhabit inside and want to express out loud. For me, the formal acting career didn't offer that – but my real life does!

Can you remember a time you found yourself questioning who your authentic self really is? What did you discover? How do you choose to direct your life from you, for you? How has this choice impacted your life ever since?

116. How Selling Fruit Door to Door Took Me to Europe

I've always been a natural salesperson. Even when I was just twelve years old, I loved all aspects of sales: meeting and connecting with all sorts of people, offering them a wonderful product, delivering the product, delighting my customers, and following up with them the following year.

When I was only in grade 9, my first year of high school, I had the opportunity to go on the senior band trip, usually reserved for grades 11 and 12 only. We had a fundraising campaign for our well-anticipated trip to Europe: selling boxes of Florida grapefruits and oranges door to door. Being a sociable, somewhat disciplined and organized person, I made a list of all the houses on my street and knocked on doors, one after another. Equipped with a smile and story about our high-school band trip, the fruit fundraiser was received very well. Many said yes, and I tallied up all my sales, determined to raise enough to go on this exciting European band trip.

I kept my files very organized, and at the end of the campaign, I was surprised and delighted to learn I was the winner! I had sold the most oranges and grapefruits, which helped me to afford the band trip to Europe, which included Germany, Holland and England.

I kept my list of customers. Every year I returned to them, and they reordered. As a result, I got to go on many band trips due to my salesmanship and tenacity.

Years later, in 1988, I started my own live music agency, called Montage Music, and enjoyed booking chamber-music and jazz groups for corporate and social events. It was also a sales job, offering various choices of musicians to suit my clients' needs. I guess those early years selling grapefruits and oranges really paid off!

We're all salespeople: selling ideas, products, services and ultimately ourselves. When there is trust and rapport, plus a great product that adds value to peoples' lives, sales transactions take place. The formula is that simple!

When in your life have you discovered you were selling something, whether it be an idea, a product, service or a vote of confidence in you? What did you learn from this experience? What role does selling have in your life?

117. An Outrageous Moment

"Cat Woman" was never a label I would have given myself. I'm no Batman fan, and I've never been an overtly sexy woman. I was an A-plus student and a "band nerd": a high-school and university student who spent most of her evenings practising flute rather than man-hunting. But one day, this all changed.

So, there I was, in my early thirties, finally dating a sexy, Scorpio guy. He told me about an outrageous party that attracted over 5,000 people in Toronto every October. It was the annual Fetish Party. Of course, there were smaller ones throughout the year, but this was the one to see and be seen at!

My inner "Cat Woman" finally found an outlet where she could reveal herself. I bought a PVC cat suit, a long black-haired wig with a fuchsia stripe of colour down the front, piled on the make-up and strutted my stuff in four-inch stilettos! Was this my alter ego, a persona that had been dwelling inside me all my life, waiting to be unleashed, seen and perhaps even, devoured? I felt my identity changing as I put on my catsuit – a sudden transformation from "nerd" to "vixen."

I'd never experienced this much attention. I was suddenly sexy! – alive, out there, but hidden behind the PVC. In my costume, no one but my boyfriend knew who I really was – and neither did I! Was I this vixen for real? Was it simply a part of me that had lain dormant in my studious persona? I was ready to unleash my inner vixen!

My most outrageous moment was when a beefy African-Canadian guy came up to me, looking me up and down, growling, "Hey there mama, you sure are sexy." Feeling mischievous, I looked him straight in the eyes and pulled off my wig! His horrified look of shock and my sheer delight my contrasting looks made my trip to fetish night worth it in spades!

Since then, I've reverted back to a more conservative, less "cat-like" existence. I'm more of a flutist than a feline these days.

It was definitely fun while it lasted. And I still know that an "inner Cat Woman" dwells within me.

When have you shocked yourself, and perhaps others, with a change in your regular day-to-day persona? What have you retained from this experience?

118. Loving it Hot and Sour

One of my favourite loves was in DeLand, Florida. I was only twenty-two, and although it had been around for years, I just discovered it then: hot and sour soup. I've never craved a food this much.

I've always been a fan of Chinese food, and love sweet and sour sauces – but the idea of combining hot with sour, that was something very different. It was downright outrageous. Despite its unusual taste, hot and sour soup became my most palpable craving: more than salty chips, vegan ice cream, spaghetti, French fries or anything else for that matter!

I was hooked on hot and sour soup.

It's funny how foods can evoke certain emotions, such as elation or even euphoria. I was fascinated to discover a book by the neuroscientist Alan Hirsch called *What Flavour is Your Personality?* It compares people's snack-food proclivities, such as those who prefer salt over sweet. Or, with ice cream, which personalities most frequently correspond to vanilla, chocolate and strawberry flavours. I was shocked to learn that people who prefer vanilla are considered higher risk-takers, and more daring than those who prefer chocolate or strawberry – interesting!

Other happy food-memories include the years when we visited our family farm for the summer holidays. Mom would fill a big pot with water, and while it boiled, we went out to the vegetable garden and picked fresh corn. We would husk it, boil it, then eat this most incredible corn on the cob! Both a delicious food, and an enduring delicious memory. As well, Mom's hot potato salad and fresh cucumber salad, German-style, were two of my favourites. My grandfather had been a Swiss chef, and Mom's wonderful cooking had his culinary flare.

Then there were those car rides up to the farm. First stop: Dooher's Bakery, in Campbellford, Ontario, to pick up a box of the best tasting homemade donuts I'd ever had. I can still remember how they tasted, thirty-five years later.

Box lunches were also a favourite. My brother and I ate them as we travelled to the farm on Friday nights, or when we took trips with Mom across Canada in her Volkswagen camper in the 1970s. Mom would lovingly fill these boxes with our favourite foods and snacks. She was so thoughtful and her wonderful box lunches always helped the time go by.

It's amazing how food can spark so many good memories and feelings of love.

What foods spark happy memories in your life? What are your favourite foods now? Have your taste buds changed over time? Are there foods do you desire now that repelled you in the past? What are they?

119. They Told Me He Loves My Music

I'd never met this young man – but had simply discovered an online request, by one of his brothers, for people interested in meditating together over Zoom for his brother who was in a coma. Somehow, this spoke to me, since I had dated a younger man around his age many years before, and he too was a jazz guitarist. Curiously, although this young man was thousands of miles away, I felt somehow connected to him. His name was Oliver.

It was during the Covid-19 pandemic, so we were on Zoom, participants from all over the world, meditating together, to invite healing for this young man. I offered to play flute during the meditations. Since often a family member was in the ICU with Oliver, their iPhone on speakerphone, I could play my flute for him by his hospital bed. Sometimes, after the group meditation, I'd play him a private bedside concert over the speakerphone. I chose to play him some jazz standards I thought he'd be familiar with, along with some gentle and recognizable classical melodies.

He had several reactions. A few times, a single tear ran down his face. On another occasion, he did a sumptuous big yawn, then a satisfying full body stretch, after that, snuggled himself back into his cozy sleeping position. On at least three occasions, his heart rate went down to an even more relaxed state. Some of the jazz tunes I loved playing for him were *Autumn Leaves*, *The Swinging Shepherd Blues*, *Bésame Mucho*, and many others.

This performance experience was like no other I had ever had. I have played for seniors, for babies, and for adults alike – but never, ever, for a young man in a coma! What an experience, sharing a circle with fellow meditators and playing flute for a very special young man – a talented jazz guitarist.

His family often told me how much Oliver loves my flute music. I hope to meet him, and play flute and guitar duets together one day.

Have you ever experienced an event that was so unusual and transcendent? How did you deal with it? Has it changed you? How?

120. Stumbling Upon a Twelve-Step Meeting

It is often said that life is stranger than fiction. I completely agree. In fact, it can even be funnier than some sitcoms, too!

I had a friend who regularly attended Al-Anon twelve-step meetings in her neighbourhood. I often dropped by her home since we lived nearby. One such evening, I knocked on her door after dinner to see if she would like to go for an after-dinner walk. She said she could go for a short one, if I didn't mind walking in the direction of her twelve-step meeting that evening.

I was happy to walk with her and even asked if I could attend. I was up for an adventure, and I was curious about how these meetings go anyway. Since it was only an hour out of my evening, I tagged along with her. Before meeting with her, I'd just done some shopping, including a quick trip to the liquor store to grab a bottle of wine. All items were neatly packed into my cotton tote bag, over my shoulder.

When we reached the meeting, at a church nearby, I saw a group of twelve-steppers standing outside, taking the last drag on their cigarettes and gulping down some accompanying coffee. I've always marveled at the fact that people who have addictions and attend twelve-step meetings for their particular vice often continue other addictions outside, including smoking and drinking coffee. These seem to be the permissible addictions.

When we got seated, I carefully placed my tote bag safely under my chair. Feeling rather self-conscious since I'd brought a bottle of wine into the meeting, I sat quietly, politely waiting for the meeting to begin. I reassured myself that it wasn't my fault that I happened to be carrying wine, since I hadn't planned for this meeting, anyway.

As usual, there were announcements and congratulatory remarks for those who have been clean and sober for various amounts of time – starting with several years, then months, then weeks and finally, days. The recipients of the sobriety success pins would then go up to the front and receive a warm applause for their abstinence.

Right at the moment when the host of the meeting asked if anyone in the audience had just today had become clean and sober, I accidentally kicked the bottle of wine under my chair, and it loudly rolled out of the bag! I was horrified, yet found the ironic humour in the situation. I had to hold back a sheepish grin – and my friend was not impressed.

I also chose not to go up to the front, as that would have been both inauthentic and an unexpected performance. I loved my wine and didn't consider myself an alcoholic, anyway.

Soon, we left the meeting, my tote in tow, my friend annoyed with my inopportune moment! Since then, I've avoided twelve-step programs and have enjoyed a glass of red, every night with dinner.

Have you ever experienced your life mimicking a sitcom? How have you reacted when you make a bold and accidental move in public?

121. Power Nap at My Therapist's

I realize that therapists get an all-day-every-day earful of patients' dumping. From relationships to divorce issues, to pathologies like OCD, depression and anxiety, or a death in the family, they have to really listen deeply, while offering emotionally intelligent feedback.

I've seen therapists off and on all my life. And unlike my on-again-off-again relationships with men, therapists have been a steadier presence in my life, even if at times I was fine without one.

In the summer of 2018, I had over twenty retirement and nursing home flute concert engagements booked. My boyfriend at the time really wanted to move out of Toronto to the West Coast: to Victoria, BC, to be exact. Although I'd visited Victoria with him the summer prior and loved its quaintness, I felt it was too small for this big-city girl.

The decision to go back on my own and perform concerts for ten days gave me the ability to see what it would be like living and working on Vancouver Island. I could put it under my test without feeling any pressure to acquiesce to my boyfriend's wishes or preferences. Like before, it had a quiet charm about it, but this time, I sort of fell in love with it. I could even imagine the possibility of moving there one day.

A week into my flute tour, I received an envelope at my Airbnb. The return address was from my boyfriend, but there was no note or card in the envelope, just the keys to his apartment in Toronto. I'd been staying at his place for the last year, although I still had my own apartment nearby. Curiously, I wondered, why the keys? Perhaps since I was returning home at 2 am a few days later, he was sending them for my convenience getting in, if he were asleep.

After finishing my second performance of the day, I phoned him. I was standing at an empty bus-stop at 8:30 pm, as dusk settled. It was dark outside, and my surroundings were unfamiliar. When I heard him breathe, I knew something was up. Then, when he spoke with a flat voice I'd never heard before, I definitely knew something was very wrong.

When he said, "I'm leaving you, and I won't be there when you return," that explained it. In complete shock, I buckled over, my stomach in knots, feeling nausea from the news I just received over the phone, the street spinning. I couldn't believe what I was hearing.

That night, I couldn't sleep a wink: I just stared at the ceiling from ten o'clock till dawn, watching each hour slowly crawl by and the morning birds chirp the arrival of dawn. Was this a horrific dream? It wasn't—the keys were still there, sitting on my Airbnb dresser on top of the torn-open envelope.

I had just under a week of concerts ahead of me I didn't know how I would get through them. I prevailed, since I knew my show had to go on. During some of my concerts, I shared the fact that I was just dumped and how, and a few ninety-somethings said, "Well, dear you're well rid of him. He doesn't deserve you." Somehow words coming from such sweet, elderly and wise women helped me begin processing my grief.

During this surreal period, I had a sudden flash of a thought: I chose to journal every single day before returning to Toronto. I made a list of what I may have done to contribute to our relationship breakdown. I listed what I loved about him and what I didn't. This helped me to see the situation more rationally, if that is even possible during such an emotional upheaval. But it seemed to.

Next, in my healing process, I made a double appointment with a therapist, two hours in length, in Toronto, for the day after my return. I'd never taken such responsibility for my healing and relationship recovery. I felt proud of my efforts and really prepared since it had only been a week since he announced our breakup.

When I arrived at the grief counsellor's home office, I was greeted by a dishevelled, sloppy, overweight woman with a cat. Her office was in the back of her house and we sat in the solarium with a sliding glass door, looking over her backyard. Her cat sat like a sentinel by the glass door throughout my session.

The therapist was very impressed by my preparation for our therapy session, and said she thought I was far along in my healing process and may not need to see her again for a while. Instead, she suggested a helpful book. She told me to call her after reading it, and if I felt I needed another session, I could book one then.

As I continued talking, I watched as her head drooped forward, chin down on her chest, and she drifted off! With mid-afternoon summer sun streaming through her back window, combined with my talking, she must have lulled herself to sleep. I could hear her snoring gently. I didn't know what to say. But I did know how I felt: disregarded, and treated unprofessionally. I realized I was a better therapist to myself than she. I didn't go back, ever again. I gathered my purse and things, and ended my session.

I've never had this happen in a therapy session before, and never since. That day, I learned that I can take care of myself – and also that my stories can be either so soothing or so boring that they put some people to sleep!

When in your life have you had a very unexpected response from a professional? How did you feel? What did you do or say? What did this teach you?

122. Heart-To-Heart Wisdom in the Hot Tub

Soaking in a hot tub is always a treat – so warm and relaxing. Usually, my hot tub moments have been purely about pampering, and in no way intellectual. But on this particular occasion – at the Ritz-Carlton Toronto, in the pool area – a very intelligent-looking man eased his way down the stairs of the tub into the bubbling hot bubbles and joined me.

He was in from New York, a cardiologist attending an international conference held in Toronto. His practice was on Fifth Avenue, in New York, and he mentioned he'd been a cardiologist for well over forty years. I asked him if he had two surprise pointers about good heart-health habits for someone like me, one not in the medical profession. He answered with:

- Jogging is not good for the heart. It's much better to walk.
- Drinking a glass of red wine everyday can be good for the heart.

I was relieved to know this, as I was a jogger. I instantly stopped the jogging habit and started the drinking habit! However, I kept it to one glass of red wine a day. (Apparently white wine isn't beneficial: according to Dr. Michael Greger, who wrote the book *How Not to Die*, red is the only wine we should drink, as others can contribute to gene mutation of breast cancer cells.)

When have you learned something so simple but easy to apply in your own life? What was it? Have you continued doing it?

123. "Portrait Of Your Mind": A Captivating Sign in the Window

I was curious seeing an unusual sign in the window of a medical clinic that day. What could "Portrait of Your Mind" mean? I walked in and met Dr. Mark Doidge, doctor and innovator.

Working with Electroencephalogram (or EEG) technology, he discovered that people's brain-activity looked beautiful. Captured in a millisecond, the image of a brightly colour-coded brain looked beautiful on a black background. I got very excited about his "art" and approached Moses Znaimer, an innovative Toronto-based broadcaster and entrepreneur, to see if a presentation of "Portrait of Your Mind" could be included in his upcoming annual show, *IdeaCity*. Fortunately, Moses Znaimer said yes, and Mark and I were thrilled.

I even had a "portrait of your mind" experience myself, with the EEG, and did an experiment. With one photo, I had my beloved Ito, my Pomeranian on my lap. Next, a track from my flute CD, "Dreamland" was played as I sat there with all the EEG gear attached to my head. The outcomes of these two photographic moments were amazing. It was possible to see the unique brain activity during both moments – the one with Ito, and the other with my own flute CD playing.

Acting as Dr. Mark Doidge's informal publicist, I promoted him to Moses Znaimer's annual Toronto-based Ideacity conference, where he was invited to display his work in 2015. It was a role I really enjoyed since I loved the product: Portrait of Your Mind.

Have you ever invented something or admired innovation in your own world? What was it and what inspired you by it?

124. Valentine's Day at the Castle, for the New Millennium

Casa Loma – an imposing Gothic mansion in the heart of Toronto – has always been one of my favourite venues to play music. From weddings to corporate events, it's been a magical place, with its high ceilings and great acoustics.

One day in late November, 1999, I was performing flute with my chamber-music trio for a corporate Christmas party. I could see large, graceful snowflakes floating down on the castle's windowpanes. It was both elegant and enchanting – the perfect fairy-tale setting.

All of a sudden, in that precise moment, I had a vision. It was to produce a concert evening at the castle, all by myself. Of course, I would hire musicians to perform, but the idea was mine to manifest. I could envision a beautiful snowy night in my mind's eye – with lots of joyous voices, drinks flowing, *hors d'oeuvres* being passed around and exquisite music being performed. I tucked this vision away somewhere to be accessed in my future; I didn't know when it would come to life.

Then, when January 1, 2000, arrived, I knew the time was right. My plan was about to unfold, in perfect timing and in divine order. My New Year's Day breakup was a startling shock after celebrating, the night before, at the top of the CN

Tower. Just a few hours after midnight, the harsh breakup news was announced to me by my then-boyfriend. How could this be? Celebrating one moment, drying my tears the very next?

I decided in that instant that I wanted to celebrate the first Valentine's Day of the twenty-first century in a positive way. It was the year 2000, after all. I didn't want to start off the millennium without hope, and in despair – I was sure of this!

Then, I had a flashback: and remembered performing with a string trio at Casa Loma castle for a corporate Christmas party back in November, 1999. I vividly recalled seeing the fairy-tale winter wonderland come to life, with those graceful snowflakes cascading down on the castle's windowpanes. I remember how I'd imagined how amazing it would be to put on a concert of my own, some wintry day, and call it "Concert at the Castle."

This vision became a reality that February 14, 2000. Laughter, music, food, wine and joy filled the castle – and it all started with a vision and a breakup!

One thing I learned from this experience is that there's strength and power in our imagination. Our minds and hearts are potent – full of fresh ideas, inventions and new realities.

From a potentially sad start to the year 2000, I envisioned a happier time on Valentine's Day for both myself and others. In less than two months, from idea to inception a memorable Valentine's at the Castle – with 200 guests, a group of musicians, and a fine caterer – came to life!

When we have a disappointing event in our lives, we can choose to be creative and change our outcome. I found that by sharing joy with others, it changes the whole trajectory into something positive and meaningful. What gifts and resources can you call upon to help yourself and others at the same time? When have you turned around a disappointing situation – and in doing so, brought joy to yourself and others?

125. Meeting Kelly: The Unforgettable Homeless Man

There he was: seated cross-legged, head bowed down, on the subway platform floor at St. George Subway Station, with a cardboard sign reading, "Homeless and Hungry." I walked over and said hello.

Up lifted the head of the sweetest man with the softest, most sensitive blue eyes I'd ever seen. He had a sparkly twinkle in his eyes, yet a deep sadness in his heart. His eyes really touched me. I could feel him in my heart. I offered to go home and get a tent, blankets and other aids, since he told me he lived in Dufferin

Park, in downtown Toronto. Many homeless people set up tents and live there in the park. Kelly was one of them. Despite his unfortunate situation, he had a special twinkle in his eyes, like a leprechaun.

Kelly also had a chronic lung condition, and he told me that he had to have them drained weekly at the hospital. Due to his weekly hospital visits for his lungs, he also would get weekly Covid tests.

I returned the next day, rolling my prized purple suitcase filled with helpful stuff for dear Kelly. With tears in his eyes, he told me both his parents had died in the past year. I felt helpless. How could *I* understand what it's like to be both homeless and parentless at the same time?

What is life like if you are Kelly? I couldn't even imagine it. I'd often think of him, and whenever I was at the St. George Subway platform, I would look out for him. Some days, I would see him sitting in his usual posture.

When he heard my voice, he would wake up, look up and *light up*. I would light up, too! It was a ritual. We were genuinely happy to see each other; there was a feeling between us like kindred spirits. I loved going and getting Kelly his favourite lunch: chili from a nearby Tim Horton's and a large hot chocolate. I'd often wonder, "How could I have a three-bedroom apartment, yet Kelly be homeless?" Where's the justice and fairness? (I long ago realized that life isn't fair. We have to do our best with our circumstances.)

I've been grappling with this and still don't have a clear and practical answer. My heart knows the answer, but sadly the system isn't run by the heart. Maybe someday it will be.

Have you ever met someone so kind and humble, in a vulnerable life situation that emotionally moved you, beyond words? What did you do? How has this changed your life and perspective?

126. Senior Moments

These aren't "senior moments" as in moments when we are forgetful, but rather they are some of my most unforgettable times with my favorite people: seniors.

They often seem to live life "at peace," in a profoundly calm and contented state of being: been there, done that, and now let's just "be." I don't see the "shoulda, woulda, coulda" running them as much as others. As someone closer to forty than eighty, I've felt privileged playing flute for this special population of people for over thirty years. They are so full of grace, dignity and have so many interesting stories to tell.

One particular senior I will never forget was a sweet elderly man named Kurt. Since my own father had been a Berliner, I could easily recognize this accent in Kurt. A happy man, perhaps the oldest man I'd ever met, Kurt also sported a contagious smile, sitting attentively on his walker seat, listening to my flute concert at his retirement home.

I couldn't help but be curious about how he maintained such a positive attitude. After my concert, I asked him what he believed sustained him at his ripe age of 106. He simply looked at me and beamed, saying, "Smile!" I asked him if I could have a photo with him, as I was exactly half his age at the time: just fifty-three. He agreed.

As we spoke, I learned that all of his family had predeceased him. He told me that it made him feel quite sad and lonely at times. I couldn't relate to such a story, and I don't think many could – Kurt being 106 – but I sympathized with him that he had experienced this. Being with Kurt, having that special conversation, I knew deep down that connecting with him was a very special moment I'd cherish forever.

Two months later, I returned to play another flute concert at Kurt's retirement home. Intuitively, I had already wondered: Would Kurt still be here? My intuition was confirmed. Kurt had died just the month before. How fortunate was I to have had that special exchange with him that day. What I also learned from this experience is the value and fragility of life – we must value and seize each moment, as both life and people are transient. We never know when either will be gone.

Another senior moment I experienced was with a couple who were in their nineties. Still visibly in love, they'd been married for over sixty-five years. To me, that seemed like such an accomplishment. It also demonstrated to me the power of love.

This sweet couple was Irish, and adorable. They had a shared passion: ballroom dancing. To my utter amazement, they hadn't missed one Saturday night dance in sixty years. They said that was what kept them happy, young and healthy. The husband even said that ballroom dancing is great conditioning and particularly good for mitigating a fall, since dancing is a great way for the feet and ankles to get exercised and build resistance to falling!

I love and respect my elders and know, deep down that they won't be here forever.

Have you had a joyous experience with elders that also gave you wisdom and insights? What did you learn? What have you added to your life because of this experience?

Chapter Seven

Friends and Lovers

What defines a true friendship? For me, I believe it's compassion, loyalty, shared joy, and ongoing growth and fulfillment. What about lovers? I've been in love many times, and always learned a lot from my experiences. Some have been tougher relationships than others, but they've all added value and lessons to my life. I'm forever grateful to all the friends and lovers who've come into my heart – and left me with a fuller, richer life.

127. Acting on the Lawn, With Ann

I suppose there's always been an actress-entertainer dwelling within me. My very first special friend was named Ann, and she lived just across the street from me. At age four, we played a lot together. Like besties do, we laughed, we cried and we argued. Both of us being Taureans, the bullish stubbornness that goes with being a Taurus couldn't be understated when it came to Ann and me.

Despite our fun and feuds, we had very creative and innovative spirits. One thing we loved to do was knock on neighbours' doors and ask them if they'd like us to perform a play on their lawn. Mind you, these were all neighbours both we and our parents knew – no strangers. So, lawn-theatre began.

This was one my most joyous times: theatrically improvising on grassy lawns with my best friend. I suppose I can really thank Ann for her creatively partnering with me and inventing skits right on the spot. This early-life experience was great training for a life full of improvised living and creativity. I have continued to enjoy generating new ideas and creative expressions throughout my life, and will always remember our theatre on the lawn at age four.

Now, as women in our fifties, we enjoy our annual birthday lunches, catching up with each other, since we have gone through several decades out of touch. There's something very special about knowing someone for so many decades, since we share so much rich history and memories. Our friendship has spanned over half a century!

Do you have fond memories of a close childhood friend? What stands out in your mind about your times together? Have you stayed in touch?

128. Cindy: My Best Friend Forever

I've been so fortunate to have a best friend since I was seven years old. Her name is Cindy. She's always been supportive, caring, and is super-smart. I so admire her: She was the president of the debate club at high school, the president of the school newspaper, and got ninety-nine percent when she graduated from Queen's University. She's totally impressive, and someone I admire for so many reasons. Cindy's also a wonderful mother of two.

It's amazing to look back and realize that our friendship has endured half a century. No one knows you as well as your best friend: someone with whom you go through life, in all its phases and stages. From high-school crushes on boys to failures and disappointments, to relationships to breakups, Cindy and I have always been there for each other. No one knows you deeply and understands you as well as your best friend, the one who has been there with you through good times and bad.

Even when I was suffering with OCD, and ruminating about what negative, imaginary things people at school might be thinking about me, Cindy was always there as my rock – the one to talk logical sense into me, to reassure me and encourage me not to worry. That meant so much. Even now that we are mature adults, we counsel each other. It's so comforting to know each other inside out. We trust each other. And that means a lot.

We have many happy memories together: from picking wild strawberries at the end of our street as youngsters, to times at my family farm, to holiday times at each other's homes. Cindy has and always will be such a significant person to me.

My life has been nourished, fortified and filled with my best friend, Cindy. I am forever grateful to her for all she is and has been.

Have you kept contact with your childhood best friend? How has it impacted your lives? What is most special about this lifelong connection?

129. Deena Loves All Living Beings

If it weren't for dear Deena, I wouldn't have my South Korean rescue dog, Kito. Also, if I hadn't seen Deena at the Free Korean Dogs booth at the outdoor Dog Tales Summer Festival Fundraiser in King City in 2017, I wouldn't have been so aware of the plight of Asian dogs and the cruel dog-meat trade. Or known where I would adopt my next door from, when dear Ito passed away.

Deena and I went to the same high school over thirty years ago. Although we were in the same grade, we weren't close friends at the time. Now, with our interest in animal welfare and activism, Deena and I have become good friends. I'm so blessed to know someone who embodies so much compassion toward all living beings.

I've always admired Deena, and found her to be both fun and deeply aware. Her IQ and EQ always seemed to be in alignment with each other. Deena is person with deep consciousness. She's a vegan, a kind soul, a cancer survivor, and a great role model, whom I cherish.

Do you have a friend whom you admire for their world view and principles? How have you been influenced by them? Have you transformed because of this friend? How?

130. Susan: Gifted and Sensitive

We met in high school when I was seventeen and she was fifteen. A gifted, sensitive pianist, Susan partnered with me as flute-and-piano duo. We entered the Kiwanis Music Festival and made it to the Ontario Finals. We shared the victory of winning the Ontario Finals one year, playing a beautiful *Concertino* by a female composer, Cécile Chaminade.

Susan was shy, studious and very talented. Her interpretations of J.S. Bach piano music were captivating and transcendent, full of deep, subtle sensitivity.

I've always admired Susan. Sadly, in her late twenties, she experienced a personal crisis, but has recovered beautifully. She teaches piano to as many as forty students a week, during the school year and in the summer months. She also has a beautiful daughter who, following in Susan's academic footsteps, has achieved very high grades in her high-school studies.

It's a gift to have an old friend for so many years, sharing challenges and triumphs.

Do you have a friend whom you admire? What challenges have they overcome? Has their triumph over obstacles taught you ways to approach your own?

131. My Angelic Friend Angeline

I never knew that I'd meet a real-life, angelic, mermaid in my life, who became one of my very closest friends. Angeline is one of the most spiritual friends I've ever met. A pure, gentle soul, beautiful inside out, I feel so privileged to have her in my life.

We met at the very first Nintendo event in Toronto way back in the 1990s. Now that's really aging our friendship! She was a hostess, hired for this exciting launch event; I hired to provide live music for the reception with my musician colleagues. Back then, I was doing lots of wedding trade-shows – and Angeline was the perfect model to do promotional work at the booth for my business, Montage Music. With her green eyes, high cheekbones and lovely flowing golden long hair, she actually looked like she could be a bride on the front cover of a wedding magazine.

We became friends instantly, then roommates. A few years later, she got pregnant with twins. She moved out to get married and become a wife and mom. She later had a third girl. All are as beautiful as she. Her radiance, deep and enduring kindness, along with a raw and uproarious sense of humour, make Angeline such a special soul in my life – a living mermaid and truly angelic friend.

Do you have a friend whose beauty and essence seem unique and otherworldly to you? Why? How did you meet? What does your friendship represent for you?

132. With Lisa, Passion Is Fashion

I love fashion. And so does my dear friend Lisa. She even made a business out of her passion for it. I'll always fondly look back at over my twenty years of shopping with Lisa's "Passion Is Fashion Ltd.", a private fashion business she ran. So much fun, always.

Lisa would greet shoppers with open arms, sincere compliments, and an excitement for our shopping sprees. She was so gracious and enthusiastic for us shoppers. Lisa and her well-appointed staff would assist us in choosing clothing that would suit our particular needs and wardrobe. (If there could be a unique way of describing the feeling I had shopping with Lisa, it was like an impeccably organized midway: rollercoasters of joy and excitement seeing bold and outrageous fashions, including fun hats, scarves, accessories. A delicious delight of sartorial splendour.

Lisa ran a wonderful fashion business. She was a true entrepreneur – a professional in so many ways. She had certain designers and suppliers she bought from, as well as very high-end individuals who sold to her. That was the most fun: having couture at my disposal at a fraction of the price. She made us ladies look like a million bucks every time.

With Lisa, confidence, style and graciousness go a long way.

When have you met a gem of a person, whose caring personality and business helped you to feel your very best? How has this impacted your life?

133. Artistic and Supportive Erin

I met Erin way back in the mid 1990s, at a Neuro-Linguistic Programing course in Toronto. We were both interested in personal growth, and have continued to be friends for over twenty-five years. Her upbeat spirit, her caring ways and sheer support have all been qualities that make up my friend, Erin.

Erin was always there, helping me promote my music CDs at places like the One-of-a-Kind Show in Toronto, the Victoriana Show, and at many of my concerts called "An Elegant Affair," held in Toronto's Heliconian Hall.

Something Erin said to me about my music that I have never forgotten: "Laura, you are the one person who has really made me able to feel music for the first time." What a compliment! As a flutist, I've always hoped that what I feel while playing music reaches those listening to me. Erin confirmed this in such beautiful words.

Erin has always been a solutions-focused person rather than problem-focused. I've always admired this about her. Even her car license plate says, "NJOY NOW." She also is a gifted artist – creating beautiful mosaic pieces and other unique creative expressions. She embodies both business-like and artistic qualities, and always stands up for justice. I admire her very much for all of this.

I am forever grateful to Erin for all her support and friendship over the years. She's helped me with some of my most difficult times: getting over breakups and with personal tasks, such as decluttering and letting go of stuff.

Erin is a talented, heart-centered, spiritual being whose ideas, insights and sheer uniqueness make her a very special friend.

Do you have a friend who has helped you overcome some of your most difficult challenges, and stood by your side as your biggest cheerleader?

134. Renate: Original and Upbeat

My friend Renate is a cheerful, intelligent, upbeat, book-lover and adventurer inside and out – a supportive, whole-body listener, and a whole lot of fun. My German-Canadian friend taught me the word *"Lebenskünstler,"* meaning someone who leads a life that is itself an art form. (She told me that there's no direct translation in the English language.)

When Renate complimented me with the label *Lebenskünstler*, I felt understood, seen, heard, and more. She really got me. Renate is a true soul, a deeply feeling humanitarian, vegetarian, and really kind person. I consider her to be one of my very best friends. Whether on the phone or in person, I always feel better after our visit – so uplifting, meaningful and fun. I admire her inner strength, she's a consummate optimist – she seizes each day and lives it to its fullest.

I must say that she embodies compassion and kindness. I'm a better person for knowing my dear friend, Renate.

Have you experienced a friend who "really" knows and your inner workings, so you don't have to explain yourself – you are understood implicitly? Who has gifted you with making you feel visible, seen and deeply understood?

135. Dancing Home with Erica

Erica is a unique artist, dancer, creative spirit, whom I've had the privilege to study with. Her "Dance Our Way Home" method is one of the most memorable mind/body/spirit practices I've done in my entire life. A fully embodied experience of "coming home to ourselves," by expressing our innermost beings: raw, truthful, uncompromising, vulnerable, and beautiful.

I loved the ecstatic dance, the guided meditations Erica did; the journaling, sharing, and more. It was all about sharing from a place of compassion and connection. I've never quite experienced anything like it, before or after this amazing practice.

Erica has a magic about her that invites your innermost being out to play – to be visible, to bubble up from the depths of privacy and deep vulnerability, to open-hearted sharing and fully, authentically, being.

The deep dive into the soul, guided by Erica, left me and others opened, seen and fully present. And it has significantly changed my life for the better: opening me up more and more, allowing in and out, who I really am, who I'm meant to be, and tools to express myself authentically.

Have you ever been so moved by a person or practice that it changed your energy, your life, and your perception of what is possible, when it comes to loving yourself and others unconditionally? What brought out your most authentic self? How do you use this practice now?

136. Dr. K., My Shrink

There are some people who are good listeners, whose very presence assures you that you stories are being fully heard and understood. One of those keen listeners, who happened to be a professional listener, is my therapist, Dr. K.

Dr. K. is retired now, but was a favourite among musician-clients, since he understood the music scene, fraught with competition, favouritism, clichés and the "business" itself. He, too, was an amateur cellist – and I wonder if his innate musical ears helped him to listen well, and be such a gifted therapist.

I felt so fortunate to have his undivided attention, with both his alert eyes and ears, taking in my life. He made me feel seen, witnessed, truly listened to, and mostly, understood.

As the wonderful therapist he was, he was able to offer great insights and feedback that helped me solve and deal with my biggest challenges, like romantic relationship breakups, and my ever-present anxiety and OCD.

One of the greatest insights he brought to my attention was an understanding of anticipatory anxiety. He told me that often the things we fear in advance ("anticipatory anxieties") may never come into being in our future, or are often less intense than our imagination suggested. I have taken this advice to heart, and it's had great impact on my life.

I would also take my dear Pomeranian, Ito, to my therapy sessions, and Dr. K. welcomed him, as he was an animal lover himself.

I owe so much gratitude to a kind, gentle, wise man, named Dr. K. – who changed my life for the better.

Have you known someone who was able to relieve your stress and anxiety through their kindness, compassion and expertise? What did you learn? How are you changed because of their impact on you?

137. Indulis and Ilga, My Music Partners

Through them, I witnessed the most beautiful example of deep love and perfect partnership, both musically and personally. I felt uplifted, joyous, and deeply connected, playing and recording music with them: Indulis, the virtuoso violinist; and Ilga, the sensitive pianist.

There was a beautiful spark between them – both musically and as a married couple who'd been with each other since their teens. They'd been concertizing musicians and music professors in Riga, Latvia, and also in Russia. I saw them grow from starting out as Canadian subway musicians to having over ten beautifully recorded CDs. Their charm, humility and honesty were traits I so admired in this rare musical and married couple.

We recorded a CD of some of my favourite baroque pieces, and entitled the CD *Passionata*. We also performed many concerts together, along with musical engagements, including weddings, corporate events, holiday parties and celebrations of life.

One of my saddest days was learning that dear Ilga passed away suddenly, shortly before their fiftieth wedding anniversary. I always saw them as a unit of one soul. My heart went out to Indulis, whose life without his other half, dear Ilga, continued for just a few years, before he too passed away.

Do you know any couples who are so interconnected that they seem to share one heart? Are you in such a relationship yourself?

138. Nicola, My Sister-In-Law

I've always wanted a sister. And when my brother got married, twenty years ago, I got one: a sister-in-law. And what a beautiful, talented, original she is! A modern dancer and choreographer, with kick-ass moves that bear her personal signature, Nicola is a force to be reckoned with. I have so much respect for her discipline, her process and her creativity. Her vision – and putting it into action – has won her several Dora awards (presented by the Toronto Alliance for the Performing Arts.) She's a phenomenal choreographer and exceptional modern dancer.

One thing I really love about Nicola is how she makes my brother feel. I watch the two of them laugh, like friends who have known each other forever, and that warms my heart. She is also a wonderful cook, and is so gracious, making meals for my boyfriend and me.

I'm so fortunate to have my sister-in-law, Nicola. Her sense of curiosity and wonder make her playfulness and wisdom perfect "dance partners" in life.

Is there someone in your family or extended family whom you admire? What qualities come to mind? What have you learned from this person? Have you told them?

139. Monica, a Natural Healer and Friend

I met her at Nehemia Cohen's Alexander Technique Centre in Toronto. I felt her therapeutic fingers on me as Nehemia coached her and other students how to be practitioners of Cohen's Mitzvah Technique. (This was the technique he created out of Alexander Technique.) I looked up at Monica from the massage table and said, "I want to have sessions with you."

I knew by her sensitivity and touch that she was a gifted body-worker. I went regularly for Mitzvah classes and private sessions with Monica. She'd been a modern dancer, touring internationally with Toronto Dance Theatre. She has the embodiment of power, strength, gentleness, and wise intuition.

I've learned so much about life through my friend, Monica. A meditator, a mom, a friend – Monica is a gentle soul with an inner roar.

Have you ever been "friends at first sight" with anyone? Did your initial intuitions blossom into a beautiful friendship?

140. My Talented Friend Shane

There's no definitive way for me to describe Shane in his wondrous entirety. Shane is like no other: intelligent, deeply compassionate, a talented artist, a misunderstood man with Tourette's syndrome, and a close friend I cherish.

I met Shane in the mid-90s, at the opening of the film *Awakenings*, featuring Robin Williams as Dr. Oliver Saks, the famous New York-based neurologist. In this film, we see the Parkinson's patients "wake up" due to various stimulations. An eye-opening experience for sure, giving hope to those suffering from the Parkinson's disease.

(At the very opening of this film, I was introduced to Dr. Oliver Saks, the guest of honour. I was *honoured* to meet him. He told me that if I were to play upbeat, fast tempo pieces for the people with Parkinson's, it could slow down their tremors. Wow, I was being given guidance right from the horse's mouth: Dr. Saks!)

Shane and I became great friends, and even dated for a while. I admire his many talents and accomplishments, including a Black Belt in karate. He's a phenomenal artist, painting exquisite big canvases with tigers, butterflies and more, along with sculpting beautifully, often with a deeply meaningful social commentary. His sculptures are heartfelt, emotionally moving and transcendent. Shane and I have remained friends all this time – and I consider him to be a true genius. I am both privileged and honoured to know dear Shane.

Have you met someone whose gifts and talents are mind-blowing to you? What impacted you the most about this person?

141. Beautiful Bill B.

One of the kindest souls I've ever met is the legendary Canadian guitarist, composer, producer Bill B. Humble, highly gifted, and also one of the best friends I've ever had.

I'm told that he became a professional guitarist at the early age of fifteen out West, in Alberta. I met Bill in Toronto when I was thirty, when my then-flute teacher referred me to him for a wedding gig. He's been such a pleasure and delight to play and record music with for many years of my life. I've learned so much about music, people and life itself with Bill.

He also happens to have one of the most beautiful souls I've ever been fortunate enough to meet. He's got an amazing, understated, witty sense of humour. Behind his clear, sparkly blue eyes, and sweet, cherub-like face, Bill is full of witty jokes, unique ways of seeing things, and really great advice. He understands people – and is probably the most gentle, relaxed, down-to-earth person I've ever met.

Over the years, I've loved going to the recording studio with Bill, coffees in hand, to record and mix our music. Bill's composing, arranging and guitar performing are superior and beyond beautiful. His many years of experience in the recording studio and live on stage, along with his great ear and sense of humour, made working with him a sheer dream.

When I think of my dear friend, Bill, a smile comes over my face, since he is such a kind and wise soul. He has felt like both a friend and second father to me, with his helpful advice, reassuring words, deep wisdom and supportive, loving ways.

I'm blessed to have had a friend like Bill. Everyone should be so lucky to as well.

Do you have a special figure in your life who feels like family, despite not being a blood relative? What are his/her special qualities? What has he/she taught you?

142. My Magic Carpets

As a flutist, visual artist, writer and actor, I've been an "artist" type all of my life. I've always loved artists, both for their creativity and for the things that they create. In the case of my wonderful friend, Nima, he's the carpet-dealer who shared with me the most beautiful carpets I've ever laid eyes on. A most kind and generous soul, I deeply admire and respect him as a person. I also have a special appreciation for him as a "curator" of finely made carpets.

Nima also happens to come from a very rare religious faith: he is a Zoroastrian, and there are under 200,000 of them in the world, nowadays. I love their philosophy, with the maxim: "Good thoughts, good words, good deeds." It's so simple yet so profound. Nima exudes this custom. He's always so positive, and never a pushy salesman. And he has always appreciated the artist in me.

From time to time, I would visit his shop, just to converse. They were always fascinating conversations about life, people and philosophy. Surrounded by carpets in his shop, I'd tell him that I couldn't imagine standing or stepping on them, since they were such incredible works of art. Some of his clients choose to hang them on the walls, admiring them from that vantage point.

Selecting one of his carpets can be difficult, since all of them seem to have their own unique beauty, and even personality. I loved hearing his stories about the different styles of carpets from different towns in Iran. One of the incredible carpets I bought from him was from the 1970s, and was exquisitely detailed: it took six different women over two-and-a-half years to make by hand. I've been so fortunate to acquire this one for my living room.

I forgave myself for not hanging it on the wall, and appreciate it as a foundation of beauty on the floor. Somehow, having this work of art beneath my feet in the living-room, has brought such a special joy and beauty to playing my flute. I feel as if I'm standing on a special artifact, my "magic carpet."

I am so thankful to Nima for his generosity, knowing I too am a freelance artist, and my paycheques aren't always frequent or dependable. His generosity and open heart are truly memorable. Nima has given me reasonable prices for several exquisite and unforgettable carpets: unique pieces of art, coming from a precious and unique soul: Nima!

Reflect upon your experiences with art. What types of art and beauty move you the most? Do you experience the same awe doing art or having art from others? Has anyone gifted you with art? What happened?

143. My Long-Time Friend Glenn

Some friends are there at the right time and the right place. In Glenn's case, he was more than that.

Fast-forward to 4:20 am on January 22, 1996, when I received that inevitable phone call from the Toronto Grace Hospital to hear the nurse on the other end of the phone. Mom had just passed away.

Only two hours before, my best friend, Glenn, a waiter, finished his shift at the French bistro and showed up at my doorstep with my favourite soup: butternut squash. I was shocked, since it was 2 am – and he was so thoughtful, as he often was. Tonight, it was very different: He told me he just knew – just knew that tonight was the night my mom would pass away. Not only was I so amazed with his intuition, but it was filled with his love and caring toward me.

For many years prior, Glenn had been my best friend, the one I would tell all the important events to (after calling and telling my mom first, of course). Glenn, an exceptionally sweet gay man, had such a sensitivity – almost psychic in nature. We were on such a wavelength together. Sometimes I didn't need to utter a word, and he would know exactly what I was thinking. What a privilege it is to have had a friend that knows you inside out. I can say that I've never met a person quite like Glenn.

Sadly, we had a breakdown in our communication about ten years ago and have lost contact. After five deliberate attempts to reconnect, by mailing him birthday cards and letters, I've let it be.

I truly hope that one day we will reunite as friends again. Glenn had been such a gift in my life.

Do you have a former friend who you want to make amends with? Have you attempted initiating contact with them yet? Will you?

144. The Harlequin Romance that Never Happened

As the saying goes, "life is stranger than fiction." My life has been full of these unusually strange moments and encounters. That day meeting Bobby was no different. It was the late '80s, and I was clothes shopping in Toronto at a particular boutique I enjoyed visiting.

As I walked in, a man with a glowing smile like a ray of sunshine welcomed me into the store. I did a double take. Approaching me was an unusually handsome salesman who had a heart of gold and the look of a top model. He offered to help me find what I was looking for. I wasn't sure. I was more caught up in him. Not just his fine looks, but his energy. His steely blue eyes, high cheekbones, and kind ways were refreshing, but definitely unusual in a big city like Toronto.

He introduced himself as Bobby and we became friends. It's strange that I didn't feel the desire to pursue a romantic relationship with him. He was my type, but something was stopping me. I have to say, Bobby was drop-dead gorgeous, and it wasn't just me who recognized his stunning, good looks. Harlequin

Enterprises, the publisher specializing in their own brand of romance novels, "Harlequin Romances," hired Bobby for over ten covers of their books. He showed me his collection of covers – and yes, that was Bobby on the front covers.

Funny, we never became lovers, just friends with a flirtatious spirit. Bobby was Jewish and was a real "*Mensch.*" His heart was broken after a recent breakup when I met him. Seeing him in grief over this, I came to realize that both men and women can equally mourn the loss of their important relationships. Bobby was no different.

He invited me back to his place a few times, and I was both shocked and saddened to learn that he used drugs. I suppose it helped him to dull the pain of the loss of his relationship.

One night visiting Bobby, I asked him to drive me home. It was around two o'clock in the morning, and he had been using drugs. I knew it was risky getting into the car with him, but I did anyway. We took a four-lane highway. As I looked over at Bobby, suddenly, his head was drooped over the steering wheel while he nodded off! His car was veering to the left, then the right. I became panic-stricken, since I didn't know how to drive.

I felt completely out of control, like I was in a nightmare. Not knowing what else to do, I screamed out, "Bobby, wake up!" Luckily for us, he did – and he took me home, safe and sound. That was the very last time I've gotten into a car with someone who's been drinking or using drugs.

Close calls can suddenly creep up on us with very little notice, or none at all. In this case, I knew I was walking into danger, and did it anyway. I made a decision in that moment that there wouldn't be a "next time" with Bobby. We slowly drifted apart, and I didn't hear from him again. I often wonder if he's still alive.

What a tragic life for a Harlequin Romance cover model! People aren't always what they appear. I've also learned that you can't judge a book by its cover or a person by their looks or their vocation. And yes, "life is stranger than fiction," even if it's a romance novel.

Have you ever experienced a shocking discovery about a person you thought you knew very well? What did this situation teach you about people, our assumptions and how to live? What have you chosen to do differently because of this?

145. When Traditional Meets Eccentric: My Friend David

David is a true "one of a kind." They say that Libras are very conversational and easy going – and that, he is. It all started when I met him at the University of Toronto's Walter Hall, at a chamber-music concert. We met in the front row, just as the lights began to dim, and as the performance was about to begin.

David had just arrived back from China, visiting his girlfriend. He reminded me of my father: conversational, tall, easy-going, and someone who listened with his whole being, just like my dad. He would lean forward, look you directly in the eyes and nod and smile. I could really feel his presence. Dad had just died two months prior, so it warmed my heart to meet someone who reminded me of my dad's ways.

David had a good ear and a great appreciation for music, and we met many times at chamber concerts. We expanded our post-concert social group, and we would all go out for drinks afterwards at the Duke of York, a local Toronto pub, just around the corner from the concert hall.

David claimed to have been shy as a young boy in England, but certainly displayed bold, conversational finesse. Somehow, I've noticed two distinctive things about my experience with British people. First of all, anything they say seems right, since their accent carries a sense of bold accuracy and certainty. The other is they have a great sense of humour and way of looking at life. British wit is unparalleled, in my books. I find their choice of words to be utterly hilarious, and often either quite tongue-in-cheek or boldly animated.

Such a fun man! Colourful and full of surprises – from wit to eccentric life experiences. I learned that he'd met his current girlfriend under interesting circumstances: she was a call-girl who became more. I was fascinated by his story, by his seeming so straightlaced and British, yet having such an interesting past.

We've been friends for years – and David always surprises me with his daring and shocking experiences and stories.

Who has been a special unexpected friend in your life? Have you ever been shocked by their choices, stories and experiences? How have you dealt with their surprises?

146. My Happy-Go-Lucky Friend Rick

My friend Rick is American, but has spent many years living in Toronto. Into healthy lifestyle as one of his biggest focuses, Rick looks at least twenty years younger than his years, laughs non-stop, and is compassionate and spiritual.

Rick is the go-to guy when you have questions about health, since he knows so much about health and healing. I often think of him as the living "human experiment" as he is often trying out new health remedies and therapies to better his health and wellbeing. His love for beauty and nature has taken us on many beautiful nature walks, noticing the butterflies, flowers, rivers and skies.

He's also been a good ear and shoulder to lean on over the years. One question he's asked me that has left an indelible mark on me is: "How's that working for you?" It would stop me in my tracks and help me to review my actions.

Always a straight shooter with an uproarious sense of humour, Rick has added so much awareness and appreciation to my life. As a lover of peace, beauty and life itself, I'm better off for knowing him.

Do you have a friend who inspires you because of something they are completely committed to? What have you learned from them?

147. My Beautiful Miracle Friend Shawn

As the saying goes, "some people come into your life for a reason, a season or a lifetime." I agree.

I wouldn't have ever dreamed that Shawn would have been such a change-agent, as well as a friend in my life. I wouldn't have met members of my birth family if it weren't for him. In retrospect, I must say that meeting Shawn was both for a reason – a very important one – and also for friendship for our season and beyond. I have cherished the walks, talks and laughs we've shared for many years.

I feel so honoured to have him in my life – and I appreciate the initiative he took that day in December 2019, buzzing the apartment of an aunt I'd never met. That day was the first of many days, connecting with my blood relatives, and I have Shawn to thank for this initial meeting. After all, I was already fifty-five-years-old, and to date, hadn't met any of them.

Shawn and I have shared many personal stories, and one that I shared with him was the story of my adoption. When I showed him a picture of my aunt on Facebook, he recognized the background – it was a senior's apartment building across the street from his mother's nursing home. What a coincidence!

I am forever grateful for Shawn's bold, courageous action: taking it upon himself to contact my aunt. As a result of his bold action, I've met her, her daughter (my cousin) and my cousin's daughter (my first cousin once removed).

To know some of my blood relatives has settled a deep part of me that had been unsettled for most of my life. I haven't met my birth mom, her kids or grandkids, but that's okay. I have two lovely cousins and a sweet and welcoming aunt – who fortunately was at home the very day Shawn buzzed her apartment.

When has a friend changed your life in ways you could have never imagined? What were the circumstances in which you met and your life changed?

148. Keith's Middle Name is "Talent"

Bubbly, like a crisp glass of sparkling water, my friend Keith has been a true source of energy and inspiration in my life for many years. Originally from England, Keith has been a drummer, music producer, composer, author, entrepreneur, black belt in martial arts, and a true friend. I've probably left something out, since every day he seems to be recreating himself and his life. When I think of the terms *"joie de vivre"* and *"carpe diem,"* Keith comes to mind.

Every single time I've met with or spoken with Keith, I've always felt lighter, uplifted and inspired. Refreshingly positive, what a gift Keith has been in my life.

I'll always remember my entertainment lawyer suggesting Keith and I meet, since he had an entrepreneurial venture, creating CD greeting cards: blank cards with themed CDs inside. Keith asked me if I had any flute recordings of wedding music, Christmas music and lullaby music. The only one I didn't have was lullaby music. With an entrepreneurial spirit, I boldly asked him if he could give me a week.

He did.

Three years later, the CD I created for Keith – called *Lullababy* – was picked up by a big Canadian distributor. And four years later, it became a certified Canadian Gold CD!

Keith and I have remained good friends for over thirty years, and always share positive, upbeat conversations. He continues to astound me with his latest creative projects: During the pandemic he wrote an entire musical, to be performed on concert stages once the restrictions are lifted.

Keith truly treats his life as a gift, and a true gift *he is!* I wish everyone had a Keith in their lives.

Have you been introduced to someone who became a very important and special friend in your life, either for personal or professional reasons or both?

149. The Dancer Is Sitting Right in Front of Me

I have a very special friend named Cate, whom I've met with for lunch from time to time. All of our meetings are inspiring, and the conversations deeply spiritual and philosophical. Such enriching talks, I've always looked forward to what we will discuss next.

We originally met in the magic section of the Omega Bookstore in Toronto, a store full of books on esoteric subjects, including astrology, numerology, and various types of mysticism. At our first meeting, a book actually fell off the bookshelf in the magic section – which seemed appropriate to the auspicious quality of our encounter.

My friend is a unique mix of intellectual and mystical. We always had fascinating conversations when we got together. We delved deeply.

At one particular lunch, we were sitting outside at a local restaurant patio. She had tears in her eyes and a tremble in her voice. Although she had a good administrative job, and loved dancing in her spare time, she really wanted to dance more. She told me she wanted to *become* a dancer. I looked over at her compassionately, but feeling astounded with what I perceived.

I took a deep breath and said, "I am speaking with the *very* dancer you claim you want to be. You are speaking this persona into the future, almost like it's out of reach, and you are in a constant state of reaching for it. But, instead, I am looking at you, the dancer, with tears in your eyes, knowing that you already are the dancer you speak of. You are seeking and reaching for her, but you *are* her."

Her big blue eyes opened in wide amazement – like she was suddenly digesting a new point of view. She *was* the dancer across the table crying about wanting to *be* a dancer.

I shared with her a few spiritual expressions I'd heard, "The seeker is the sought," and "You are the one you have been waiting for." These quotes had really impacted me, and I hoped they would her, too.

Only a few years later, I went to see her one-woman show: a solo dance piece at the Toronto Fringe Dance Festival. She had both choreographed and danced her piece. Her costume was colourful and beautiful – and so was she. She'd transformed. The dancer that had always lived within her was dancing for us, now, fully, unapologetically and with abandon. I was so thrilled for her! I always knew she *was* the dancer speaking to me across the table that day.

Can you think of a time when you felt like something you wanted to be was out of reach, and later you discovered that you were that already, you just needed to shift your perception? How did that discovery help you?

150. The Living Goddess: Lisa Van Stygeren

One of the most beautiful human beings I've ever met was Lisa Van Stygeren. She was beautiful inside and out. I first met her at her art exhibit in Toronto, at the upscale ladies' club, 21 McGill. Her show was made up of beautiful, angelic bronze sculptures along with framed photographs of them too. There was something otherworldly about them – they looked so real, yet seemed mystically beyond. The exhibit was aptly called "Modern Day Goddesses."

I approached Lisa in a state of pure awe. I couldn't get over how life-like her sculptures all were – and that she didn't use any live models or photos as references for her creating them. As I continued talking with her, I looked at her sculptures and asked about them. She had named them all. Then it struck me: There was no model or photo reference, since *she* was all of the goddesses, herself! I don't know if she realized this consciously, but many of her fans could see her symmetrical, angelic face in all of them.

I was completely blown away, and in a deep state of awe and wonder. Two of her sculptures really spoke to me: *Bliss* and *Surrender*. *Bliss* is a long-necked beauty with her eyes closed, looking peaceful and blissful. She was simply a sculpted beauty from the neck up. Magically, depending on how the light shines on her, and from which angle you are looking at her, she seems to have a subtly different emotion on her face.

Surrender is a full-body sculpture kneeling in a state of what seems to be rapture, bliss and surrender, all at once. I love her because she is unapologetically feminine, with strength and vulnerability, all at the same time. Looking at *Surrender* gives me a powerful sense of what it can feel like to be a fully expressed and empowered woman. I wonder if in some way, *Surrender* has helped me to be both powerful and vulnerable at the same time? She's been a role model for me, for sure.

Despite loving all Lisa's art, I couldn't afford to buy it on the spot, paying in full. I asked Lisa if I could pay her a deposit for both sculptures, along with some of her beautiful, framed photos, since I wanted to be surrounded by this sheer beauty in my home. For over twenty years, these inspirational beauties, *Bliss* and *Surrender*, have lived in my home.

Lisa moved to Santa Fe a few years later, and I had the pleasure of traveling to see her in Galisteo and visiting her gallery on Canyon Road, in Santa Fe. Santa Fe is known as an artist's paradise, since the light is so unique and sparkly, and the skies are beyond exquisite. This is also the home of Georgia O'Keefe.

One remarkable thing I learned about Lisa was that she decided to start sculpting after her daughter, Kim, a professional artist, urged her to. Lisa was about fifty at the time. What a gift – to step into such a sensually beautiful expression of herself at this sage age. Lisa had done many things prior to creating her modern-day goddesses, including modeling, so she was familiar with beauty.

Sadly, Lisa passed away in June 2020 – yet her beauty, celebrated in her sculptures and photography lives on. So do memories of this bold, talented, original human being, Lisa Van Stygeren.

Have you been moved or rendered speechless by beauty? What was your experience? What made this experience so unique?

151. Yanka, Power of Self-Image, a Magnificent Soul

I met Yanka for the first time at WEC, "Women Entrepreneurs of Canada." As members, we attended monthly meetings with all sorts of women entrepreneurs. It was so inspiring to learn from each other. I even remember one meeting when the famous entrepreneur responsible for Miss Vickie's Potato Chips, was speaking, and inspiring us with her story. To this day, I remember her spirited talk, and consider her potato chips my very favourite and superior in their taste, crunch and overall experience.

When I met Yanka, I realized that women can be positive forces of nature. She personified boldness, courage, frankness, charisma and fun. Her huge heart poured out into all our conversations. Yanka, a Dutch-Canadian, former model and self-image coach, also happened to be married to one of the three founding members of the Toronto International Film Festival (TIFF), originally named the Festival of Festivals, which started in 1976. I got to know Yanka, her husband Henk, and her daughter Yolanda quite well over the years.

I loved going over to their studio for photoshoots. Greeted by their beautiful black Bouvier dog, white orchids decorating the space, I always felt wonderful and alive there. It was Yanka and Yolanda who, as a mother-daughter team, took my promotional photos. Yanka was a skilled make-up artist, who also coached clients in front of the mirror about intrinsic beauty and essence – a very natural and intuitive spiritual coaching that just seemed to spontaneously and effortlessly come out of her mouth prior to the start of the photoshoot.

These encouraging and beautifying remarks would continue throughout the session, making it one of the most transcendent, uplifting experiences I've ever had. As Yanka continued directing and coaching me, her daughter, Yolanda, would photograph. What a perfect pair, encouraging the best out of all their photography clients. But, as I mentioned, it was more than a photoshoot: it was a delightful self-empowerment session!

Another gift I experienced was every September, when the Toronto International Film Festival ran, Yanka would call me and generously take me as her guest to galas and world premieres, and offer me pairs of tickets to films she couldn't attend. We had so much fun experiencing many films together and meeting movie stars.

A kind, thoughtful soul, Yanka is a very special friend I will cherish and love forever.

Have you ever met someone who is so interesting and humble, and opens your eyes and heart to your truest potential? This is a special gift, when someone sees who you really are and what you can be. How did you transform because of this special person in your life?

152. My Talented Friend Dyniss

A true friend, who listens with the ears of a skilled musician, engineer and producer, Dyniss has been my friend for over twenty-five years. I was fortunate enough to have had him as our engineer on my improvised CD, *Above the Sound of Gravity*, with my dear friend, sound-healer and multi-instrumentalist, Michael.

Dyniss is a vegan, a true animal lover and a critical thinker. He's also a very fair-minded person whom I respect a lot. Some of his songs are soulful, some are funny, and others are animal- and environment-focused.

I enjoy how deep and honest Dyniss and I can go together, when we talk. I can discuss almost anything with him, and I feel listened to and considered – and he gives great feedback. He's a wonderful balance between being logical and emotional. (I've found this to be rare among my male friends.) We also share a quirky sense of humour and always enjoy our times connecting. Our conversations are always fulfilling and emotionally satisfying.

Speaking deeply, honestly, and from the heart is a real privilege. Do you have any friends with whom you share this quality of sharing? Who are they? What do you treasure the most about your connection?

153. My Heart-Centred Friend, Charmalee

I call her "Charm" – and indeed, she has been my friend and my "Lucky Charm" for many years. A true heart with a soul the size of the universe, Charm is generous, supportive and full of amazing ideas. Whenever I'm with her, we creatively fuse, and delve into interesting projects. She's an Aquarian, and according to astrology, this sign is very innovative, and that's Charmalee for sure.

Charm has been the designer for the cover artwork on many of my flute CDs, for most of my websites, and has generously donated her time to some of my animal welfare fundraisers. And, if that's not enough, she's also my accountant!

One year I was being audited by the Canada Revenue Agency, and was particularly stressed. She cautioned me, advising me to have her reply to them on my behalf. That was the greatest advice and support I had ever received. The audit was smooth sailing because of her.

In so many ways, Charm has lightened my load, helped me change my perspective from stress to tranquility, and has been a human elixir of creative inspiration. Always an inspiration, Charmalee is full of inspiring ideas and perspectives, and her generosity is over the top. I've never met someone so kind and Buddha-like as Charmalee.

She also happens to be a wonderful mother of four, a grandmother, and a friend to many!

Who in your life has helped soften the sharp corners of your life? Who's helped you to live more creatively and with more peace and tranquility?

154. Caitlin, Friendship on the Beach

I met this lovely South-African woman at the Toronto Islands. I knew instantly that we had something in common: a sense of joy and wonder, and living the moment. It was a weekday, and my dog Ito and I were at the shoreline of Ward's Island beach – and so was Caitlin. We smiled and said hello, recognizing a similar sunny spirit in each another.

It was a perfectly sunny day, not a cloud in the sky. Just this moment in time. The waves wafted up at water's edge. Life felt both alive and gentle at the same time. We smiled again. We introduced ourselves. We became friends. As a musician, the sound of someone's voice has always had a big impact on me. Caitlin has one of the most melodious and beautiful voices I've ever heard. This intrigued me, as her accent sounded like a hybrid of British, South African, and something I couldn't quite define.

We had rich conversations and really enjoyed the pleasure of life: walks, talks, curiosity and discovery. But sadly, soon after meeting, her father fell ill. I learned more about what it means to live life with joy and gratitude every day – a tenet her father carried within his soul, as was so clear to all who met him. A few years after, her father passed away.

Several years later, my own father passed away. It's interesting how friends can come into our lives, around themes, life passages, unbeknownst to us at the time. But later, when looking back, we see the mystical parallels and serendipities.

Have you experienced a friendship where a lot of mutual themes and life stages were experienced together? How has this friendship helped you through some of your most challenging times?

155. Saying Hello and Goodbye to Elizabeth on the Phone

Elizabeth is one of the brightest human souls I've ever met. Meeting her in a rush line for an evening chamber-concert at Toronto's Royal Conservatory of Music, we immediately hit it off. She had a splash of fiery red hair, a face that welcomed me with her open smile, remarkable cheekbones, and melodious voice. She was eighty-seven at the time, I later learned. She had a flair for fashion and looked twenty years younger. I later found out she had modeled in earlier years – a natural beauty.

We hit it off immediately. We learned that we were both Taureans, loved beauty in all its forms, including classical music, nature, pets, fine food and beautiful flowers and adventure, galore. We also enjoyed being absolutely silly and childlike with each other. I felt a natural bond with Elizabeth and she with me.

I later learned that dear Elizabeth had unfortunately lost her only daughter to cancer when her daughter was only thirty-three. She had been a modern dancer with her own dance company. A tragedy to lose such a young daughter. Coincidentally, I'd lost my mother to cancer when I was just thirty-two. Elizabeth and I further bonded over our mutual losses. We joked about her adopting me as her daughter. Based on our similarities, we actually could be mother and daughter.

We definitely had some life-experience synergy. Elizabeth could be my next adoptive mom – not to devalue my love for my original adoptive mom, Nancy Nashman, which was the most amazing mother I could have ever asked for.

Elizabeth and I, despite our age difference of twenty-three years, were like two peas in a pod. Upbeat, loving music, butterflies, adventures, chatting with strangers, and simply celebrating and enjoying life. We would go to the Toronto Islands and watch the butterflies in the well-manicured gardens, we'd attend

Toronto Symphony concerts, and nod to each other at the deeply emotional parts in the music that reached us at the same time.

Now, Elizabeth is in a retirement home with advanced Alzheimer's. It's sad, yet our conversations are still full of love, celebration and memories of good times together. My "hello" on the phone is always recognizable to Elizabeth, since she says she recognizes my voice tone. She has a musical ear, and played piano as a child, sang in choirs, and later, even taught music and other subjects in school.

One of my most favorite parts of talking on the phone with Elizabeth is how we say "goodbye." We playfully repeat "goodbye" back and forth to each other, in upbeat cartoon-like fun voices, and send each other big hugs, which we both say we are catching. I asked Elizabeth what her *modus operandi* for life is, and she replied, "Living in gratitude." And she has!

With two grown boys, many grandchildren and great-grandchildren, I wished her an extra Happy Mother's Day, noting that if it weren't for her, none of these people would exist. In her classic joyous laugh, she agreed!

I will always think of Elizabeth's beautiful smile, twinkly eyes, contagious laugh and generous soul. Elizabeth – what a genuine gift to my life and the world.

When in your life have you appreciated hearing "hello" and savouring the "goodbyes"? It may be a rare occasion, but with some people, simply saying "hello" can open our hearts and how you say "goodbye" can sustain the joy, long past the visit or after they are gone.

156. The Pink Floral and Fragrant Sky

I telephoned my dear ninety-year-old friend Elizabeth, in her retirement home. She was feeling isolated and lonely because of the Covid-19 lockdown. It had already been almost one year. I sympathized with her, emphasizing that all of us were feeling very isolated, but we needed to continue to socially distance due to public safety.

Elizabeth is both a very emotionally aware and logical person – her IQ matched her EQ. She could see that the lockdown made sense, but emotionally, it was no fun at all. Like many people in her situation, she felt sad and depressed and very alone.

Because I loved her so much and wanted to cheer her up, I got inspired to create a visualization for her right there and then, over the phone. I asked her to close her eyes on the bed, and lie comfortably on her back. Next, I asked her to breathe in through her nose and out her mouth. She was happy to do so. Next, I started the visualization in a completely improvised fashion.

Without effort, in my mind's eye, I saw a soft and dreamy sky. I then gently asked her to imagine a gentle, pink-coloured sky with puffy cotton ball-like clouds wafting by. Next, with each breath, I invited her to imagine inhaling fragrances of some of her favourite flowers. The sky had become a fragrant bouquet: gentle breezes of jasmine, rose, peonies, lilacs, hyacinths, freesias, and more! She loved it. She was amazed at how this made her feel. She exclaimed that it cured her loneliness, right then, right there! What a gift – to help a friend feel happy again.

Another time, I brought her two of my original paintings from my "Spa-on-the-Canvas" collection. She said, "Your paintings literally saved my life!" She described her despair, staring at her four walls, and feeling so depressed – but she told me that the oceanic colours of one painting and the sunset colours of the other brought her so much joy. Bringing gifts to her delivered a gift to *my* heart.

By just knowing that my heart had reached hers through my paintings and fragrant visualization made my heart sing.

Have you used your senses to help calm or uplift your spirit or the mood of others? Do you continue to use this tool? How has it helped?

157. "Dr. B": A Blissful Soul

One of my all-time favourite people is Dr. B, a neighbour of mine, two floors down. A retired English professor, with a charming wit, old-fashioned politeness and humility that always exuded from him. He's a true gentleman, in his late nineties, always insisting on getting up to see you out of his apartment after a cordial visit, and opening the door for you. In 2021 he turned 100 years old!

During the Covid-19 pandemic, whenever I would ask him how he felt, he would boldly exclaim, "I'm in rude health." I had no idea that this was an old-fashioned way of saying, "good health." Dr. B. was full of such surprising prose. I found myself amused, entertained and warmed by his presence like no-one before and no-one to follow. He's such an original.

I admire his fierce work ethic. He dedicates at least five or six hours to writing *every* day – and would tell me with the accuracy of a self-satisfied accountant that he exceeds at least eighty-five hours of writing per month. He goes to bed at nine o'clock and gets up at five, quite the opposite to the average working person, who works 9 am to 5 pm. (I fall somewhere in between: more like noon to 8 pm.)

A remarkable man in so many ways, during the Covid-19 pandemic in 2020, Dr. B. succeeded in writing three books. Many of us didn't even read a book. I've noticed there are many people who like to say, "I've always wanted to write a book," but still haven't. In a way, I understand, since it's a commendable goal – yet more often than not, they never end up doing it. Their mantra of "someday I will write a book" is more constant than their sitting down and starting. Dr. B. is the opposite: with three books written in 2020, he is a role model I admire.

Knowing Dr. B. has been a gift: such a kind, old-fashioned elder, as well as being an "open door" to scholarly life with a heart-centred connection. I will forever cherish our richly satisfying talks and his humility.

Have you ever met someone whose wisdom and years made you feel like you were in the presence of a wise soul? What did you learn from this person? How has it changed your life for the better?

158. The Brains of My Boyfriends

I've definitely had unusual and unexpected experiences with boyfriends with unique brains. Fascinating thoughts, words and actions were all part of our times together.

One boyfriend in my early twenties, named Shane, was a painter, sculptor and karate black belt – and he happens to have Tourette's syndrome. He was and is an extraordinary human being. Sadly, with Tourette's, he experienced a lot of ridicule due to his ticks (involuntary movements), and was often misunderstood. He was taken to police stations, wrongly accused of being on drugs, when his Tourette's presented with many sudden involuntary movements and vocal utterances.

I loved spending time with him, absorbing his keen observations, and experiencing life through his unique and fascinating lens. With him, life felt so alive – a "technicolor," wondrous experience of all the senses. Every sound, sight and observation seemed amplified, and worthy of attention and fascination.

I remember him telling me about that day he visited the Toronto Zoo, and many people were looking at a majestic tiger. Uncannily, the only person the tiger looked at and continued to acknowledge was my friend, Shane. Did the tiger have a special instinctive sense? Were my friend's ticks attracting the tiger's attention?

After Shane and I parted ways, I felt as if all of life's vitality left life itself – like the bottom fell out! It suddenly went back to black and white, returning to its normal ways. No more technicolor world, no more delicious life. Traffic went by, people went to work, life went on, but it all paled in comparison to how I felt when I was with Shane.

Tourette's syndrome. What a true gift it was dating a person with such extreme talents and unique neurological wiring.

About ten years later, I met Michael, another fascinating individual: a multi-instrumental musician and sound healer. His brain wiring was unique too: Asperger's syndrome, which is high functioning, on the autism spectrum.

Experiencing life alongside Michael was always fascinating and eye-opening. It seemed like he had an extra ability with perception. It appeared that he could see things more intricately, in great detail – and he became an amazing nature photographer. He was able to hear things with the sensitivity and precision of a dog's ears, and could sense things spiritually and intuitively with the ease of a wise sage. In fact, he is also an astute astrologer.

I remember the time we would sit down to dinner and he'd simply eat, facing his dinner plate. I felt frustrated since I wanted to converse and look at each other while we ate. Michael, explaining his Asperger's dilemma, said: "I can either put my fork down and talk with you, or I can eat dinner, and focus on that, but not easily do both." I didn't understand this phenomenon: not being able to easily do two things at once. At the time, I was utterly frustrated, since I felt such a disconnection that sadly wasn't Michael's fault. It was his brain wiring.

Now, looking back, I realize that Michael's Asperger's has been a true gift all along. In fact, single-minded focus is advocated when living life in a state of mindfulness. Perhaps, in a way, Michael's inability to speak and eat easily and simultaneously was a gift in practising mindfulness at the dinner table!

My current boyfriend has a unique wiring, too. He's introverted, experiences life inwardly, rather than outwardly. In a way, his high IQ makes him what some would call a "brainiac." He composes modern classical music, plays – and even invents – board games, and thinks a lot. He's a published author, with two books and hundreds of articles in international magazines and newspapers. His written words are clear, crisp, pointed and witty.

I often find myself asking him what he's thinking about. I've gotten used to his quietude. I understand him a whole lot better.

Highly gifted and intelligent, he can also be quite eccentric. I've often heard him talking to himself in the shower, practising music passages and conversations. He seems more engaged with his phantom conversations than real ones at times.

Perhaps introversion brings conversational ease both in the shower and inside the head.

Have you experienced people with unique neurological wiring who fascinated you? What did you discover and learn being with them? How has your life been enriched by them?

159. Falling in Love with My Special Friend, a Gay Man

My first boyfriend, John, wasn't really a boyfriend, but rather a very special music partner – which, at the time, was the most important role I could have had in my life.

I was just seventeen. He was sixteen. My life as a teenager was all about practising the flute for four-to-five hours a day, listening to flute recordings with earphones, even when I nodded off to sleep, and rehearsing with John. I had such a crush on this handsome Spanish-Canadian pianist. He played with so much beauty and passion, and we musically fused together.

Every Monday night, I would go to practise with John at his place. Sometimes, we would put a tape recorder on the keyboard and simply improvise. It was sheer magic, since we would create melodies on the spot, and somehow John always knew what chords to play. It was almost like we were meant to be – as musical partners.

After our concerts, audience-members would come backstage with tears in their eyes, showing how moved they were by our music. This was the greatest compliment a performer can receive – bringing listeners to tears, reaching their hearts and souls. I felt privileged to be part of this.

On the life-partner front, sadly for me, John was gay. I had dreamed of the perfect life: being married to this wonderful pianist and having a lifetime career of concertizing as a flute and piano duo. This magic bubble was burst when reality reminded me that this could never happen.

What *did* happen was years of performing concerts locally in Toronto at Heliconian Hall. We put on a series of concerts called "An Elegant Affair." The performances were followed by welcoming *hors d'oeuvres*-and-wine receptions. We gained an audience following, and some people even told us it was their favorite concert series, since it had that special social component after the concert. We ran this series for about six years.

We also made many CDs together, some containing music John had composed. Ironically, years after we'd originally met, we created a CD of John's compositions and called it *Remember When*. The title fit in several ways: for one, it was a personal title for us, remembering those Monday nights at his place, improvising original flute and piano music on the spot with the tape recorder. Also, *Remember When* invites the audience to reflect and think of times that the CD's melodies evoke.

We recorded many other CDs, including a lullaby disc entitled *Lullababy*, that became a certified Gold CD in Canada in 2000.

As musicians, life was fortunate for us. We played concerts, received quarterly royalties and recorded CDs. What a perfect time and place to express ourselves together musically from our hearts.

There's love everywhere. Love expresses itself in so many ways. Sometimes it is meant to be friendship and collaboration as musical partners. What partnerships have you had that have nourished your life and your spirit?

160. Junji, My First Lover

My first lover was Japanese. And with him, I experienced a lot of firsts. I experienced sex for the very first time (on a shag carpet, to Shostakovich's Fifth Symphony – an intense musical and sensual experience). I also communicated with someone where English was his second language – and I broke up with someone for the first time. These were a lot of firsts, and I was just twenty-two.

We first met at the University of Toronto's Faculty of Music, both budding flutists. He'd flown all the way from Japan to study flute with the famous flutist Jeanne Baxstresser, then the Principal Flutist of the Toronto Symphony. (She later became Principal Flutist in the New York Philharmonic.) I was studying flute, but more interested in studying this fascinating fellow from Japan – standing six feet, two inches, with spiky, coarse, jet-black hair, a sly smile, sexy eyes, and a cigarette in his mouth, casually, like the Marlborough man at the back of 1970s magazines. He was an Asian sex symbol, at least to me!

I noticed everything about him, including his cologne: "Devon," a men's fresh and crisp citrus cologne by Christian Dior. Junji, with all his mysterious allure was also was full of philosophical wisdom – in broken English. I loved his curious spirit, his sense of fun, his studious approach to the flute, and our exquisitely sensual moments together.

One challenge I had that sadly became the deal-breaker was his drinking. He would sport that tell-tale "drunk red" complexion so common on Asian faces. I told him it scared me when he was inebriated, but he didn't really take me seriously. I decided I needed to give him an ultimatum. I gave him three chances to respect my wishes and not come over drunk – but the third time, he lost his last chance with me.

I broke up with Junji. He cried, he begged, he pleaded. Although it broke my heart, I stuck to my guns and said a firm "No."

Junji returned to Japan that summer, heartbroken, but a better flutist. Every year for at least fifteen years, he remembered to call to wish me a happy birthday. It broke my heart to think he held a candle for me from the Orient. There was only one other person I've broken up with since – the rest have broken my heart.

Have you experienced a special relationship, lover or friend, that left you with an indelible print of them in your life? What made it so?

161.   Mensa Peter Meets Hunky Armando

I never thought I'd fall in love with two men at the same time. But I did.

They couldn't be farther apart in looks, values, intellect and life trajectories. I first met Armando when I was hired with my classical chamber-music group to provide elegant dinner-music for a corporate banquet at the University Club, a posh, ultra-conservative private club in downtown Toronto.

One of my favorite activities is people-watching, and it's even more fun while playing flute. I find that the time seems to go by much more quickly, too, when there is something else, or *someone* else, to focus on, in addition to playing the music for the usual three-to-four-hour engagement.

People-watching went up a level that day. Armando was one of the most beautiful, tall, Spanish men I'd ever laid my eyes on. Standing six foot, two inches, with sparkly dark eyes and grin with a hint of mischievous bad-boy, he would sashay by us, delivering delicious *hors d'oeuvres* and champagne with the charm of a movie star.

Armando caught my eye several times and I knew that this mild flirtation had more fire behind it. I hoped I'd get to experience his delicious Spanish charm in person on one of our music breaks. Fortunately for me, we did.

Discreetly, Armando gestured to me to follow him up an elegant winding staircase to the second floor. We were the only ones up there. He led me to a closed door and slowly opened it. The coast was clear. Without blinking an eye, he grabbed me, picked me up with his strong arms, propped me up on the beautiful dining-room table like a doll on display. I gasped in utter shock and delight. I'd never experienced such a passionate scene in a movie, let alone my own life!

I heard my sheer black pantyhose rip as he lay me down on my back. Then, he held me down gently by my wrists and started kissing me passionately. I was euphoric, yet nervous that someone would walk in. That was part of the tease and thrill.

Looking down at my watch, I realized I needed to get back, since our break was over in just one minute. He took out a sharpie marker, reached into the back of my black silk blouse and quickly scribbled his phone number on the back of the shirt tag. What a sensual business card! By far, this was the sexiest way any man has given me his number.

I called him a few days later. He and his approach were utterly irresistible.

My times with Armando were childlike and fun. He would often piggyback me down the sidewalks of Toronto, traffic zipping by, and I would feel like a kid again. When I'd telephone him to wish him a great day, his usual reply was often, "It's not over yet," with his telltale sexy Spanish accent.

Our times together were unparalleled. But there was an unfortunate flaw to this fairy-tale. One day, I found out he was dating another woman, an older woman, in her late forties. I'd discovered one of her earrings on the seat in his car. I could only imagine what they'd been doing for her earring to fall out! Despite the evidence, I didn't want to know the details. Since I was only twenty-seven at the time, I thought I may have had an advantage over her.

My "Baryshnikov look-alike", Peter, also came into my life around that time. He was a green-eyed "prince," with a tanned, Mediterranean complexion and blonde hair. His background was Croatian, and he turned heads. A Scorpio, with all the seductive gestures and bedtime prowess, he was the opposite to youthful, boyish, Armando. He was a science guy, worked as a sales rep for a pharmaceutical company, and happened to be a member of Mensa. Some people refer to it as the "egghead club," since you need to have an IQ of a high level to be a member.

What was remarkable was this Croatian heartthrob was so sensual, so smart, yet so traditional and conservative. He even proposed to me one day. I will never forget how he did it. I was in my tiny office downtown and he called me from his car, saying how he believed we could really be a great married couple.

Almost like it was yesterday, I can remember myself putting on red lipstick, plum-purple eyeliner and nervously brushing my hair, mumbling to myself, "I'm getting made-up to say goodbye." I didn't tell Peter this, but I knew this is what was about to happen. It was a surreal, bittersweet moment, waiting for Peter to arrive, to tell him I couldn't marry him – at least at that time. After all, I wasn't ready for marriage with anyone, neither Armando nor Peter, nor anyone else for that matter. I wanted to experience life's freedom, feeling autonomous and boundless.

It was all very exciting! But at the same time, I was tormented and in conflict, deciding who was best suited for me, at the time – even if that meant just to date, but not marry. Peter was the best lover of the two, shorter, gorgeous, and had a typically European style. He was traditional, had more rules and seemed to try harder with life. He was an achiever, took his life seriously, and was definitely more of a "grown up." This seemed less childlike, less joyous, and quite frankly, not as much fun.

Armando, on the other hand, was tall, debonair, fun-loving, flirtatious, curious and playful. He was full of many surprises. One surprise, of course, was learning that he was seeing another woman.

One day, in my desire to be completely honest and transparent, I invited them both on a date, to meet each other – not to have a *menage à trois*, but to experience honesty and make amends. We went to a bar, ordered a beer, and the three of us played an awkward game of pool. I was trying to make things right.

Sadly for me, both relationships fizzled out quickly. Peter ended up leaving me for a University of Toronto Dean's Executive Assistant, and got married soon after. Armando ended up getting deported, back to Mexico, since he was in Canada illegally.

It definitely was fun while it lasted – and I had been honest with both of them. What was even more, I was also honest with myself. I felt too young to get married, and stayed true to this inner conviction.
This experience was an example of my not being able to make a decision, and because of this, choosing both and inevitably losing both!

When have you had an adventure in your life when you had to make a very difficult decision? What happened? Were you being challenged with opposite choices? What made it a difficult decision for you? What decision did you end up making in the end?

162. Jim, My Love, My Mentor, My Rock

If we are lucky, we meet someone who changes our lives, and we are forever changed because of them.

When I was in my early twenties, I was fortunate enough to meet such a person. Jim helped me to redefine my identity, and differentiate between who I am and what I do. I learned that how I speak about these two aspects of myself made a big difference in my life.

This was the very first time that I considered the difference between saying, "My name is Laura, and I'm a flutist" and "My name is Laura, and I love playing the flute." The fine distinction was between "doing" and "being". Jim explained to me that often people equate their significance or self-worth with what they *do,* rather than just *being*, and having interests, preferences, vocations and talents.

We are not what we do; we simply *are*. Jim always emphasized to me that we have many aspects to our beingness. If we identify with being what we do, that can often get us into trouble. In fact, many people only identify themselves with *what they do* and don't know who they are without it. It took me a while to peel myself away from introducing myself as "a flutist", rather than, "Laura" who does various things. Big distinction.

This explains why many people experience an identity crisis when they retire, go on sick-leave or have major life changes such as a divorce. Jim helped me to mitigate this by getting clear with who I am, not just what I do. For this alone, I am so grateful to Jim.

He also represented unconditional love in a human form. I had experienced it spiritually with my faith and I would later in life experience it with my dog, Ito. But so far, I hadn't come across a person with whom I could just "be," and just be *me*.

Jim also instilled in me the idea that being in a relationship with a beloved doesn't mean you own or control each other. You are actually interdependent, autonomous people who care for and about one another. For this reason, he suggested an open relationship, if that was something I wanted.

Since I was five years younger than him, and really hadn't dated that much before, I agreed. Jim was accepting of my going on dates with others and I felt free as a bird. Ironically, he didn't date anyone but me. He believed so strongly in the theory of open relationship at the time, but didn't act on it himself, for whatever reason. I will never know.

I remember coming home to him, my primary relationship, and telling him about the wonderful dinner or coffee date I had. There was both a trust and intimacy in being completely honest and not sneaking around with others. In a strange way, it strengthened us, since there was no overt jealousy at the time. All was out in the open.

It didn't seem to upset him at the time – but later, due to some of my selfish behaviors, he chose to leave me for someone he loved. They shared the desire to be monogamous, and soon after, got married. I wasn't ready for this. I was shocked and desperately saddened, since I thought we'd always be together.

Earlier, I thought the idea of an open relationship was good: freeing and uncontrolling in nature. Later, when Jim left me, I was devastated and heartbroken. Had I known how I'd feel having him leave, I wonder if I would have ever gotten into an open relationship with him. Hindsight is definitely twenty-twenty.

There were so many gifts in my relationship with Jim: his unconditional love, and his support in starting my first business, Montage Music. He supported me by loaning start-up money, and over time, I completely paid him back. He was also a vegetarian and yogi. I learned so much from him about healthy eating and healthy lifestyle.

He loved making pasta and putting brewer's yeast on it. He said he refused to eat anything with eyes except potatoes – and was often found hanging from special ropes in certain inverted yoga positions. I was so smitten by Jim and his unique ways.

Jim was a fine singer, pianist and composer, and producer of many original songs. We'd often play music together at retirement homes and other places. He also was the engineer who recorded and mixed my CD, *Lullababy*, way back in 1994. I will forever be grateful to Jim for his enduring love and support, his vegetarian lifestyle and his many life lessons. His love and belief in me instilled in me a sense of worthiness I had never known before.

Have you had a person in your life that left an indelible mark on your heart? What was the nature of your relationship? If they are no longer in your life, what would say to them in a letter to thank them for their profound impact on you?

163. Cherub in the Doorway; Devil in the Media

That perfect summer day – June 24, 1995, at Toronto's Future Bakery – marked the beginning of a series of events that I will never ever forget. A cloudless blue sky, sun beaming down on the café patio as I sipped my coffee and took in the morning.

Then, a drop-dead gorgeous tanned young man in his late twenties, blond ponytail, dimples and sparkling brown eyes, carrying a well-worn guitar case covered in stickers from concert destinations, asked me if I'd watch his guitar as he went in to order a coffee.

He beamed with beauty, and my heart almost missed a beat. I felt a bit shy, but sheepishly smiled and nodded. While he was in the café ordering, I decided to think of some questions I could ask him. Three instantly came to me. Since he seemed Californian in his appearance, yet was here in Toronto. I thought to ask, "Are you Canadian or American?" Then, "What do you love most about playing guitar?" After that, I told him I was a flutist, my third question. "Do you want to go back to my place and jam together?" I was eager and poised to ask him all three questions when he got back.

He returned, but so did my pre-pubescent giddiness. He said he was a dual citizen, since his dad lived in Napa Valley, where he'd just been. That made sense, since his tan and ease seemed more West Coast than East Coast. To my second question, he answered, "I love song-writing and singing."

Then, the answer to the third question. I was so relieved and elated when he said yes! I tried to contain myself, since I didn't want to seem too eager. We walked for twenty minutes in the summer glow, I basking in my sudden infatuation with Californian-Canadian lover-boy.

As soon as we got to my place, we started kissing passionately. Could this really be happening? I was amazed that such a gorgeous guy would find me attractive. I always felt like a bit of a band nerd. We took our instruments out of their cases and starting jamming – musically, then romantically – kissing some more. My heart fluttered like a hummingbird – humming with a sparkly joy I'd never felt before.

All of a sudden, I looked down at my watch and discovered it was already 4:30 pm. We'd been at it for over four hours: that is, the music and the smooching. I excused myself to listen to my voice mail: "Laura, it's 12:30 and we are in the chapel waiting to walk down the aisle. Where are you? We are waiting for you to play the processional on your flute!" This was the voice of a bride who had booked her wedding music with me over a year ago. The venue was the Old Mill, a forty-minute car ride away.

My heart skipped a beat, and I felt a queasiness in the pit of my stomach. I had actually forgotten the wedding I had been hired to play at. So swept up by the unexpected spontaneous infatuation at the café that Saturday morning, I missed the wedding. And I had already cashed their 50-percent non-refundable deposit! Yikes!

I wanted to cry, turn back time, and apologize – but all I could focus on was that sick feeling in my stomach. There was no rectifying the situation. It was too late. The wedding would be over by now.

What surprised me even more was Jon's response to my oversight. He grabbed me and hugged me, looking down into my welling up eyes, "Laura, you're a good person. Everyone makes mistakes." He was so gentle, loving, forgiving, reassuring, and I had only known him four and a half hours! I'd never experienced such compassion and forgiveness before. My shame and despair were somehow alleviated by his warmth and encouragement.

To my amazement, after contacting the married couple, apologizing profusely and refunding their deposit, I wasn't sued. What a relief and a true gift. I was so terrified they would have taken me to court.

Jon and I continued our budding romance, but I was jolted out of this living fantasy by some very bad news the very next day. My mom had been diagnosed with a brain tumour. I was mortified. What was also curious was the day after her diagnosis, which was June 26, I was supposed to be flying to San Francisco myself. My mom's diagnosis was the day in between Jon's arrival from California and the next day, my departure for California! Our trips were the bookends on either side of her bad news.

I cancelled my flight, and Jon moved in with me.

Not only was he a heartthrob, he was also a gifted macrobiotic chef. He told me that he had wanted to cook for his dying uncle years before, but that didn't happen. It was disappointing for him, since he really wanted to help his uncle heal. He was relieved when my mom said yes to his offer to cook healthy food for her. This became our daily project. We'd take a taxi two times a day, transporting lunch and dinner to mom's hospital room – and removing the unsavoury tray of hospital food. We'd replace it with a colourful, fresh, organic, macrobiotic meal. Much more appetizing and nutritious, to say the least! Mom loved her meals.

In fact, when Mom first saw Jon standing in the doorway of her hospital room, she exclaimed, "Laura, who is that cherub in the doorway?" Clearly, Jon had a beauty that was quite angelic: a sweet round face, dimples, big brown eyes and a splash of sunny blond hair pulled back in a ponytail. Kind of an "angelic rock-star."

He was definitely a rock-star of the heart and soul; tenderly helping my mother, and reassuring me when I forgot the wedding with his sage-like wisdom. Spirituality oozed out of Jon.

Sadly, a short seven months later, Mom succumbed to her illness, and passed away. Shortly following this, Jon left me for another woman. He traveled with her and her four-year-old son to Maui, Hawaii. Choosing to do this may have been Jon's way of compensating and trying to make amends for a "mistake" he made. He felt like a "deadbeat dad," since he'd left his pregnant girlfriend in Belgium, a few years previously. He didn't want to be a father, ran from the responsibility, but felt guilty about it, anyhow. He'd refer to his young Belgian son as his little "Brussel Sprout." Despite his sunny nature, he had an underbelly of shame. He tried to fight his inner demons, but they ate away at him.

Then, when he met a red-haired dance-kinetics teacher, it felt to him like a way he could sublimate the responsibility he ran from, evading fatherhood with his own son. Unfortunately, he smoked some very potent marijuana on Maui, which most likely contributed to his arriving back to Canada with latent schizoid disorder. His father, a clinical psychologist in California had this condition too, but was medicated and managed it well.

This is where the story changes direction. Jon entered the psychiatric ward of a hospital in Brockville, Ontario, where he lived for years, managing his devastating disorder. One tragic day in September, when he was out on a day-pass, Jon took his stepfather's life in a heinous act of uncontrollable schizophrenic rage. It was that pervasive voice in his head that forcefully misguided his actions. A true tragedy.

I knew he'd been suffering with auditory hallucinations, directing him to "take a sacrifice or the world would end." I adamantly encouraged him to take his meds, but he complained that he would feel emotionally flat, and wouldn't feel inspired to write songs and do his music. Despite this, I kept encouraging him.

He told me that some days he would put his meds under the mattress, pretending he took them. He confided in me that if his psychiatrist knew this, "he'd never get out of the psych ward." I was perplexed, and between a rock and a hard place. If I told the shrink, could I trust him not to tell Jon? If he did tell him, would I be the one murdered? I was scared, so decided to emphatically continue telling him to take his meds.

I saw Jon's name the newspaper, for murder – and my heart sank as I read the report. Murder is final. Murder evokes images, defines the murderer, casts an evil and dark image on him. Murderers are feared and vilified. But that's not all they are.

Jon had been Mom's cherub in the doorway. He had cooked healthy food for her, while she experienced the despair of cancer day in day out. He had wiped my tears that day, reassuring me and reminding me that I was a loving soul, despite missing the wedding that day. He gave me the forgiveness I couldn't give myself.

He had loved. He had lived. He had suffered. He had killed. He committed an unspeakable crime – and I wanted the world to fall silent, since I knew more about that "murderer" Jon than anyone reading a newspaper report.

Then I got to thinking: Every murderer was at one time a little baby, innocent and pure. Every murderer had a mom and dad. Some had brothers, sisters, cousins, aunts and uncles, grandparents. Murderers are humans with deep problems, but they aren't *just* murderers. In my case, Jon was a blessing, an angel in my life and in my mom's. May Jon, the cherub in Mom's hospital doorway be remembered for his kindnesses too.

Life itself can rock our worlds. Turn it upside down. Make us think. What appears one way can appear the opposite to others. The lesson I took from this profound experience with Jon is that people are complex beings. We need to give people compassion and understanding, no matter how difficult or severe the situation. When we offer compassion to ourselves and others, I believe there can be greater understanding and forgiveness. This, I think can heal the world.

What moments in your life were complex and could have been looked at through different lenses of awareness? What would you see with different perspectives and clarity? How would this change your life?

164. NCR: After My Cherub Became a Murderer

NCR, which stands for "Not Criminally Responsible," is an award-winning documentary by Canadian film-maker John Kastner, about the mentally ill, living in high-security hospitals in Ontario, who are labelled by the courts as not responsible for their crimes. It premiered in Toronto in 2013. As a documentary film fan, I chose to go see this movie at Toronto's Hot Docs film festival. Also, because I'd known someone whose murder sentence was labelled NCR, I was even more intrigued.

Arriving just in the nick of time, I entered the theatre as the lights went down and quickly grabbed a seat halfway from the screen. Unbeknownst to me, I ended up sitting right behind the filmmaker. He was asked to stand up and the audience applauded him. I leaned forward and quietly tapped him on the shoulder, asking him if, in the course of making his film, he'd ever met Jon, my former boyfriend, and Mom's cherub in the doorway?

There was an awkward pause, and then an acknowledgment, as he answered, yes. What he was about to tell me was so creepy that it made my hair stand up on my neck.

The filmmaker told me that when they were interviewing patients for the movie's central role, Jon was considered. But since he'd demonstrated such unsavory qualities, he thought that the audience wouldn't sympathize with Jon, or his mental illness leading to murder, if they saw him interviewed. I gulped. What a dilemma. He had been my special friend, and Mom's Cherub in the doorway, who cooked healing macrobiotic meals for my dying mother. He'd been cut from the director's choices for a suitable central character. He was simply too scary to put on the silver screen. This was so hard for me to imagine: it sickened me.

Jon was someone else back then. I had a very personal relationship with him while my mom was dying. The *NCR* film felt to me like an arm's-length from my own Jon saga. It seemed so unfair. The audience wouldn't have known all the caring acts Jon had done. I felt like Jon's identity now was psychiatric patient, an experiment, and a potential documentary subject to be studied and understood. And he didn't make it to the film.

His disease had dramatically changed him from the person I once knew. Had he become a monster? I would never know. As I sat watching the documentary, *NCR*, it felt so strange seeing the inside of his psychiatric hospital, yet not see him, nor have communication with him anymore. I felt like a peeping tom, secretly peering into his private and devastating life. It all seemed so surreal.

I didn't know at the time of the 2013 screening that Jon would die only three years later. I was shocked to learn that he was only fifty-two. What a tragedy. The devastation of mental illness touched my life, his life and his family's. To this day, I still don't know the cause of his death. In my attempts to reach his mother, Emily, I was told by Jon's funeral home that she has dementia and even if I were to reach her, she probably wouldn't be able to remember. I am left wondering; what happened to Jon inside the maximum-security psychiatric hospital, Waypoint. How did he die? Did he overdose, did he die by suicide? Did one of the other patients kill Jon? What actually happened? These questions still haunt me to this day.

I must admit that from 2008 to 2016, those eight years were riddled with thoughts and fears of Jon somehow getting released from Waypoint, the maximum-security psychiatric hospital near Penetanguishine, Ontario. Every year, there was a Review Board hearing, and Jon would get a chance to be seen and heard by the board.

Every year I shuddered, wondering if he got released, would I end up his next victim? After all, he knew my address – he'd sent me a Christmas card and accompanying hand-written letter from the hospital – and he even apologized for leaving me, saying he wanted to get back together again with me. I shuddered, realizing that I was probably one of the only people he remained in contact with.

I didn't like looking at Jon through this lens of a not-criminally-responsible murderer. I knew him as someone else: a friend, lover, cherub to my dying mom.

But now that he's gone, I can finally take a deep breath of relief. I now know I have no reason to fear being killed by Jon. But every day, I live with the mystery of how dear Jon died. I hope that one day, finding out this last piece of the puzzle will help me put the Jon saga to rest. Forever, I will always remember Cherub, Jon.

We are all different characters or personas to people in our lives. Is it possible to accept and forgive people? To deepen our compassion and see people with our eyes and hearts more? Have you ever had a shocking experience beyond your wildest dreams, which caused you to look at this person, situation differently? How did you treat the situation? What did you learn about yourself, your ability to forgive others and yourself?

165. When Love Isn't Enough

"I love you, but not enough to marry you." I will never forget the way these words landed in my ears and on my heart. It was crushing. I couldn't believe what I was hearing. There I stood in the modern condo kitchen of my twenty-five-year-old German boyfriend, Markus. He was almost in tears giving me our "breaking news" of the day. Standing tall like most Germans, blond and stylish, today, he was delivering me a heartache.

We had met in New York City about four months before, at a record industry conference. It was my very first time to New York. I was young and "fashion-forward" – I wore mini-skirts and cowboy boots, and I was ready for excitement.

As a bit of a packrat, I ended up collecting a bunch of unnecessary brochures at the conference: too many for my small carry-on suitcase. Like a well-mannered European, Markus, who said he lived in Toronto, told me he would be glad to take my stuff back home in his large suitcase, and we could meet again back in Toronto. What a clever ploy to take me out for a date. I had to give him credit for his originality! I was excited to pick up my new beau, not the brochures.

Everything about Markus was sexy, exciting – or very well organized. He was six feet three inches tall, with blond hair and big brown cow-eyes, and his kisses remarkably tasted like freshly baked cookies. He wore a range of tasteful colognes, ranging from sensual, to fresh, along with nice shirts. His sexy accent made me weak in the knees. He must have had a collection of at least 1,000 CDs, and meticulously filed them in alphabetical order, on beautiful shelves made especially for them in light green Italian glass. Andy Warhol hung on his walls, his décor, tasteful. Like many Europeans, he often bought fresh flowers.

Every weekend, we'd take his Jeep up to cottage-country near Bracebridge, and stay in the middle of the forest. Always a thrill. His eccentric friend, Reiner, would have us up to his property, where we stayed in the one cabin and he slept in the shovel of his tractor. We would stay up late by the campfire, just the three of us plus the night animals: loons, coyotes, wolves and mosquitoes.

Then, suddenly, after just three months, it was over. I knew something wasn't quite right when he hadn't called me in a few days. I phoned him but no answer. I tried again and again. When he finally picked up the phone, I was met with a different voice than I had ever heard before. His tone was flat, sad, and had no life in it. Even his German accent didn't seem bold and charismatic – it was distant and lifeless.

I went over to see him and he had tears in his eyes. "I love you, but not enough to marry you," he said, adding, "You're just not *the one*." He explained to me that there was only *one* who could be *the one*, and used a strange German logic, suggesting that I was in a camp of many, all having one thing in common: we were all not *the one*. I will never forget his teary-eyed attempt to explain this concept.

During this time, I was in my sixth year running Montage Music, my live music agency. We were doing weddings every weekend, and during this year, three major hits were being played on the radio, at weddings, everywhere.

One was Whitney Houston's *I Will Always Love You* (written by Dolly Parton, I found out later). Another song that touched me much was *Unforgettable*, sung by Natalie Cole in a duet with her deceased father, Nat King Cole. The concept of doing a live recording with an already recorded version of a deceased person seemed so bizarre to me, but was deeply moving. The duet was beautiful, despite its strange production.

But the song that had the biggest impact on me during this heartbreaking year was by the Canadian artist Bryan Adams: *Everything I Do, I Do it for You*. During that year, it had achieved number one in sixty countries. Needless to say, *Everything I Do I Do It For You* got in deep into my heart and breakup wounds. Every time I heard it, I would mourn for the loss of relationship with my heartthrob, Markus.

Years later, after he'd been married and living over two decades in Germany, a fifty-year-old Markus reached out to tell me he was going through a divorce, after having been recently diagnosed with multiple sclerosis. Sad. It's strange how things turn out.

I felt very sorry for his plight. He seemed like such a "Wunderkind" when I knew him over thirty years ago in Toronto. He was a German hot shot, amazing record company A and R director, and very talented in many ways.

A while later, I experienced my own breakup. Markus invited me to Germany, and in his wildly exuberant way said, "Come visit your ex, and let's paint Europe red." He then went on to paint a brilliant picture of his invitation. "Laura, I will take you around to Italy, Berlin and all over Europe." It was that old Markus I had fallen in love with years ago, beckoning me come and reunite our connection, maybe not our romantic relationship. He said, no pressure. Let's see what happens.

I carefully weighed the odds, and decided that my heart had been recently broken – and had been broken by Markus in the past, too, over thirty years ago. What if I got vulnerable, got close to Markus again, and he breaks my heart again? I didn't want to go through this again. Also, Markus had a serious illness and was divorced, and I was afraid of being vulnerable and falling in love and not being prepared or equipped to be with him at this stage of our lives.

We did stay in touch for three more years. Then, as I was visiting his Facebook wall, checking to see if he had posted any more of his original art there, I was stopped in my tracks.

I read, "R.I.P Markus," and my heart missed a beat. How could this be true? My German boyfriend, the one who broke my heart three decades ago had died. The most shocking part was I learned it on his Facebook wall. No phone call, but who would have my number? It seemed like a strange and impersonal way to learn such heartbreaking news.

I walked around my home like a zombie for the next few days, disbelieving the news I had just read.

Markus was a warrior spirit with a soft sensitive heart and a kick-ass edge that I will never forget.

Have you learned about someone's death in a very shocking way? What happened? How did you process this discovery? When has your life had an ironic turnaround? When did you think you were losing something and later found out the other person ended up losing, too?

166. Mystical Michael

A friend, a former boyfriend, a music collaborator, an astrologer, artist, sound healer, photographer, and so much more – that's my friend Michael. Michael has Asperger's syndrome, a mild form of autism, which (despite challenges) has given Michael some very unusual gifts and proclivities. His immense sensitivity makes him one of the most fascinating people in my life.

Michael has enriched my life with so many of his gifts: opening my mind to new perspectives and ways of seeing the world. A deeply compassionate soul, Michael is a natural sage, full of heartfelt wisdom. Some of my most favorite moments with Michael have been collaborating musically. Sound healing is one of his greatest gifts, and improvising on my flute with his many world instruments has been a huge treat. Since I am a trained classical musician, improvising with Michael has opened my mind and heart to a whole other world of music-making and healing. In fact, many health practitioners use Michael's and my music for their treatments and modalities.

Michael's astrology sessions are another favorite activity for me. His deep knowledge, interpretation and spiritual guidance all combine to offer a very specific, easy-to-follow astrology session that's not hard to understand. His sessions are deeply transformational and have helped many on their life paths.

Another thing I've loved doing is looking through Michael's lens on life, through his exceptional nature photography. He sees things most people don't and they are visible in his photos – such exquisite perception and precision. A true gift.

I am so grateful to Michael for all his gifts and the sheer joy of collaborating with him musically.

Do you have a special friend whose many gifts inspire you and bring you closer together? Have you collaborated with any of your friends?

167. Dating A Younger Man: They Said I Shouldn't, But I Did Anyway

It all started one day when Bill B., my amazing guitarist friend and colleague, wasn't available for a gig. I asked around to find a substitute player, and a young *"Wunderkind"* was recommended to me by a friend. Lee arrived at the hotel ballroom with his guitar, in an oversized suit-jacket, shoes with holes in them, a sheepish grin, and – I soon learned – a killer jazz technique. His dad was a famous bass player; and he was a young guitar wizard. He was just twenty-two at the time, and I was forty. I was astounded by both his humility and his immense talent.

After the gig, I invited Lee back to my place to meet my three-year-old Pomeranian, Ito. I wanted to share the game of "volley-dog" with my new guitarist friend. This was a game I'd invented to play with Ito that was a dog version of volleyball. Ito would grab the small, soft air-filled beach ball in his mouth, flip it up in the air and volley it to me with his dainty front paws. Pure joy!

Lee had quicksilver thinking and was funny, sometimes in an abrupt but witty way. Jazz musicians' minds work very quickly and because of this, often have this style of immediacy and enthusiasm, while maintaining a "cool" persona. I suppose their quick jokes replicate the facility of their minds improvising music on the spot.

Lee and liked each other, were connective and playful. People have always told me that I have a youthful spirit. I felt ignited and alive with Lee, although seventeen years older.

I broke up with Michael for Lee, since I'd been craving more emotional connection, enthusiasm and lightness. I loved being with Michael – it was a very spiritual, sage-like experience – but I found his Asperger's very challenging to deal with on a personal level.

My turning forty-two just two days before Lee turned twenty-four was a remarkable coincidence. We had already been dating for almost a year. Of course, my girlfriends were both fascinated and discouraging. Some said, "Good for you, Laura," (wink, wink), while others bluntly said, "You are really wasting your time. This is going nowhere." I would butt against this advice. I knew we had a profound age difference, but my friends didn't know how much fun we had together.

There are a few jazz tunes whose titles convey how I felt with him: *You Make Me Feel So Young*, which Frank Sinatra made famous, and *Easy to Love*.

At this point in our relationship, he was still a bashful *ingenu* and a phenomenal jazz guitarist. I found his humility endearing, along with his wit and charm. Sadly, as he got older, his ego became more developed as he became more popular. I think that's when things started going downhill for us. He also had his eye on a few younger women – not just younger than me, but younger than him! He was definitely getting attention – and enjoying it. Wouldn't any man?

I acted so insecurely, probing him with questions that were fuelled with jealousy. My friends said, "See, told you so." Not only was I upset with him for his change of heart and developing ego, but I was even more upset with my friends. They didn't believe in love and all its possibilities: its boundlessness, its uniqueness, its many shapes, sizes and original expressions. I never wanted to be a disgruntled older woman, saying, "There are no good men left."

Older woman-younger man relationships were scorned by many, along with my well-meaning *single* girlfriends. Were they jealous, jaded, or simply being practical? A bit of all of the above, I think.

I'd insist that just because a relationship may not turn out in the long term, it can still have value in the present. This was completely ridiculous for many of my girlfriends: a counterintuitive idea, staying in a relationship that was "doomed."

Disagreeing with them, I set out to ask myself if I truly believed in staying in the relationship, since the writing on the wall said it wasn't forever. I then asked myself a very philosophical question: "What actually lasts forever?"

I remember my dear father once saying to me, "Laura, the only thing constant is change." That stuck with me for years. This profound statement needed to marinate within me for the rest of my life.

What is *forever*, anyway? It is a construct that actually suggests a destination. But there really is no such thing as time; I remember a wise friend from Mumbai, whose popular expression was, "Enjoy it while it lasts." I like how that sounds, since the act of enjoying is a present tense activity, not a worry about the future.

Incidentally, my relationship with the jazz musician ended six times – and each time it started up again, the gap between our endings got smaller. Finally, after two trips to Thailand to visit him at his hotel music gigs, and many fights pleading we stay together, he ended it with me.

My friends were right, but so was I. Through the experience of dating a much younger man, I came to a conclusion: You can still enjoy something even though you have the foresight that it won't last a lifetime.

Enjoying the moment has profound value. The present is the *present* – and is a gift to cherish, no matter what the future brings.

Has there been a time in your life when you did something you loved, even though you knew it would not turn out in the future? What did you tell your well-meaning friends? What have you discovered about yourself and your relationship with time?

168. Bill, My Older Man

I never imagined myself dating a man thirty years my senior. But I did.

Bill (*not* the "Bill B." mentioned above) was a successful businessman: a book publisher and author. Bill was six foot four. Bill was fifty-nine and I was twenty-nine. Did I say Bill was an older man?

Well, not in spirit. In fact, Bill was fun, playful, mischievous and daring. He even brought hash home from Amsterdam in his trench-coat pocket and we made hash brownies before going to the movies. Yes, his years were older, his experiences rich and international, but Bill was an original. And I love originals!

Throughout my life, I've been one to ask myself a lot of questions, test myself and put myself up to challenges. With Bill, I made an experiment, consisting of just two questions:

- Could I walk down the street with this executive, rich-looking man, and not be self-conscious or concerned with how people may judge me, even if they may perceive me as a gold-digger?
- What would sex be like with a man almost sixty, and I still in my twenties?

I was up for my personal challenge. I didn't tell anyone, but these questions were top of mind for the next few months I dated Bill. I learned that I could choose to be comfortable in my skin no matter what others thought my intentions were. Only I knew it. That was a refreshing insight that grew into a major theme in my life – not being concerned with the opinions of others. I always remember the expression, "Your opinion of me is none of my business." It really stuck.

When it came to sex with Bill, I was pleasantly surprised. I thought it would be clumsy and awkward, but instead it was passionate and very natural. In fact, it was the most effortless sex I'd had in my twenties. What is said about older men was true in his case: sensitive to the need of others and experienced with women.

When our relationship came to an end, I was sad, but not traumatized. He was mature and willing to discuss and process it with me, so I didn't feel abandoned. I even became friends with his new lady friend, and the three of us would have meals together. It was one of the best breakups I'd ever had.

So, yes, I can be with an older man, and it can awaken fresh perspectives, like a newborn life. Quite unexpected.

Have you ever had a relationship with someone you never dreamed of dating and it turned out surprisingly? What did you learn or discover? How has this experience shaped your outlook about relationships and future relationships?

169. Karrie: I call her "CARE-ie"

I've never encountered a soul quite like this remarkable woman, Karrie. I've also never made a best friend over the internet. I haven't yet met her in person – just on Zoom during the Covid-19 pandemic, while baring our souls in writing and sharing at Tracey Erin Smith's Soulo Creation Lab.

Karrie is an expressive, multi-talented, heart of gold human angel. Her partner is a photographer, turned quadriplegic, due to a freak accident. As he was knee-high in the water, wading ashore he was pulled backwards by an undertow. Tragically, he was rendered quadriplegic, with a spinal-cord injury similar much like the late Christopher Reeve's.

Karrie – who had known of him while they were both in New York, acting – read about his accident. When she learned this startling news, they were both in L.A.: he, an award-winning photographer, and she, a sought-out voice and theatre actor.

Now, she found herself compelled to visit him in the hospital, keeping him company as a sympathetic friend. She would read to him and watch movies with him by his hospital bedside. Sadly, few of his friends and family came to visit. He felt sad and lonely, and Karrie was the only consistent friend in his life.

Four-and-a-half years have passed, and she has been primary caregiver to him, devoting herself to keeping him alive at home, with homecare nurses, and keeping him out of institutions. I don't know how she does it. What a huge heart Karrie has, taking on such a monumental task of overseeing his wellness with such an extreme injury.

I admire Karrie for so many reasons. She embodies all the qualities I admire and aspire to: She's vegan, (so am I), loves all living beings, is empathetic, a kick-ass innovator, super sassy and fun. Plus, she's an energetic and resilient solutions-finder, and does what it takes in all aspects of her life, complaining rarely.

When I meet Karrie in person for the first time one day, I will give her the biggest hug. I feel so connected to her soul and want only the best for this living genius and bearer of light and compassion.

Sometimes, we are blessed with the opportunity of meeting unusually gifted people: people who shake up our world, and show us what real compassion and staying power look like. I found this in my friend, Karrie. Can you remember a time you met someone whose qualities you admire profoundly? What ones stood out for you the most? Have you modelled after this person? How has this changed your life?

170. Colin Before, Colin Now: Recycled and Upcycled

I believe there is something very special about meeting someone again after many years. This is the case with Colin. A composer, author, and music critic with many talents and gifts, he's a person who revisited my life and has stayed.

When we were both in music school, we had part-time jobs in a call center and sat close by. We were in our twenties. Thirty-plus years later, after Colin has had two books published and a CD of his own original compositions, and after writing hundreds of articles for various newspapers, magazines and publications, he met me again! He said I hadn't changed at all – but he'd grown to a big cozy teddy-bear size, and had silver-fox looks. I barely recognized him at first!

We started dating and I felt a comfort with him that usually only exists between people who've known each other for a long time. Colin and I have been together for over six years, but with a short intermission of a year. Time to rethink, regroup and re-appreciate. Now, we are in "Version Two" of our relationship, and things are great. I feel so supported by him, loved, and he believes in me. I support him too, and hope I make his life better.

We also have a rescue dog from South Korea, named Kito, who makes the family ever better. The expression, where something makes a house a home applies to our little family unit: having Kito and Colin in my life makes our house a home and life an ever growing gift.

This is a destination I would wish on everyone. There is nothing like having someone who has your back, and you, theirs.

My former boyfriend is my future "husband," whether it's a formal union or a union of our hearts. Sometimes, we need to take breaks from our relationship to work on ourselves, reassess, regroup and appreciate what we have. Think of a relationship in your life that needs or needed some time for wisdom to take hold. How has this time benefited the relationship? Have you recycled or upcycled a relationship? What is different, better about it now?

171. Colin: the "Handburger," and MRI Love

My boyfriend Colin is a soul I love with all my heart. And, on a couple of occasions, he's won my heart a thousand times over.

One brilliant summer day, I had attended Toronto's Outdoor Art Fair at Nathan Phillips Square. I loved to go each year – so many talented artists! One particular booth had a huge painting leaning against its wall, but wasn't fastened to it securely. When a rush of wind came in, I was suddenly hit on the back of my head by the pointy corner of the painting.

I didn't have any instant reaction to the impact, but knew something about concussions. The effects could occur within moments, hours, or even days, weeks, or years. Because of this, I asked the artist to immediately accompany me to the Art Fair office, which was about a five-minute walk away. By the time we arrived, I was dizzy and nauseous – and suddenly fainted, I am told. Apparently, my eyes rolled back and my head moved back and forth rapidly. By all accounts, I looked like I was having a seizure. I could have died.

Thank God there was an ambulance right there and it was a very short trip to St. Michael's Hospital, just around the corner. Upon arriving, Colin was called by phone. I felt instantly reassured knowing he was on his way. He hurried to the hospital and came to my bedside, lovingly placing one warm bear paw-sized hand under my weak hand and one above, making a kind of a "handburger." He reassured me that he'd stay by my side until I was released. We awaited test results, from bloodwork to CT scan and then Colin took me home. I felt safe because of his loving presence.

Another memorable time with Colin was my experience getting an MRI on my shoulder in Buffalo, New York. I had a frozen shoulder, and it had been so persistent that it was time for an MRI scan. In Ontario, there was a waiting list for MRI scans, so we decided to go to a private clinic in Buffalo and pay for it: about $900 Canadian, but no wait. But there was another challenge to overcome: I was claustrophobic, and the thought of being inside an enclosed tube scared me. Since some of the machines at the Buffalo MRI clinic had open sides, this made it all the more reason to go to there, this one time!

The MRI clinic in Buffalo looked like a cross between a spa and a funeral home. Each little waiting room had silk flowers and a hospital pastel paint colour on the walls. When we were finally taken in for my MRI, Colin asked if he could be there with me. Fortunately, they said yes.

He lovingly held my ankles as my reclined body was wheeled into the noisy, clangy MRI machine. The sounds were sporadic and erratic. The procedure went on for just over thirty-five minutes. Colin's warm hands were the only constant.

When it was all done, I asked Colin if he had been brought a chair. No, was his answer. He told me that he also didn't want to leave me in order to get one, since he figured that I wouldn't know where he had gone and when he was coming back. What an angel! I've never met someone who cared so deeply about my welfare and did what it took to ensure my comfort and sense of security.

Yes, Colin's a keeper.

People say love is a feeling, or a state of being. I say, love is all those things and more. It can also be actions we do for the ones we love. Have you had a life-changing experience where someone was there for you beyond what you could imagine? When have you been there for someone else? What did you do?

Chapter Eight

Mystical Moments

Coincidences, auspicious and serendipitous events, synchronicities, and intentional moments – my life is full of them. In fact, some of my favorite, most fascinating times have been experiencing life in its fullness and most mystical. The lens I've chosen to look through, along with my perceptions, have added a kaleidoscope of magical experiences to my life. By experimenting with life itself, I've found many answers, and many discoveries have been revealed to me.

172. The Power of a Single Rose on My Desk

The power of intention and believing in manifestation have always been central in my life. And many years ago, I decided to test this theory myself.

I've always loved nature – and living life impulsively and spontaneously, not in an orderly or scheduled way. Life has felt fresher and more alive to me this way. However, I did need to make a living. As a flutist and owner of my own entertainment agency, Montage Music, I decided that I wanted to earn a living from my music: my entertainment bookings and recordings. Equally important for me was spending lots of time outdoors in the fresh air. The child in me wanted to play, while the adult knew I needed to make a living. I discovered a novel way to beautifully synergize the two.

I simply bought a single red rose and strategically placed it on my desk beside my phone, along with a thin pile of two or three blank Montage Music contract forms. I would go outside and have a long walk near my apartment, but only after gently placing everything on my desk: the rose, the contracts and most importantly, my intention to invite in prospects. I imagined that while I was out enjoying nature, prospects would call and leave me voice messages for gigs. I was thrilled and astounded to see that this seemed to work! I could go out and play, while I intentionally invited in prospects to call.

Another important detail is the rose and its role in calling the prospects back. I would dial the prospect's number while gazing at the rose, and imagine I was transmitting its beauty in my voice tone. It seemed to help the connection and sales process.

Over the years, I've discovered that being in a state of ease and flow can really magnetize and draw in what I want. By just believing and feeling my intention realized in advance at a sensorial level, it seems to attract its manifestation. This technique has been taught for over a hundred years, in the foundational works of Napoleon Hill, in his many books, such as *Think and Grow Rich* – as well as our modern-day manifestation heroes, seen in the book and movie *The Secret*, and more. I took this secret to life literally and have been fortunate in seeing a lot of my dreams manifest since I believed that they could!

Have there been times you've intended something with all your heart, and it came true? Have you continued to think and behave in this way? How has it changed your life for the better? What is your manifestation sweet spot, your life formula?

173. My Mirage Moments

Have you ever experienced mirages? Maybe on the highway, where they look like glistening puddles in the distance – and then all of a sudden they disappear? My mirage moments have been mystical for me, since they symbolize something mystical. How can something exist in the near future, in our present, but disappear once we approach it? That is the mirage phenomenon. I love mirages.

Life seems to offer us symbolic mirages in many forms. One such "mirage" is our fears. We may anticipate things going wrong in the future, we imagine them, we anticipate them, and boom, they don't happen. That very thing we're fearing never comes into being. Isn't that mirage-like? It exists in our imagination and seem real, but then disappears.

When I suffered anxiety and depression in my teens and early twenties, my therapist would always say that anticipatory anxiety feels worse than the very thing you're fearing, and often it doesn't even come into being. And if it does, often we have the resources to deal with it. But when we have anticipatory anxiety about it, we feel overwhelmed and unable to imagine ourselves coping in the future. Fortunately, often the things we're fretting never come true.

Isn't it strange how our minds work? I like to remind myself of my many literal highway "mirage" experiences, since they reinforce the idea that things can actually disappear as you approach them – like worries dissipating, once we know that anticipatory anxiety is usually way worse than the thing we fear, and which may not even come into being!

When have you had the "mirage experience," when what you imagined in your mind's eye disappeared as you approached it? When have you experienced anticipatory anxiety and discovered the thing you were fearing never came into being? How has this informed your coping strategies with anxiety and fears?

174. My Distorted Experience of Time

I do believe that time-distortion exists, since I've experienced it, played with it, and enjoyed its subtle nuances.

Have you ever been in the "zone," when time stood still, or seemed to slow down and expand for you and your focus in the moment? Or have you ever felt it race by, and you didn't feel it traveling? Have you ever been in a bank lineup, and felt like you'd been waiting for fifteen minutes, but only two minutes had passed? I believe these are all forms of time-distortion. I find the concept fascinating.

Many say that time is an energy. When we're stressed out, the energy can feel heavy, like it's taking up a lot of space. Then, at other times, we can feel like there's never enough time to get things done. We've all heard people say, "there is never enough time in the day." Is this mostly our perception, and the energetic state we are plugged into at the time?

One interesting experience I had with time was doing a one-hour, timed productivity exercise in a group. The first part was to declare out loud to the group what we were going to do, then in the hour do it, and come back and discuss what we did. I chose to practise scales and arpeggios on my flute.

I was completely absorbed in it, staying focused on the job at hand, with no distractions. When I went to check the time, thinking our time was up, it wasn't. There were still twenty minutes left! What caused time to seem to slow down? Was it the extreme focus that secured each second that passed with purpose and intention?

This exercise got me thinking about ways I can use time more efficiently and "bend" time, so it works for me.

Time-distortion: what a fascinating phenomenon! When we're feeling at peace, sustained, satisfied, on purpose, fulfilled and authentically ourselves, I believe we can shapeshift our time and our lives quite magically. We can stretch it and expand it, along with contracting it, and making it shorter and faster.

Have you had any unique or interesting experiences with time, and time-distortion? What happened? What did it teach you?

175. The Tree-Trunk Rings of My Life

Often, when I see a tree-trunk sliced cleanly and notice the many rings, I think of my own life. Isn't it similar: a series of rings, or years of experience? I am who I've always been, and always will be intrinsically. But my life has been full of different experiences, like rings in a tree-trunk.

When I look at my life as "now," this is all there is, and the past and future are simply rings encircling the essential me. Perceiving life this way is very different than the linear past, present, future frames we're most accustomed to. The tree trunk ring idea puts me in touch with my essential nature, my soul, my eternal self.

Our souls have always been with us, but are expressed out loud in our lives, through our thoughts, words and actions. How we express them is very unique to each and every one of us. When I've been most authentic to myself, my soul feels nourished and expressed. Over the years, I have grown more and more aware of ways my soul feels most authentic. Giving it a voice is vital to my growth and fulfillment.

When have you perceived your life as all-inclusive: past, present, future, rather than sequential? How has this influenced how you live and experience your life? Do you give more attention to your past, present or future? Did you always look at your life this way? If not, what changed and how? How may this have benefitted you?

176. Life Measured in Hours

When I was very young, it seemed like a long time before my age would get into the double digits. For example, when I was just twelve years old, and had been living for only 104,832 hours. I was having the time of my life, riding and showing horses, and getting ready to start playing flute: my soul-calling.

Now, having played the flute for over forty-four years, or an astounding 384,384 hours, life seems very fulfilled and fulfilling. It's hard to believe that if I make it to eighty-six years of age, I will have lived 760,032 hours! One of my very best friends, Elizabeth, has made it past ninety years of age: 786,240 hours. And a dear scholar I have known for years is 100 this year: 873,600 hours. The oldest man I ever met was 106 years of age, or had lived 926,016 hours – close to 1 million hours!

When I look at things this way, my life takes on a very unusual perspective. Perhaps doing this makes me appreciate my life even more – by the passing of years, months, weeks, days, hours, minutes, and moment to moment seconds!

I've noticed that when I measure time using a timer, the passing of time seems so visible – like watching the sand in an hourglass. This technique has been very helpful for me when doing a task – simply watching the seconds go by. For me, it really helped me to respect time even more, and make the most of the seconds, minutes, hours, days, weeks, months and years to come.

Have you ever experimented with your perception of time? What has worked for you? What did you discover?

177. When "Is" Becomes "Was"

Nothing has changed my perception more than when "is" becomes "was," almost overnight. I noticed it so prevalently when my dear Pomeranian, Ito, passed away. For sixteen years, I referred to him in the present tense: "Ito is my calm Pom," "Ito is a therapy dog," "Ito is my best friend." But as soon as he passed away, the present-tense verb "is" suddenly became "was." It was a shock to my system. It just didn't feel right, at all.

I wasn't ready to refer to my beloved Ito in the past tense. How could he be living all these years, and one day become a being of my past. I found myself saying, "Ito was a great dog," and "Ito was my soulmate" – and it just didn't feel right to say these things. I returned to the present tense, yet something was profoundly different. Ito was no longer here. Yet, he was still in my heart, in my soul, in my memories. In my everything.

I just couldn't see him, hold him, play with him, cuddle him anymore. One day, something very odd happened. I visited a very reputable psychic a week after Ito passed away. I wasn't crying or experiencing any symptoms of grief I had expected myself to. The psychic matter-of-factly said to me: "Ito is right beside you on your left side, like always. He's still here, in spirit."

This was reassuring, and also made sense. My calm was authentic. I wasn't having shock or denial, or even delayed mourning: I realized that I didn't need to, since Ito was still with me, non-physically.

I've continued on, treasuring our memories, feeling full and fulfilled by my years with Ito. I haven't experienced any intense grieving or mourning periods since he died. I'm okay with this, since I know he has and will always be with me. Ito, my soulmate forever.

Has changing from present tense to past tense about someone, after their passing been a strange and uncanny experience for you? Were you surprised by your own grieving process? How was it for you?

178. Surreal Subway Door: Mourning Mom's Morning

Mom died at 4:22 am on January 22, 1996. It seems like so long ago now. I even remember that cold gray, January day, saying to myself that the raw pain of this deep wound of losing my dear mom, would hopefully soften overtime. Maybe it wouldn't be so unbearable and painful. I asked myself to imagine twenty or twenty-five years into the future – and looking back to the very day I was suffering through. From this future point of view, I knew the pain would lessen. Just not today.

Everything felt surreal. I would see people going about their business, like nothing out of the ordinary had happened, not knowing my mom had just died. It seemed like the weather, the world, the traffic, everything was indifferent to my personal, and astounding life-changing event.

Where my apartment was situated, it was possible to see the street entrance to the closest subway station. It was about 150 feet away. I asked God, "If Mom's spirit is still with me, could you open the subway doors as I arrive in front of them, when I'm approximately five feet away?" It was a very specific prayer.

I began to walk down the street toward the entrance to the subway station. There was a hushed silence in the air. All remained still. It seemed like a pale impressionistic painting that morning. The sky was grey, the colours of life, muted. No door opening or closing at all. I kept watching very carefully for my entire walk to the subway. Still no door opening or closing.

Then, as I arrived precisely five feet away from the subway entrance it happened. The door opened, in a big gust of wind. I felt both mystified and satisfied. My prayer had been answered. I quietly thanked God and knew Mom was with me. This very mystical event uplifted my heart. This was the beginning of my life without my physical Mom, but sensing her spirit around me.
Having that very personal sense of knowing has helped me throughout my life during all sorts of challenging events. It restored a sense of faith and trust in my heart.

I believe that prayers do get answered. When they are, we are fortified with more belief and faith. The morning of my mother's death was a true turning-point in strengthening my faith. What events in your life strengthened your faith or belief in something bigger than you? Did you feel relief? How have you integrated this knowing into your life?

179. Subway Suicide Aborted

I was getting off a subway train in Spadina Station that late Wednesday morning, around 11 o'clock. As I was walking toward the escalator to go to street level, I witnessed the scariest thing: A young woman dressed in black, long dreadlocks, back to me, hopped down onto the subway track, after my train left the station.

There were about three of us passengers on the platform witnessing her action. We all shouted out to her, "Come up! Don't go into the train tunnel!" All this was happening as I could see the lights of next train approaching our station. It was about 100 metres away, and it was difficult for me to judge the time it would take to arrive at this platform.

What was I to do? Should I remain there screaming at the top of my lungs to encourage this woman to hop back up from the track level to the platform, or I should also remain there waving my arms in a panic to signal the oncoming train of the imminent danger?

I had another idea. In an instant, I mustered up my courage and ran up the escalator, to the closest streetcar in the subway station, and yelled through the protective glass shield to the driver, "Please stop the oncoming train! Call the train operator and have them stop the train; there's a woman on the tracks!"

I was shocked by how easygoing and calmly the driver called the station. She seemed unfettered by my real panic. I worried that her seeming lackadaisical way might lengthen the time getting into contact with the station and the woman would be hit by the oncoming train.

Fortunately, as I left the station, I knew she was safe. I knew this since there were no sirens, no police cars, no ambulances, and there was no shutting down of this subway.

Whew! Did I actually help save this poor woman's life? I hope so.

Have you experienced a panic-stricken moment when you had to muster up your courage to make a choice what to do in an instant? What happened? What were your choices? What did you decide to do? How has this event affected you? Has it built up any extra trust and confidence in yourself? Has it increased your faith in God?

180. Giving and Receiving: Serendipity in My Mailbox

I will never forget that young woman panhandling outside the Second Cup coffee shop at the corner of Spadina and Bloor, in Toronto. I happened to have a twenty-dollar bill on me that day. I wanted to help her and, at the same time, not flaunt my money. I didn't want her to feel "less than." So, I asked her if I could buy her some lunch at the coffee shop. She graciously accepted. After lunch, I offered her a twenty-dollar bill, asking if I could offer her this. She happily accepted my twenty, telling me that it would help with this month's rent.

When I got home, I opened my mailbox and discovered one of my quarterly royalty cheques from my most popular CD, *Lullababy*. I eagerly opened it as I entered my apartment – alone, in privacy. My jaw dropped as I looked at the amount on the cheque: it was the biggest cheque I had yet received! Of course, this cheque was for both myself and my pianist – but the staggering amount shocked me, since I had always heard that when we give, what is given back is multiplied. Here was living evidence of it.

When have you helped someone, and without expecting it, received a tangible or intangible gift in return? How has giving impacted your life and others?

181. "Zooming" in on My Flute for a Guitarist in a Coma

I've rarely been one who loves the internet and social media – but during the Covid-19 pandemic, I learned to enjoy using Zoom, Facebook Live, Instagram and some other social media platforms. One day I was online and saw a post on Facebook. As I read it, I became more and more intrigued.

It requested people join a meditation Zoom call for a young jazz guitarist twenty-seven years old named Oliver, who had experienced a sudden heart attack and was then put into a medically induced coma. He was living in Austria at the time, but was an American, having graduated from the prestigious New England Conservatory of Music. I decided to join the group, and offered to play soft flute music during the meditations.

I've never had such an unusual experience. Over the years, I've played at weddings and funerals, and even celebrations of life – the happier type of funerals. But playing flute for Oliver's healing felt very unique and a bit surreal. I knew no one in the group, but felt, in a strange sort of way, that I already knew Oliver. His family was so beautiful and supportive to their brother. Taking turns leading the meditation daily, Oliver's family was a testimony to love and undying devotion to his well-being.

I continued to zoom into the Zoom meditations daily, led by his compassionate older brother, Albert. One day, I performed Debussy's *Clair de Lune*, which apparently Oliver loved to play on his guitar. His mom was in the ICU with Oliver, and tuned into the Zoom meditation on her cell phone, on speaker phone. As I played *Clair de Lune*, I wondered if, on some level, Oliver could hear me. Was the flute making it into his consciousness? I wonder if I would ever find out?

I was also curious if one day Oliver and I would meet, and would get to play music together, celebrating his life, alive and recovered. The idea of this lit me up.

A few days later, Oliver's heart-rate went down and a tear came out of his right eye as I played three pieces: *Clair de Lune*, Leonard Cohen's *Hallelujah* and *Greensleeves*. It warmed my heart knowing that my flute playing was calming for Oliver.

Research says that music can heal on many levels. Also, that intentional prayer can be felt and heal non-locally, too. Have you experienced a time when you felt deeply connected to people you didn't even know, where the very experience left you speechless? What happened? What did you make of it?

182. The Spontaneous Dance out of Bed

I've always believed that we have the ability to heal ourselves and others. And, we don't have to be doctors to do so. One of my first experiences with healing myself was with playing my flute when I had bad headaches as a teenager. After playing my flute for only about twenty minutes, my headache would miraculously but predictably subside. My flute became something of a "music-ceutical" for my physical and emotional ailments. When I was sad, anxious, or depressed, simply playing flute made me feel lighter, lifting me out of my darker moods.

One day, when I knew that Glenn, my best friend at the time, was in bed sick, I decided to see if I could help him feel better from a distance. I didn't tell him a thing. I ended up doing this from my shower: I had to take a shower anyway, so I used this tranquil setting to experiment. I'd heard about quantum physics and distance healing before, and wondered if I could do any of this. I simply stepped into the shower, letting the soothing hot water cascade down my back. Then, while thinking of him intently, I placed one hand on my heart, the other palm out – imagining I was sending him love and healing from the palm of my hand, while sending him loving energy from my heart. I focused on this alone, and then got out of the shower, towelled off, and got on with my day. Throughout the rest of the day, I wondered what may have just happened in the shower. Was it possible that my focused intentions of healing actually reached Glenn?

About four hours later – after not being able to remain in suspense any longer – I phoned him. I was so curious to know how he was feeling. To my astonishment and relief, Glenn was incredulous. His voice suddenly got very animated. He told me that something very strange had happened to him – around four hours before my call, he suddenly got out of bed and started dancing for no apparent reason.

When I explained to him that I was sending him intentional healing, it all made sense. Now, more than ever before, there are scientists, doctors and many researchers finding that "non-local" connection with others is completely possible, and that distant healing can occur.

My little experiment in the shower that morning is being proven relevant and plausible, and is believable.

When have you experienced something intangible but so real at the same time? Were you surprised? Who did you tell? Have you continued doing it?

183. From the North Pole to Maui

That snowy, winter-wonderland evening at home in Toronto: I'd just finished writing twenty-five Christmas cards to my Montage Music clients. Every year I would send out cards thanking them for booking us musicians for their parties.

And as a reward to myself for completing this two-hour long task, and to satisfy my curiosity, I spontaneously decided to search Craigslist to see what it would cost to stay at an Airbnb on Maui, Hawaii. I'd always dreamed of experiencing Hawaii like a Maui resident, rather than tourist. This would be a chance for me to act on this deep desire. And I knew that dreams can come true, since, years previously, I had visited Maui under serendipitous conditions.

So, on this particular evening, I decided to call the phone number on Craigslist for Maui Vacations. A very friendly person, named Melinda, answered the phone in a sparkly, sunny voice: "Aloha, Maui Vacations." In my usual bold style, I told Melinda that I owned my own live music booking agency, and was accustomed to being on the phone, doing bookings. I asked her with an optimism that has helped me often, if she might need someone to help her take vacation bookings over the holiday season?

Well, she was amazed with my timing. As it turns out, her mother was planning to come visit from California and the two of them were planning a trip to Kauai, the most lush, green, undeveloped island in Hawaii. Without hesitation or consideration, she immediately said yes. She must have trusted me. She also said that she liked my voice. I loved her sense of adventure and spontaneous risk-taking. After all, she didn't know me from Adam.

The very next morning, I booked a flight to Maui for early January. I would stay for ten days: five days were barter and five were $120 a night – a far cry from the "unaffordable," "unattainable" Maui holidays most people put on their bucket lists. Somehow, my life has circumvented these posh options, yet I've always had the time of my life.

I ended up sharing Melinda's beautiful bungalow in paradise with her and her three cats. What a miracle that the ocean was just a five-minute walk from her place.

One day, while taking bookings, I got the most curious call. A man's voice on the other end of the phone, explaining that he needed to extend the trip he'd already booked on Maui by three days. He'd had an injury and was having trouble getting a flight that could accommodate his special needs: two seats side by side on the plane. I felt badly for his predicament and did my very best to help him out.

As usual, I took down the client's info, including his name and full address. When he said he was from the North Pole, I thought he was joking. But he wasn't; he was from the town of North Pole, Alaska. How oddly coincidental it was for me to have landed a five-day vacation bookings job on Maui, after desperately getting out of cold Canada, to then be taking down the details of a client who lived in a place called the North Pole!

Life truly is stranger than fiction. Especially on Maui!

When has your life seemed stranger than fiction? What happened? How have you expressed the boldest part of you? What did you do? What surprises did you encounter along the way? How has this experience impacted your life?

184. Home Sweet Home, Sight Unseen

I felt totally at home with my own live music entertainment business, Montage Music, located at 5 Charles Street West, in Toronto. My office was a tiny little ten-by-twelve-foot office space in a quaint, old townhouse. Seven West Café, a hip and trendy 24-hour restaurant, was conveniently located next door.

At the time, I was enjoying my role as business owner, manager and flutist, booking musicians for social and corporate events. I played most of the flute gigs myself – but sometimes I'd get double-bookings for the flute for the same Saturday. Usually, they would be for summer weddings.

Since I couldn't be in two places at once, I called a flutist colleague I knew from university, to see if she could substitute for me at one of the weddings. We hadn't been in touch for over three years. Fortunately, she was available.

Before hanging up the phone, something inside compelled me to ask her if she knew of any available apartments downtown. I don't know why I felt so strongly to ask *her*, but I did: it was a gut instinct, and I'm so glad I did. Coincidentally, just the day before, a huge three-bedroom apartment had come up for rent in her building. The price was right, so I told her to please let the property manager know I'd be right over with first and last month's rent within the hour. It was a bold promise I made over the phone, sight unseen.

She complied and I was so relieved that I got to rent this large space, conveniently located on a beautiful, old tree-lined street, close to the subway and right downtown!

It wasn't the first time that I acted upon my intuitive impulses. After that, a few years later, I rented a Montreal sublet, and ended up bringing my Pomeranian pup, Ito home to Toronto. It reminded me of how I also had rented my office at 5 Charles West without really seeing it – merely seeing the "for rent" sign in the window.

What has given me the confidence to do things and act upon decisions, site unseen? I think it's a certain trust in God/the Universe that everything does turn out.

When have you acted upon impulse, intuition and felt glad you did? Has this informed your decisions further to trust your gut? What moments stand out for you the most?

185.   Tom Coffin Playground: A Portentous Parkette

My dear father, Tom Nashman, was staying at a nursing home near Georgian Bay, nestled in the beautiful Ontario countryside. Each wing had its own name, like Pine Villa or White Oak Manor, making the place sound cozy, quaint and hospitable. The staff were very nice, and my dad seemed as happy as he could be in this home away from home. He had many health conditions that required 24/7 nursing care. It felt bittersweet putting him in the home, but knowing it was the best thing for him with his various health concerns.

I was three hours away from my own home in Toronto, visiting dear Dad, knowing he was experiencing many medical conditions at once, and particularly some memory issues. One of the gifts of his memory issues was the way it caused Dad to live in the moment, every single minute. Dad, being an optimist and appreciator of beauty, would often comment in his armchair by the window about how beautiful the clouds looked wafting by, and how tranquil and calm it was. This warmed my heart, since he was experiencing the moment. *Every single moment* he was experiencing his own profound state of mindfulness without even trying.

I remember those days in my childhood with Dad: our special days walking in nature, listening to the cardinals, chickadees, blue jays, and all that was beautiful. His appreciation of life continued even in his armchair at the nursing home looking out from his eyes at *his* world of beauty.

One visit, I decided to take a break and go for a short walk. It was a perfect sunny day: blue sky and birds singing gleefully all around. With the strong sunlight shining right at me, I squinted my eyes and crossed the street. I was stopped in my tracks.

I couldn't believe what I saw before me: The parkette was called "Tom Coffin Playground." First of all, my dad had emphatically said he didn't want a funeral or big production when he died. The fact that the parkette had the same name as my father was not only coincidental, but also perhaps portentous.

"Coffin" was a bit foreboding, and the word suggested to me that Dad's passing might be imminent. The "Playground" part gave me pause. Was this a spiritual nudge, to suggest that once we go, and leave this world, we are lighter, somewhat like innocent children in playgrounds? All of this was quite unnerving, and at the same time, strangely reassuring.

I also heard the most beautiful songbird in this Tom Coffin Playground. It had three parts to its song, each one distinctively different than the one before. I was in awe, both by the name of the parkette and the unusual beauty of this exquisite birdsong.

I returned to Dad's bed and kept this whole story to myself. I looked over him, knowing he was close to his passing. I had researched the signs of a person physically starting to slow down, and finally shut down. It was all so sad, yet I was relieved to be prepared, as much as anyone can be, for that ultimate moment: Dad's passing.

The very next morning, when I arrived once again at Dad's nursing home, a series of events occurred that really prepared me for what was about to happen that day. I looked up at the sky, and unlike yesterday's pure blue sky, there was a puffy cloud right above me, oddly looking like Dad's profile. Dad had a pronounced nose and a beautiful smile. This face in the sky was Dad's!

I heard birds boasting the arrival of morning in their brilliant cacophony. But something else happened that shocked me to the bone. It was both auspicious and somewhat like a warning. That unusual bird that I had heard for the very first time the day before at the Tom Coffin Playground was singing at the top of its lungs right at the entry of Dad's nursing home. What could *this* mean?

I took a deep breath and entered the nursing home, greeting the receptionist behind the glass window with a phrase that came out of my mouth automatically. It was almost instinctive, spoken with matter-of-fact certainty. "Hi, my name's Laura Nashman, and I'm here to see Tom Nashman. He's my father. He's going to die today." I couldn't believe what I'd just said. Was I uttering the truth?

I didn't wait for a response from the receptionist, and quickly walked through the lobby to the elevator. I pressed the button for the fourth floor, where my dad was. In my gut, I felt a sense of urgency.

That evening, at nine o'clock, my dear father passed away. I held one hand and my stepmother held the other. It seemed as if I had mysteriously been warned the day before with my visit to Tom Coffin Playground, and this day with the cloud of Dad's face in the sky. What about that bird in the park that I'd never heard before? And on the day of my dad's passing, why did I hear it as I entered the nursing home? All these signs seemed to point to my dad's passing being imminent.

I had an inner knowing that he was going to die soon, and I was prepared. I will always remember Dad, his enduring love and endless support – and those two very portentous days in Georgian Bay.

When have you had a series of mystical, auspicious events occur that suggested to you that there may be something more? How did you respond? Who did you tell? How has it changed you?

186. "Radiance" Is One of My Favourite Words

When I think of what inspires me, it's those radiant moments – those uplifting, elucidating ones. Rainbows feel like radiance to me; also, that day I signed my CD contract with Solitudes for their very first lullaby CD, *Lullababy*. Mystically, after shaking hands with the president and owner of the company, and leaving their building, I looked up and saw an actual rainbow arched over it. How magical. I had to do a double-take. Was this real? I ran back up to the Solitudes office on the sixth floor and invited them down to witness this magic, deliciously and beautifully, extended across their building!

The rainbow was auspicious, and only four years later, *Lullababy* became a Canadian Certified Gold CD!

Radiance can also be simply a feeling; a sense of merging with life itself. You know – those sparkly spring days, when the sky is steely blue, the buds are on the trees, and the robins are hopping around the ground looking for worms, while the squirrels are flirting with passers-by for peanuts. Puppies scampering by.

It's those sparkly moments that have an immediacy to them. You want to experience them right then and there before they vanish. I've always been intrigued by those special, fleeting or transient moments of beauty and life itself.

Radiance for me, is also a state of mind. A state of abundance, fullness, boundlessness. Sparkle.

What are some radiant moments in your life that have stayed with you? What made them have radiance for you? Did they happen to you or did you create them?

187. The Spiritual Surfer

"Breathe, ease, release, ease." Somehow, this phrase came to me one day: the idea of breathing with ease, then releasing with ease, over and over. Life doesn't have to be a struggle. After many years of trying to figure things out, I realized that life can be approached deliberately but lived with ease. In fact, my best moments have been filled with a delicious ease and flow: a state of positive expectancy of things turning out. At these times life is without struggle. There's a simplicity about it. I also noticed a placard with the saying, "Inhale the moment, exhale the past." That has worked for me, too.

I've tried many things in my life, but I've never surfed. But, in a way, I've been a spiritual surfer: riding the waves of life with as much ease as I can muster up has been a life-long practice. The holding and letting go is my learning. In fact, one wise friend once said to me that it isn't the *letting go* that is so difficult, but rather the *holding on* that is so trying. That was one my life's biggest aha moments.

I noticed this contrast between *letting go* and *holding on* when experiencing relationship breakups. I used to have such a difficult time adjusting to my life without my boyfriends. I must have had attachment issues. My *holding on* like a dog with a bone was so painful, but when I realized I was capable of making another choice – *letting go* – I realized *letting go* was the easy part, and *holding on* was the real pain.

I've taken this distinction seriously, and tried my best to apply it when it's best that I transition out of a situation. More and more, *letting go* helps make my life have more ease and flow.

Has there been a time in your life when you have been aware of struggle vs ease? Were you able to consciously choose ease over struggle? How has this approach or perspective helped make your life better? How do you apply it?

188. Book Expo America: A Playground for the Bookish Folk

One of my favourite "life sandboxes" has been the second-largest book exhibition in the world (second only to the Frankfurt Book Fair). It's Book Expo America, known by seasoned regulars as BEA. Since I used to frequent New York City with my Pomeranian and best pal, Ito, for six years, and I love books and socializing, this seemed like the perfect place to be in the first week of June.

On one occasion, I was invited to perform on my flute at a private breakfast meeting with the renowned Dr. Masaru Emoto. This Japanese man discovered that frozen water-crystals actually respond by forming dramatically different shapes, according to words that are being spoken to them or written on the beaker lid. It was astounding to me that words like "I love you" created symmetrical formations, while "I hate you" or heavy metal music produced jagged, irregular shapes. They were like snowflakes; no two alike, but the pattern existed: love, positive statements, classical music, and harp music produced beautiful shapes; while hate and negative statements produced asymmetrical, jagged shapes.

Even when I wasn't playing flute at the conference, I loved going to Book Expo America, BEA. I've never experienced quite the same type of "buzz": that mix of literary agents, publicists, book publishers and their sales and marketing staff, plus new authors, legendary authors, and celebrities touting their vanity projects. One bonus has always been the free books and autographs at the book signings.

One year, I decided that in order to seem "legit" at such a literary conference, as I wandered the trade show floor, it would be most appropriate to have my *own* book under my arm. I created a picture book called *Doggie Bliss with Ito*. Each picture of Ito had a descriptive slogan and life wisdom written under it.

Since I named my dog Ito after a Japanese jazz guitarist I heard at the Montreal Jazz Festival, I thought it would be most befitting that I seek out a Japanese publisher. I know Japanese women love cute dogs. Perhaps if I found a Japanese publisher, *Doggie Bliss with Ito* would take off in Japan. It was worth trying!

BEA is a huge conference, taking up most of New York's Jacob Javitz Center, which is many football fields in size. I heard that the fifth floor was where I might find a Japanese publisher. Confidently, with Ito under one arm and his book under the other, we eagerly took the elevator up to the fifth floor. Unbeknownst to me, this was the allocated floor for international rights procurement.

After the doors opened, we were politely yet officiously greeted by flight attendant-like hostesses. They were slim, young and attractive – and I suddenly felt uncomfortable, and out of place. They were all wearing similar navy-blue suits and matching yellow and orange silk scarves. I felt like I was about to get on a flight – perhaps, in this case, a successful flight to my Japanese publisher!

No such chance here. With a professional smile, I was asked if I had an appointment. I didn't. I was politely uninvited to stay on the fifth floor. Apparently, only lawyers and publishing executives were allowed here, with their author clients, for pre-scheduled appointments. This was where the big deals were being made. The floor had an air of "happening" and success.

Quietly and bashfully, I escaped the fifth floor quickly and inconspicuously. A quick ride down six floors, the elevator doors opened, and we ventured back to the massive trade show floor: an overwhelming place, with aisle upon aisle of booksellers and publishers.

As I reached the first aisle, I saw a man walking toward me. There were no other people in this particular aisle at the time. His laminated name badge was swinging over his colourful tie, tucked under his navy-blue suit jacket. As he got closer, I could see that he was a Japanese man. But I still couldn't read his name. I squinted, but still couldn't.

As he got even closer, I was stopped in my tracks. His name – no word of a lie – was Mr. Ito! I introduced myself and my Ito, marveling at the fact that my dog had the same name as this Japanese publisher.

I showed him my book enthusiastically, but unfortunately, he didn't respond in kind. Instead, in a typically Japanese, polite way, he bowed at me and said sorry that his company only published financial and economic books. Disappointed by the aborted serendipity, I sheepishly walked off, Ito in one arm, our book in the other.

The synchronicity of this moment was astounding. How funny that I had gone up to the fifth floor to seek out a Japanese publisher, and the very fist person I met re-entering the tradeshow floor was Mr. Ito! I chuckled inside, tickled by how life is truly stranger than fiction! What a coincidence, or was it serendipity?

Even though Ito was a small dog, and I was an inexperienced author, being at BEA and sharing Ito's joyous book was a big deal to me. Bigger deals were happening at BEA all week, but my biggest deal was having dear Ito at my side.

Can you recall a coincidence in your life that caused you a moment to pause, giggle, shake your head? How did that moment affect you?

189.   The Hidden Mysteries in My Names

At birth, I was named Michelle by my birth mom. Apparently, the meaning of the name Michelle in Hebrew is "close to God" – and it's the feminine form of Michael, which means "who is like God, or gift from God." What a privilege to be given such a spiritually based name! Over my lifetime, I've gotten closer and closer to my version of God, and I listen more carefully to the guidance I receive.

When I was chosen by my loving adoptive parents, Nancy and Tom Nashman, they changed my first name to Laura, and made Michelle my middle name. Apparently, Laura means "the embodiment of victory and strength – and is the feminized form of Laurus, which in the Greco-Roman era, was used as a symbol of victory, honour or fame."

If the essence of our names gets energetically embedded into us and our lives, I wonder how my names have affected my identity and life? I've always been much more interested in spiritual things than materialistic ones, that's for sure. Having said this, I love beauty in all its expressions: birdsongs, flowers, sunsets, music, art and animals. Those are all spiritual things. I've never aspired to the monster-mansion lifestyle, or to keeping up with fashion trends and designer clothes. I've always enjoyed expressing myself with my unique sense of style.

My adoptive last name, Nashman, means "gifted with an analytical mind and an enormous appetite for the answers to life's hidden questions." Apparently, I have "a strong interest in exploring scientific matters, philosophy and even mysticism," as well as "clarity and persistence in the search for truth."

At a core level, I really resonate with all of these above definitions and descriptions about myself. All my life I've sought out answers, and have been interested in philosophy, psychology and self-development. I've studied with Tony Robbins, Richard Bandler (co-founder of Neuro-Linguistic Programming) and with dance teachers Margi Gillis, Gabriele Roth, Erica Ross, Martha Randall and Jennifer Hicks. (The expression, "Let the dance move through you," has been particularly impactful, for me – simply letting go, and allowing the dance to arise from within, spiritually.)

Always as satisfied searching for the answers as I am finding them, I've led a life full of curiosity and abundant discoveries!

Do you know the definitions and original meanings of your first, middle and last names? What did you discover? Do you names suit you, or rather, do you and your life fit in with your names? What are the most prominent qualities that represent the authentic you?

190. Living the First and Last Day of My Life

Life is so many things: astounding, incredible, mystical, ever-changing, serendipitous, painful, memorable, fleeing, fragile, unfair, and more.

One perspective I've chosen to live with for many years is the gratitude for my health, and the privilege of waking up each morning for a new day. Not everyone gets this opportunity. With the Covid-19 pandemic, this statement rings even more true. Life is ever moving and flowing, and the only thing constant is change.

I've often experienced my days as if they are the very first day of my life: filled with wonder, curiosity, and a sense of awe and excitement. At the same time, I've also experienced my days as though they were the last day of my life: a day to cherish, with its many expressions of beauty, connections and meaning. Some moments are over in a flash, while others linger and can be stretched out over time.

For me, my life is more fulfilling when I focus on these two, seemingly distinctively opposite, vantage-points: my first and last days. What they share in common is a sense of celebration – celebrating the moment, and celebrating life itself. *Carpe diem* may be the best term for this state of seizing the moment, with all its awe and wonder.

I don't usually have boring days, since I get absorbed in each moment with a sense of wonder and curiosity – sometimes simply witnessing and just being. Life is miraculous, unfolding like a moment-to-moment birth and death.

I've discovered these special momentary gifts when taking pictures of flowers, birds, people during my daily morning walks. Looking for the source of a melodious birdsong is a magical moment for me, just as much as stopping to speak with a homeless person. Both are moments of connection and being.

When I'm aware of the connectivity of everything, life speaks to me in a language that is so magical and fulfilling.

How do you experience your life to its fullest? Have you ever imagined living your days as if they are both the first and last days of your life? How did that impact you? Are there other ways you celebrate life itself?

191. Heart Connections: Animals and Music

I heard somewhere that the palms of our hands energetically connect with our hearts. Perhaps that's why putting our hand over our heart is such a true gesture of compassion. The heart and hand actually *feel* connected. One thing I've also noticed is the curious connection that exists between a beloved pet on the end of a leash and its owner – both by holding the leash at the other end, and the extending of the heart through the leash.

Often, when I walk my dog and notice other people lovingly walking theirs, it looks like the leash is the conduit of heart energy, extending from the person to the dog and from the dog to the person. Could it be true that our hearts, both physically as well as energetically, extend to our pets as we walk them – simply connected by a leash? It's like a bridge from heart to heart.

I've also noticed that playing flute feels very heart centred. It's not just because of the sound of the flute, but because the left arm is positioned over both the keys of the flute and the heart. Also, the upper body is held so open – almost in a natural posture for heart-energy to flow out of.

So, I've discovered that both the flute and the leash are two wonderful conduits of love and heart-energy. I wonder what else is? I'll continue to explore more!

What have you discovered about your heart connections? Have you experienced any remarkable things? What does it feel like when you lead from your heart?

192. Meeting with a Celebrity Who Gardens

When I meet celebrities, I try my best to be considerate of their privacy and perhaps their bugaboos. While some would love ongoing accolades, others prefer to simply be! To me, that means don't act starstruck – and if I converse with them, perhaps keep it away from their profession. Talk about the weather and other non-intrusive things.

On several occasions, I've met a very famous Canadian author gardening on her front lawn. I say hello, ask a few questions about the various flower types, politely wish her a good day, and continue walking my dog. Since I began walking my dog past her home every morning, I've said hello to her whenever I've seen her.

One Saturday morning, my boyfriend and I were walking the dog, and there she was again, but this time carrying some plastic bins neatly stacked out to her boulevard. An auspicious moment – since my boyfriend had just bought a condo and was waiting for Covid-19 lockdown to be lifted so we could get some packing containers from the local Canadian Tire store. I asked her if she was offering them and she insisted that we take them.

Here we were, face-to-face with the distinguished, award-winning author Margaret Atwood, thanking her for the containers that would help with the move. In the back of my mind, I wondered if any of her many manuscripts had been stored in these bins. Since I was just finishing my memoir, *Sparkle*, this seemed to add a good-luck charm to my completing the book – and my boyfriend, a composer and author himself, was helped with his move! Packing containers: practical help and auspicious gift to encourage my book completion.

Have you experienced auspicious moments when the coincidence of meeting someone coincided with a special project you were undertaking? What happened? How did you interpret this event?

193. Experiencing Altered-States

When I'm in the shower, practicing my flute, swimming or on long walks, ideas just seem to drop into my consciousness. I've also noticed that when I first wake up, creative and inspired thoughts come easily to me.

It's a strange sort of phenomenon. I've even experienced this while writing this book. In fact, while I do my morning scales and technical exercises on my flute, I have a notepad beside me, since ideas just seem to flow into me. I wonder if repetitive passages, like scales and arpeggios, kind of open up my mind for creative thoughts to appear spontaneously? I wonder, does repetition actually trigger concurrent creative thinking or daydreaming?

Fascinating.

Sometimes I think I live in altered states most of the time. It's a very curious subject, for sure. I also wonder if since I play my flute two-to-four hours a day, this seeming altered brain-state I go into remains with me throughout the day.

Perhaps this is why I don't like too much "mental confinement," or a process-oriented lifestyle. Am I in a state of dreamlike flowing in an out of states, but predominantly in a Theta state: the one experienced just before falling asleep or just awakening? It's definitely something to think about and continue exploring.

Have you ever experienced an ease of inspiration, and creativity while busy doing something else (like my experience practising scales, with ideas flowing at the same time)? What were you doing at the time? What was the inspiration and creativity that flowed from you effortlessly? When were you first aware of this?

194. Flying, Somersaults, and Breathing Underwater

Since I was a young child, I've loved to experiment in my dream-realm. I'd lie there in bed asking myself, "What do I want to dream about tonight?" At that early age, I was aware that I could direct my dreams into being, just by the very decision to do so. I looked forward to going to bed, since this is where remarkable things happened: in my dreams, while I was asleep.

I loved flying in my dreams, breathing water while swimming underwater (and not drowning – something I'd never try in waking life), plus all sorts of seemingly surreal things that wouldn't seem possible when I was awake. I particularly loved that one-second moment of transition from thinking and intending my chosen dream that night, to falling asleep and having a full-fledged dream.

Sometimes my dreams were preceded by a hypnagogic hallucination: a very fancy word for various things that can occur while we transition from wakefulness to REM (Rapid Eye Movement) sleep. One that I've experienced often is losing control and slipping down an imagined hill just before falling asleep. Many people have had this experience. I have always found it fascinating and a bit scary.

What's great about these dreams is that I'm aware I'm dreaming. They say that when you actually know you're dreaming, you're experiencing a lucid dream. I have had many such dreams. I love knowing that they're dreams. I can even nudge myself saying, "This can't be real – it must be a dream." In this moment, I can choose whether I want to stay in the dream or wake up.

I wonder if being able to do these things in our sleep opens a part of the brain that allows for more possibilities and sense of boundlessness in our waking lives? I'm not saying we should try to breathe under water or to jump off buildings and fly. But what I'm wondering is if this kinesthetic freedom during sleep informs our waking life. Does it give us a sense of freedom, otherwise not experienced before? Perhaps this belief and actual feeling of boundlessness can actually inspire more possibilities than had we not had those experiences in our dreams?

In the way that riding horses has created a horse spirit within me, carrying their boldness, their confidence and sensitivity, I wonder: Are flying dreams, along with somersaults and swimming while breathing underwater, an informant or embodiment of living courageously and boundlessly? Are we bolder and more risk-taking in our waking lives since we have had embodied experiences stored in our brains from our dreams?

When have you experienced a thin line between consciousness and lucid dreaming? What did you notice? Have you had dreams that have fascinated you, and perhaps influenced your waking life for the better? What were they? How have you benefited from them?

195. How My Voice Saved a Life

We've all heard about opera singers, and the sheer power and volume of their voices. Some have even been able to break glass by their vocal power and intensity.

Well, one day, on my way home, I experienced my own voice like never before. I actually called upon it as an aid, perhaps as a sonic "weapon," to stop a fight that could have gotten very, very, ugly.

Toronto's Chinatown, on Spadina Avenue, is a vibrant area: Busy and bustling with pedestrians, streetcars rumbling by and cyclists dipping in and out of traffic. On this day, as dusk was falling, I was waiting patiently at a crowded streetcar stop on Spadina. As I looked south to see if the streetcar was coming, my eyes were diverted to the corner, three blocks down. As the light of day darkened, I spotted a gang of teenage boys punching and kicking someone violently, causing him to fall onto the street on his back. Traffic was coming in all directions and the boys continued their assault relentlessly.

Out of the blue, instinctively I shouted out, *"Stop!"* The boys' faces were turned away from me, but I saw visual shock ripple down their backs, almost as if they were shuddering to the sound of an unexpected gunshot. But it wasn't a gun – it was me!

They then scattered in all directions, leaving the scene of the crime. In that instant, I realized that my voice had functioned like a weapon, and I had most likely saved a life. The streetcar clanged up to the stop and a bunch of us got on. I'm sure they all had witnessed my outpouring of vocal power.

I climbed onto the streetcar, my heart still beating quickly. I sat down, reviewing what had just happened, and what may have happened if I hadn't used my voice.

I will always remember that we all are equipped with intuition that knows what to do at all times. We just need to trust and follow our instincts.

Have you experienced a time when you were called to save a life? What happened? Were you surprised? How has this event shaped or changed you?

196. Out-of-Body Bubble-Bath

I'd heard about out-of-body experiences for many years – but what I didn't realize at the time was that *I* would be having one of these experiences in the bubble-bath.

Sometimes, with the candlelight flickering, and the warm bubbles making that soft delicate sound, it's easy to get so relaxed I almost fall asleep. In fact, a few times I *have* fallen asleep.

One day, while I was soaking, I had my legs bent, my knees poking out of the water, facing the ceiling of the bathroom. As I looked at my knees, I noticed that I felt very removed from them, almost like I was witnessing someone else's anatomy. I was fascinated by this, but a little scared too. I'd never had quite experienced anything like this before. And, I knew that I wasn't dreaming.

Suddenly, I snapped out of it, changing my perspective to deliberately observing my knees and knowing they were *mine*. What was most fun about this was the fact that I not only experienced an altered state, but I was able recognize it was altered. I was able to revert back to my conscious state, where the knees were part of me, and not abstract objects. I was playing with my own consciousness.

And this isn't something that only happened to me in the bath: I had a similar experience in my own bed. One night, I was lying on my back, not yet asleep but just starting to drift off. Without warning, suddenly I felt a rush of cold air on either side of my body. Then, I felt myself being rapidly lifted up into the starlit night. What was I doing up there? What caused this to happen?

All I could see were thousands of stars, magically twinkling against the dark night sky. It was a feeling I'd never felt before, (or ever again). It didn't feel like dreaming, yet looking up at the starlit sky seemed somewhat familiar. The only difference here was I was up there amidst the stars, so close to them, I could have been one myself. I felt light years away from my bed.

Was I having an out-of-body experience? I really didn't know what to think, since I had no reference point for anything like this. Wide-eyed, I was hyper-awake, but definitely felt like I was in an altered state. It felt both clear and dreamlike at the same time. Suddenly, I heard a man's voice inside my head say, "Do you want to stay or go back?" I figured he was referring to my levitated state in the stars. I quickly replied with a desire to go back. Again, I felt the cold, racing wind on either side of my body – and I thudded back into myself, lying on my back again, like before, on top of my mattress. I stared at my bedroom ceiling, in a state of sheer awe. My heart was racing.

What had just happened? It was unlike any dream I'd ever had before. It must have been an altered state and/or an out-of-body experience. Whatever it was, I was relieved to be back in my familiar surroundings. Whew! I made it back.

Have you had out-of-body experiences? Were you able to return to your habitual consciousness and know you were temporarily in another state? How did you go from one to the next? Have you had any experiences like this since?

197. The Power of Intention and the Law of Attraction

I will never forget that particular breakup. I've experienced many breakups, some easier than others. This particular relationship was so hard to separate from.

It was back in the late '90s, shortly after my mom had died. I was already quite sensitive to loss and grief. At this particular time, I had found solace in riding the ferry to the Toronto Islands – to Ward's Island, in particular. I loved it since it had such a beautiful boardwalk, long and winding, looking out on Lake Ontario.

I had woken up crying, not able to deal with my recent breakup, and decided I would go to Ward's Island for a bike ride. Before this, I would meditate, and Ward's Island would be my reward for meditating. I chose to focus on three good qualities that I wanted to feel towards my ex-boyfriend:

- Love
- Connection
- Peace

As I sat cross-legged on my living room carpet, I meditated on love, connection and peace between us. After twenty minutes of sobbing, I gave myself the reward of going to the island and walking the boardwalk. I arrived there in less than an hour.

As I rode along this barren boardwalk, not a person in sight, I suddenly saw someone on a bike, approaching me from at least 100 metres away. As the figure gradually came into focus, I could see that it was man in his early thirties. As he came closer, I could see that he had a baseball cap on, with three words listed, one word over the other: Love, Peace, Unity.

I was literally dumbfounded: it was my ex-boyfriend! I was shocked, and marveled at the fact that we were the only two people on the entire boardwalk stretch. What was even more remarkable was that he hadn't been to Ward's Island in many years. This was his first time in a long time.

What could this whole serendipity mean? We hugged. I told him I had been meditating on three words, wanting to have peace and love and connection between us, even though we were no longer together in a relationship. I guess my meditation came to fruition, since it was a thought, a feeling and then manifestation on the boardwalk. Since that day, I've always believed in the power of intention, meditation, prayer, and manifestation.

When have you had an unexpected visitor or event that seemed so serendipitous, you couldn't explain it? What events have deepened your belief in the power of intention, prayer, manifestation, prayers answered? Faith?

Chapter Nine

Healing and Reflecting

Self-reflection has been a big part of my life – my ongoing inquiry and fascination. My curiosity has taken me into the depths of my past shopping habit, into lucid dreaming, out-of-body experiences, and many more trippy experiences, without the help of psychotropic drugs! I've always loved to delve deeply and investigate how things work, and what works best for me. Healing is also one of my biggest ongoing experiences and transformations.

198. How My Psychology Hobby Became My Way of Life

When I was only about twelve years old, I loved spending hours upon hours at the local library, poring over books, meticulously sifting through psychology titles. There were no big Indigo or Barnes and Noble bookstores at the time, so the library was a very welcoming place for my inquisitive mind. It also served as a quiet place for me.

At the time, I was also incredibly anxious, and saw a therapist twice a week to help me to cope with my daily OCD (obsessive-compulsive disorder) and anxious ruminations. Dealing so early in life with my emotional challenges led me to the library often. It was a calming oasis for me, where I could dive into so many books and keep my mind off my worries.

I was fascinated with so many titles in the psychology area. I would literally stack one book onto another, making a one-metre pile of books I wanted to skim. Then I would find a private spot in the library, with its "old book" smell, sit cross-legged on the floor, and go into a reading trance. This hobby/habit filled me up, emotionally and spiritually, too.

Years later, I did a lot of adult self-development courses, including NLP, (Neuro-Linguistic Programing), hypnosis, and more. A lifelong learner, I've always felt enriched by the learning process.

Now, a half-century later, I'm writing my own book, as a kind of "self-help memoir" – offering short stories from my life, and inviting you, the reader to delve into your own stories and reflect upon them. I chose to call it *Sparkle* for several reasons: Life offers us many memories that inspire ourselves and others; some spark feelings and unforgettable situations, while others may originally have been hurdles that we overcame. These hurdles and challenges may now be light, joyous sparkles of wisdom, gems in our lives – magical transformations.

It's funny how the genesis of ideas happens. A troubled time – the Covid-19 pandemic – led me to inner work, and finally to writing about all those moments that sparkled, or transformed me, leaving an indelible spark from their experience.

When have your experiences brought you silver linings, magical moments and sheer sparkle to your life? What made you grow? Transform? Choose differently?

199. "Dr. V.L.," My Heart-Throb

They say it's common to fall in love with your therapist. I was no exception. When I was as young as eleven, I used to worry, obsess, ruminate about so many things. I would compliment friends at school for their pretty outfits and, later at home after school, call them to double-check they knew I was sincere. I was so sensitive to tonal nuance (which later helped me to become a better flutist and artist) that I thought they might hear a subtly unkind tone in my delivery, and perhaps think I had been sarcastic. This type of worry plagued me many days at school to the point that I couldn't focus on doing my homework or even relaxing and watching TV. Mulling things over things *ad nauseum* was my *modus operandi*.

This non-stop worrying became so painful that my mom sought out professional help for me. She would pick me up Tuesday and Thursday afternoons from school, and take me to Sick Kids Hospital, in downtown Toronto, to have my therapy sessions with my psychiatrist, "Dr. V.L." And what a heart-throb he was! Not only did I take an interest in psychology and read many books on it at the time – but I told him I loved him and wanted to become a psychiatrist myself one day. I've later learned that it is quite common for patients to fall in love with their therapists.

Every week I looked forward to seeing my doctor. In fact, it was the highlight of my week. Like a dog with its head out of a car window, ears flying in the breeze, I felt uplifted going to see Dr. V.L. I loved listening to him with his Dutch accent, and ever since seeing him, I've had a soft spot for the Dutch. He never medicated me, but helped me to calm down my ruminations and additional OCD habit: incessant handwashing.

That must have been one of the biggest obstacles for me to overcome, since it was a logical compulsion. You see, I rationalized that when we have dirty hands and turn on the tap, we are adding germs to the tap, and when we turn it off, we are reinfecting ourselves. Therefore, my seeming logic dictated that I turn the tap off with my wrist to avoid getting germs on my freshly washed hand. But then my wrist was dirty, so I would rewash and then turn the tap off with my elbow – and the process began all over again. I would come out of the bathroom several times a day after fifteen-minute handwashing rituals with red, chapped hands. I felt so out of control, yet felt I was doing what was necessary.

Finally, my breakthrough, and my break from appointments with Dr. V.L., occurred when I decided to turn it all over to God. I decided that God would not want people to misunderstand my intentions. So each time I ruminated, I would remind myself that God wouldn't want me to worry or have friends misinterpret my compliments. This self-directed therapy really worked. I simply reminded myself to redirect my ruminations. I stopped seeing Dr. V.L after two years of therapy, and strengthened my faith in God.

Professional medical attention is very important. I also discovered that having a strong faith in God was equally important to me. It set me free to trust and have faith and believe. What leap of faith have you experienced that made a profound difference in your life? How has your life benefited from this discovery?

200. Running In and Out of Control

When I was a teenager, my anxiety and OCD were very present. I was a chronic list-maker, bed-maker, and homework-doer. I also practised my flute daily and diligently. The problem for me at the time was my compulsive desire to get things right, as perfect as possible.

One of the ways I lowered and managed my stress and obsessions was by jogging thirty minutes every day. This gave me a mix of motivation, discipline and sense of control. I'm sure the endorphins helped, too! It gave me the "runner's high," that certain type of euphoria avid runners talk about. I felt compelled to weigh myself at least ten times a day. I was anxious at first, but always relieved to see that my weight remained the same, most of the time. This sense of being in control was so important to me. I also loved chocolate, but didn't want to gain weight, so my solution was to chew it over the garbage can and just before swallowing it, spit it out. It seemed to make sense: enjoy the flavour without the calories.

I was one step away from bulimia and definitely was anorexic. I didn't have anorexia nervosa, which I understand is the component of anorexia where you see yourself in a distorted way (for example, obese, when in fact you aren't). If I went up a pound, I would skip meals or eat lighter that day so that my regular weight would return. My days were very disciplined. Up at six o'clock, in the pool next door from 6:30 to 7:00 am, flute practising from 7:00 to 8:30, and then work from nine to five during the summer months. After work, I would jog, have my salad and practise more at night. Quite a self-regulated regimen. I was in a constant state of chasing away my anxiety.

My OCD also affected my flute practising. My playing became laboured, as I would go over and over passages, without moving forward to the next exercise. I wanted to perfect them, but it felt like an endless loop. I felt like a hamster on a musical treadmill, running in circles, with no end in sight, always attempting to get things perfect.

But in some ways, my OCD has had its upside for me, I suppose. I'm sure I wouldn't have practised my flute for so many hours, or repeated technical studies as many times, if I didn't have OCD. Somehow, it has assisted my flute development with a fastidious type of self-discipline, all in the name of perfection-seeking.

OCD can aid many art forms and tasks that demand focused, repetitive movements, such as ballet, music performance and some sports. Although OCD can be a result of great anxiety, using the repetitive approach to certain areas of our lives can help us improve. What aspects of your life could benefit from focused, repetitive attention, not necessarily OCD?

201. Overcoming Over-Shopping

I've been a shopper most of my life; everything from clothes to necessary and unnecessary items. For many years, the act of shopping definitely filled a need, I thought. But actually, it was filling a deep void. Like for many, retail therapy became a big part of my life. If I felt upset, I would simply take myself on a shopping date with myself.

There seemed to be nothing better than being in a perfectly orderly, aesthetically pleasing environment, with upbeat music changing my low mood, and salesclerks offering to help, step back, or be attentive in some way. It all seemed so orderly, unlike the feelings of despair or chaos that I was experiencing inside – those very feelings that fuelled my retail therapy. It could have been a failing relationship, an upsetting conversation, my inner critic beating me up, or anything! Shopaholism was my new route to so-called happiness and fulfillment, *for the time being.*

One day, I realized that at stores, you are immersed in the experience of getting "yes" for everything. Credit cards are the "plastic yes," even if you don't have the physical money: they offer a momentary suspension from reality. Also, for the most part, sales clerks are friendly and compliment you on how you look. What a better way to boost your sagging, deflated ego? Lifting shoppers' spirits is the name of the game.

This is where it became interesting. I blended my inner magician with shopaholic to create my own strategy for overcoming my shopping habit. I used a simple insight to trick my own shopaholic mind, by telling myself, "Laura, yes you can buy anything you want in the store." I felt a burst of joy, a permission, a shopper's euphoria. With my shopping cart, I put everything thing I wanted in it, with absolutely no hesitation, no criticism, no over thinking. It was, "yes", "yes", "yes". And that made me feel so much better than when I entered the store.

When I finally arrived at the cash register, I simply told the cashier that I wasn't going to be taking anything, and with the same boldness and enthusiasm, proceeded to put everything back. I realized that with this self-inflicted shopping trick I was able to enjoy the retail therapy process, but not end up at home, in debt and with a hoarder's closet of unneeded clothes!

Another trick I used on myself was to tell myself, over and over, that neatly displayed clothes in an impeccable boutique were a far cry from the hoarded mess they would make in my stuffed bedroom closet.

I would remind myself of that dreaded task of going through my closets every year, in the name of decluttering! It was impossible to decide what to keep and what had to go. While in the act of indulgent clothes shopping, I would often remind myself of this by flashing a visual reminder of my hoarded mess across my mind, before taking the items to the cash register.

I also learned to recognize marketing tactics. We women often get seduced by offers like "Buy one, get one free." To the shopaholic, it seems like such a sumptuous offer. But I realized that if I didn't need one of those items, I certainly didn't need an *additional* one!

Now, I shop when I need or want something, but not as retail therapy, to sublimate something else. Shopping has lost its fireworks for me. I am finally free – and I feel better, knowing I'm no longer at the mercy of my shopping habit.

Have you experienced retail therapy? Did it ever become a habit that felt out of control for you? What did you do? How did you replace the shopping habit, and with what?

202. Hiding in Bed from Life

For many of us, the bed is a true comfort zone – a place for rest, solitude, reflection, and even hiding from the world. For me, I discovered that I found tranquility staying in bed late. It was a true escape from life's challenges, my anxiety and depression. By simply putting the covers over my head, I could evade the monsters within. Eventually, I would surface, and the monsters would subside.

Many mornings, I'd wake up feeling deliciously calm and warm under the blankets. But as soon as I considered the day ahead, I would feel my heart start to race, my stomach tense up, churning uncontrollably – and my mind become a kaleidoscope of ideas coming at me from so many directions. At the time, my solution was to stay under the covers as long as I could. When I finally decided to get up, it was often a struggle for me.

I've actually heard that we create almost invisible holograms in our mind's eye – and it was possible that I was making the scary thoughts of my day appear way too close to me in bed. So, one of my NLP teachers suggested simply throwing the covers forward and off myself, almost sending away the up-close negative holograms. After that, I could deliberately get up and start my day. What a relief that solution was!

This technique really worked. Since then, I've been throwing the covers off my bed and jumping out and seizing the day – without indulging in cozy under-the-covers time.

Have you discovered formulas that work for you to combat anxiety and stress and that get yourself going in the morning? How and when did you discover these helpful techniques?

203. Going Home to Nurse My Depressed Self

When I experienced daily anxiety and depression, I found it so hard to concentrate on anything but it. After school, friends would invite me out to do things, but I often felt uneasy joining them. Why?

Somehow, I felt a responsibility to go home and nurture my depressed self – the person who dwelled under my student persona. Nobody knew *this* Laura. It was my secret self, the self that seemed to dominate my emotions and consciousness, most of the time. This is one of the strangest sensations I've ever experienced: feeling duty-bound to this secret part of myself, rather than wanting to go out and play with my friends and celebrate life.

I felt that in order to be honest and authentic, I had to respond to my sad self, and leave celebration and fun to those people who were happy. It was almost as if that sad persona was dragging me home to tend to her. My depressed self was always waiting for me, like a distinct character wanting to be taken home and looked after. She often won, and I declined get-togethers with my friends, most of the time.

Later in life, I realize now that I'm made up of many parts. Honouring the part of me that celebrates life, and enjoys being alive, is as important – if not more important – than succumbing to the beckoning of my depressed, anxious self. I understand that it's a balancing act.

And most importantly, I discovered that my sadness instantly dissolved when I allowed myself more happiness.

Have you experienced depression and anxiety? Did you experience it as another part of yourself – a distinctive self? Did you feel like you had to accept the invitation of this persona first, rather than open up to happiness and celebration? What did you do? What did you discover about yourself?

204. The Black Hole

Everyone has had moments experiencing the dark night of the soul, and I definitely have, too. Most of my dark moments have been accompanied by loneliness, self-criticism and feeling left out. In retrospect, I wonder if being adopted had any part in this. I've heard that abandonment is a big issue with adopted children.

Having said this, I definitely didn't feel abandoned by my adoptive parents. They were truly wonderful; so welcoming, loving and supportive. I'll never forget hearing them say to me that they chose me! What a gift to be chosen! I knew deep down this meant they wanted me. But my sadness, bottomless despair, and depressive, anxious moments prevailed.

I've even heard it said that, in utero, if a mother is experiencing emotional turmoil, the fetus can actually feel it too. And, at birth, the severing of the umbilical cord along with the separation from the birth mother can have devastating emotional outcomes, since so much is stored in our subconscious minds. I've often felt a sense of panic, separation, sadness and despair, but didn't understand it on a conscious level.

Adding to this, in my case, I was told that for my first five months, I was in and out of foster homes. This could have led to separation issues, resulting in my OCD and other anxiety disorders.

As a youngster in school, I would often ask permission to play with other classmates during recess, since I often felt like an outsider. This sense of needing to be granted permission to be included continued throughout my adolescent years, and sometimes even into my adulthood.

When I reached the age of twenty-five, I decided I wanted to take control of my life and develop my own business so that I would be the one in control. I'd hire the musicians for performances and recordings. No one could leave me out, since I was the one doing the choosing. This was one way of dealing with my insecurity and rejection issues – but sadly, I discovered I still felt isolated, even if I was in the driver's seat. Being in charge didn't deliver me from my lifelong sadness.

Some days, in my early twenties, I would feel such a blackness sweep over me, a type of all-consuming dark depression, a heaviness that I was lost in yet part of. It was an ongoing feeling; I couldn't quite shake it completely. My father was often perplexed by me. He complimented me on my entrepreneurship and victories, yet shook his head, bewildered and confused about why I felt so lonely, unhappy and depressed. It didn't compute for him. Quite frankly, I didn't totally understand it either.

In my efforts to make sense of it, I would explain to him that it was probably due to some very early life trauma, before I was even adopted by him and my mother. He took that in and considered my words, but by the look on his face, I could tell he was still thoroughly perplexed.

Fortunately, I have done a lot of inner work, everything from transformational courses and workshops to grief counselling, psychotherapy, NLP training and more. I've also found that the healing power of nature has really helped me throughout my life. Painting and dance, also, have brought me a sense of inner peace and boundlessness too.

Black holes and the dark night of the soul are very real. So is light at the end of the tunnel. For me, I've never forgotten the evolutionary stages of my life, and the gentle tending to my soul. I'm so grateful to have had loving adoptive parents, amazing friends and mentors, pets and a life that is worthy of gratitude and celebration.

Have you had a dark night of the soul? How did you climb out of it? Did anyone help you or did you do it alone? What are some of the tools and strategies you've used to transform these dark moments? What have the most important lessons been? Have you had the opportunity to help others experiencing the dark night of the soul, depression, anxiety, despair? How did you help guide them?

205. Roller-Coaster Love

I remember the day I said to a close friend – after a tumultuous passionate on-again-off-again romantic relationship – that if I finally got over this recent one, I would become a "flattened," less passionate, version of myself. It was a profound moment for me, not wanting to say goodbye to my passionate, sensual self – yet at the same time, wanted to get over the unbearable breakup pain.

I felt so alive and on fire with life, but when applied to my relationships, this level of emotional voltage was destroying me. I would ride this predictably unpredictable roller-coaster love, revelling in the euphoric highs, but drowning emotionally in the lows. It was addictive, all-consuming, and felt impossible to stop. I felt like a relationship junkie, addicted to these stormy ups and downs, almost compulsively wired for them. I expected them, feared them, and then, as usual, I crashed and burned.

After many years of this self-inflicted abusive pattern, I decided I needed to come up for air; otherwise, I was going to drown forever. I remember that very day – literally deciding to let my passionate, overly feeling antennae of emotions soften, dilute and become less intense, in order to move on and survive love, and even life itself.

But at the same time, I knew that when I recovered from the overwhelming heartache, I would be a different person: one who no longer functioned from extreme intense emotions – which at best were euphoric, but at worst were emotionally crippling. I decided to bite the bullet and give up on this unhealthy and unsustainable expression of me: up and down like a yoyo. I decided that I both wanted and needed more harmony and tranquility in my life.

I started to seek out healthier relationships, where there was more of an emotional balance, as opposed to my usual highs and lows. I realized that I could be so much more creative and productive when I didn't have the burden of rollercoaster relationships running my romantic life. I decided that loving myself and getting out of emotional harm's way was being more respectful and loyal to myself. I never turned back.

One realization I had during my final romantic breakup was that partners can leave us, and this can feel very lonely and empty – but if we actually leave *ourselves* when our lover leaves us, that is even worse.

I promised myself, from that moment forward, that I would honour and love myself and be true to my needs. From this authentic place, I would then find love.

As with all changes, we can feel loss, and this was no different. But I definitely gained myself back – and that made the learning process all the more worthwhile.

When in your life, have you relinquished someone or something you loved for self-preservation? How has it helped you in your life overall?

206. Peace Of Mind: *Being* Rather Than *Achieving*

For so many years, I suffered anxiety, depression and insecurities. Caught up in wanting people to like me, and worrying so often about what others thought of me, literally consumed my waking hours. Needless to say, my life was very stressful. I tried to cope with it by introducing rituals and routines – I was good at making lists, making my bed, practising my flute, doing homework – but comfort and joy were not my closest companions – neither was peace of mind.

One day, after having won several horse shows, flute competitions and other achievements, I decided I needed to create a valuable goal that would change my life and its direction. I chose the pursuit of "peace of mind." Suddenly, my life wasn't about doing, achieving, impressing, living up to others' expectations, it was about *landing* – landing in my own skin, being myself, and no longer caring so much about what others thought of me. This was a game changer. My life blossomed completely as mine – authentically, purposefully, mindfully, meaningfully, dynamically and peacefully.

It became a life of *being* more than *doing* – and that has made all the difference both inside and out.

My life was no longer a series of trajectories and accomplishments, but rather a calm, ever-present sense of "beingness." It may sound a bit flakey, but my peace of mind became the most important thing to me – the source from which everything I say and do now comes.

I remember attending a Mark Victor Hansen seminar in the early 1990s, and his reversal of the myth of happiness from the customary sequence of Do-Have-Be to *Be-Do-Have*. What a distinction! I learned that if I'm happy, content and grateful, I can *do* all the things I love to do, and *have* what I want – not the other way around.

Over the years, my life has become much more peaceful. I even look forward to getting up each morning to create my life, authentically and unapologetically. It feels like coming home to myself – the home I now know best.

When in your life did you make a major turnaround, and zero in on your essential nature? What did you discover you needed in order to have peace and happiness in your life? How do you continue on this path every day?

207. Active Wisdom from a Wise Teacher

"If you can't do something, imagine you can." This is one of the most profound statements I've ever heard. Plus, as the saying goes, the brain doesn't know the difference between reality and the imagination, so if you give it realities you want to manifest, it can treat them as true already.

The downside of giving our brains instructions is we often find ourselves feeding ourselves lies: lying about our potential, our dreams, our abilities, our innate gifts and other things. Most extreme examples are mental illnesses that include delusional thinking that is destructive to our own and others' lives. We must be vigilant in knowing when imagining is a brain-fuel that is productive, generative and healthy.

I've learned about bringing intentions into being from NIA (Neuromuscular-Integrative Activity), a dance and movement practise. It's easy to think you can't do a certain dance move, until you replace this thinking with, "If you can't do it, imagine you can!" This opens a part of the brain available for boundless possibilities and positive outcomes!

This mindset has helped me to believe in ideas, opportunities and things that may not exist yet in the material world but are in the process of coming into being: manifestation. I also love the fact that we can think, and then be able to speak something into being or becoming. There's a saying: "Our thoughts become our words, our words become our actions, and our actions become our life."

I also remember a very helpful statement I learned from another teacher, Colin Sprake. Rather than saying, "I'm trying", or "I can't do something," he encouraged us to acknowledge things not completed, formed or manifested in this manner: "I am in the process of doing, being, becoming." This has been a very useful statement to make, and I use it often as I move confidently toward my goals.

What mindsets and phrases have helped you to lift an idea from your imagination into full manifestation? Did you experience any "aha" moments or helpful revelations with these phrases and mindsets?

208. My Healer Moment

A "healer moment" that richly comes to mind is one I experienced as a graduate from a Neuro-Linguistic Programming course I took in 1997. I was studying with one of the two founders, Dr. Richard Bandler, at the time. We were practising the strategy Richard created called "Changing Personal History." It sounded interesting, since so many of us have had unpleasant events in our lives which we would love to erase and forget.

This particular day, I had one of my first paid NLP clients come to my office. He complained about having had a car accident, and all the feeling leaving his left ankle. I could clearly see that one leg was longer than the other. I asked him what he wanted to create in the session with me, and he said that he wanted to restore feeling in his left ankle and be able to walk properly again. His accident had occurred a few years ago, so he had been adjusting to a new way of walking for quite some time.

I took him back in time (in a closed-eye process, similar to hypnosis), and asked him to deeply imagine the moment, just *before* his accident. With his eyes closed, calmly he nodded yes. I got him to go right past the accident, and not register it in his body. Instead, I saw his left ankle twitch and move. A few minutes later, upon opening his eyes, he stood up – and for the first time in two years, said the feeling was restored. The actual specifics of this intervention are more detailed, and can't be covered in this brief synopsis. It's also important to be an NLP practitioner in order to do the above intervention.

I discovered I was having a first-time-ever experience, and it was a profoundly healing one. It was a powerful moment for both of us! Although training in NLP has been highly transformative and inspiring, I chose not to become a full-time working NLP practitioner: My heart and soul was with the flute, as it had been from that life-changing moment when I heard it, played by my cousin when I was only eight years old. I chose to be a concertizing, recording artist, along with painting and other passions. But to this day, I continue to use helpful strategies from my NLP days to keep learning new things and living my life to its fullest.

We are all healers. We may not know it, but we may be unexpectedly called upon by life to help, to heal, to love. When have you noticed you had a purpose helping and healing another's wounds, be they physical, emotional, or even spiritual? What did you say and/or do?

209. If You Don't Go Within, You Go Without

For me, reflecting within has more often been a satisfying experience than not. I've always enjoyed what I discover about myself and life when I navel-gaze. I once heard someone use the expression: "If you don't go within, you go without." And it stuck.

I've found that the times I went within the most were either *lonely* times or *alone* times – which I have discovered are quite different from each other. One of my loneliest times was being a teenager in high school. I was definitely not part of the "cool gang," and considered myself a classic band nerd – always practising my flute, never dating. During this time, I also found great solace in reading psychology and spiritual books, along with daily swimming and jogging. These activities took me within even though they were outward activities. How ironic: I had some of my most creative thoughts during these "flow" moments.

Recently, during the Covid-19 pandemic, I found myself taking a deep soul-dive within. My outside activities of the past, such as dancing, swimming, café visiting, traveling, going to concerts, playing concerts and visiting friends, suddenly came to an abrupt and unwanted halt. And living inside – not only in my home, but my psychological "inside" – magnified my private inner landscape from day to day.

In these circumstances, I asked myself what mattered most, and discovered some very interesting things: family, including my beloved dog, my flute practising, walking in nature, dancing, painting, sense of community, sense of contribution, animal welfare and activism and writing this memoir were most valuable to me. I also discovered I valued things much more, realizing by the example of the pandemic, that they could change or be taken away without much notice. Even the "simple things" in life seemed more delicious and meaningful.

It wasn't until the pandemic that I realized how to be my own best friend – but an even better version than before. I was literally with myself, and always am, twenty-four hours a day. It just seemed much more pronounced and unavoidable during this time.

I've always exercised self-care, but I knew there was still room for growth in this area. And being even more aware of the fragility of life gave me more appreciation for what I already do have. With some friends in their nineties, I've been conscious of staying in touch and cherishing every moment with them. I've also looked more closely at my own mortality, and chosen more carefully how I spend my time and energy.

Going within has really helped me avoid going without.

When has life called you to go within? What did you learn? Were there any unexpected discoveries? How has this experience of going within changed you? What have you gained from this magnified awareness?

210. The Nine-Second Meditation/Relaxation/Reset Tool

Calmness and stillness are states of mind so few of us can achieve readily. Those people who say they don't have enough time to meditate are the very ones who need to the most. I also believe that we always have enough time for the things we value most.

In our Western world, meditation seems to many like a peaceful luxury: only if you are inclined, know how to do it, and have enough time in the day for it. Many of us invent excuses for not having time to do it: like any discipline, such as ballet, music and sports, meditation requires discipline: a desire and a pointed focus to do it, and practise it deliberately. The results can be positively astounding.

I've found meditative states in many activities, such as a mindful walk, swimming, taking a shower, playing flute, lying in bed contentedly, daydreaming, or taking a bubble-bath. However, formal meditation has always been quite daunting for me.

I've done the classic "mindfulness meditation," popularized by Jon Kabat Zin – but for some reason, I felt irritated by the body scan. Visualizing scanning my body parts for me is a dry, detached exercise, devoid of sensuality. I guess meditation isn't necessarily meant to be sensual, but I am a sensualist.

One day, I discovered a way to deliberately "reset" my sense of calm and inner balance, and it only takes nine seconds. It's a sensorial relaxation exercise. Remarkably, it has worked for me and many others every single time. I believe the reason it works so well is that in a very short period of time, with our senses engaged, there's no time to worry or have any fleeting unwanted, or distracting thoughts.

Here's the exercise: With your eyes closed, breathe in through your nose for three seconds, imagining one of your favourite scents. This may be the scent of your favourite flower, such as a rose or hyacinth or lilac. Hold your breath for three seconds, then, still with your eyes closed, exhale for three seconds through your mouth – imagining, in your mind's eye, blowing out a flickering candle. When you are ready, gently and slowly open your eyes.

In just nine seconds, you'll feel calmer and more relaxed: "reset" and centered.

Repeat this exercise as needed. You'll find it really works in calming your nerves and resetting your sense of inner balance and tranquility, whenever you need it.

Have you discovered your own ways for recalibrating yourself into calm? What works best for you? What makes you feel most balanced and centered? How does the exercise above make you feel?

211. Enough Is Enough

After many years of pondering happiness, I realized that most of my woes and self-loathing moments are about three things: Being, Doing and Having. I also realized that if I state the three affirmations below, and both *believe* and *feel* what I'm saying, that they can change my consciousness and happiness:

- I *am* enough.
- I *do* enough.
- I *have* enough.

During the times I've accepted the above statements as true, really tuning in and feeling them inside, it's profoundly changed my attitude toward everything for the better.

Likewise, I've also noticed that when I feel like I *don't* have enough, or am *not* good enough, or I don't feel like I'm *doing* enough, these negative thoughts conjure up an image of my being at arm's-length from self-acceptance.

When I've used the word "want" in my desiring something, such as, "I want something" (whether it's to be, do, or have something), this particular something remains outside my reach – literally. Not only is there great power in words and the ones we choose, but particularly by using "want," we put ourselves into a position of it being somewhere "out there," and just out of reach. This is bit of an illusion, since we have everything within us: we just need to recognize, accept and be it.

I've also heard that what we say to ourselves, or think, becomes our words – and our words then become our actions, and our actions, our destiny. This reminds me that we need to be deliberate and mindful with our thoughts, since as they transform through words and actions, our destiny arrives as a result of them!

Day by day, I feel more and more like all is well, and I am, do and have enough – a contrast from my earlier years of worry and anxiety. This realization and deep, inner knowing have changed my life for the better.

Has the theme of self-worth been in your life often? How have you self-esteemed yourself? What have you discovered that works for you? How have you transformed by thinking, speaking, doing things differently? What new habits have you developed?

212. All You Need Is Love

Like the Beatles' song states, "All you need is love." However, that may be easier said than done for many of us. For me, love is a multi-layered phenomenon. For me to feel love, I have had to know first that I am lovable. Then, by knowing I am worthy of love, I feel I'm loved. I also feel that the knowledge that I am loving, both to myself and others, fuels my love phenomenon.

So, I created a mantra for myself, and have also shared it with my friends. It's grounded in self-esteem, and feelings of worthiness.

I say, out loud:
- I am lovable.
- I am loved.
- I am loving.

This has really worked. I refer to it often, and say it out loud to help keep myself in a state of self-acceptance – which at times can be hard for all of us – but also to fuel my feelings of loving others. I also do my very best to show them love through my words and actions. It's really very simple, but has helped me find my true essence and share it as much as I can.

Have you developed any statements, affirmations or mantras that help elevate your sense of self-worth and lovability? What has worked for you? Have you experienced others benefiting from it? How?

213. A Special Vantage-Point in My Daydreams

I'm finally here, floating on a pink cloud, a cotton ball in the sky, elevated, peaceful and taking in the view. It's tranquil and peaceful up here. So much to feel: the warm, soft, fragrant, breeze, like lilacs perfuming the sky; the sensational sunrises and sunsets. I'm immersed in it all – and I'm actually part of this dreamlike vantage point.

Oh, and the stars at night! They surround me with their flirtatious twinkly lights, winking at me and surrounding me with energetic scintillations. I'm safe up here, in my fluffy perch up in the sky.

The views are breathtaking up here: I can see exotic birds I've never seen before, the Northern Lights, shooting stars, soft, sun showers, and rainbows. The snowfalls from here are amazing to see and feel: these unique snowflakes, no two alike, softly swirling and cascading around me on my pink, puffy, cotton-ball cloud.

I'm safe; I'm "boundless." I'm peaceful, and feel connected with every living thing. There are absolutely no limitations. I have always longed for the boundless life, within and without.

Even my flute plays melodies I've never played before – although I have a slight recollection of hearing them in my dreams. I should have kept a pencil and manuscript paper on my night table back on Earth to capture these otherworldly, heavenly melodies. Curiously, up here, they come to me with an ease I've never quite felt before. I'm effortlessly birthing melodies that have gestated in my subconscious all my life.

Sometimes, I see other forms of life fly by, in magical chariots. They must be from other planets and galaxies: I wave enthusiastically and they gesture back at me with unusual sounds and lights. They are suddenly out of my view. They're gone.

From this vantage-point, I look back at my life on Earth. So infinitesimal, it seems: like a curious little ladybug, crawling through life, or fluttering like a butterfly.

Now, I've finally "landed," yet I'm in a constant state of blissful suspension, free of fears, unnecessary concerns, in pure "being." I guess that's what people have been trying to accomplish back on Earth, practising yoga, meditation, mindfulness and even Vipassana silent retreats.

This is a "spa-in-the-sky," complete and utterly tranquil; no questions asked, no answers demanded from anyone. There are no conflicts, no hurt, no pain, just pure serenity. This special vantage spot is one of my favourite places. My imagination always knows the route here.

Do you have any special happy places your imagination takes you to? What are they? How have they served you?

Chapter Ten

My Life as a *Lebenskünstler*

I've had a full life, as a flutist, music producer, entrepreneur, voice actor, visual artist, dancer and writer – and also as a lover of art, nature, animals, adventure, and all that God has blessed me to enjoy. For many years, I thought these things defined the expression of me being me: all my roles, all me being me.

But I didn't know there was a precise word to describe how I live my life, until a German friend told me I was a Lebenskünstler. *The term has no English direct equivalent. Literally, it translates as "life-artist" – and it means my life itself is my artform.*

Yes, I am a Lebenskünstler*!*

214. Who You Are Isn't Necessarily What You Do

One of the biggest distinctions I've learned is that I am not what *I do*, but who *I am*. I learned this lesson from one of my very first boyfriends, when I was only twenty-two years old. He said many of us mistake our identities for what we *do*, such as: "I am a flutist." But sadly, if we're not meeting our own expectations of what it means to be flutist – such as being a recitalist, orchestral player or recording artist – then who are we? We may have an identity crisis if we live this way. And it's very easy to let self-judgment creep in when we think that who we *are* is only what we *do*.

But, if we are who we are, and we happen to love playing flute, this doesn't make our identities dependent upon playing the flute. It also means that we don't *need* to play the flute in order be loved or have acceptance by others or status. Our identity doesn't depend upon what we do, but rather who we are as people, with our values, beliefs, and authentic essence.

This one simple distinction has made such a profound difference in my own life. It has allowed me to open up to so many possibilities of who I am and how I can joyously express myself. It gives me freedom and a sense of boundlessness, rather than being attached to the identity or label for "what I do for a living."

It's possible to extend this perception to an even broader sense: When we're asked who we are, we can say, "I am alive/love/peace/honesty/compassion/

awake/curious/grateful/full/worthy," and more. This may seem like a very unusual response, yet it may be the most real one. Essentially, I believe we are states of being, more than labels, and that's why the above adjectives may describe us even more authentically and accurately. Also, states of being are fluid, ever-transforming, and intrinsic to our nature. Who you are is your true essence, expressed in lived experiences.

Have you ever asked yourself who you are without any labels? Who are you without a professional or personal identity? Make a list of who you know yourself to be, not what you do. What do you experience reading your list? What do you discover?

215. An Artist Without Knowing It

People often say that they don't have a creative bone in their bodies: I challenge this statement. It's interesting that when I've asked them how they arrived at this conclusion, they may say a teacher or parent had said they couldn't paint, draw, or simply weren't talented. This would dissuade them from pursuing their artistic interests for years. Early childhood discouragement can really wreak havoc on your inner expressivity and creativity. It's such a shame for so many. It can even abort creativity and restrict boundlessness.

When my friends say they aren't artists, or "don't have a creative bone in their body," I always point out how they coordinate the colours of their wardrobes and accessories so impeccably and beautifully. How *can't* they say they are artists? Their bodies are their living canvases! Also, their colour sense is inspired by the same eyes that could choose paint colours. *Everyone* has an artistic bone in their body; it just may be disguised.

This realization often changes "unartistic" peoples' views of themselves in an instant. I love the look on their faces when they discover that they, too, are artists with artistic abilities. They simply express and embody it in their dress, accessories and unique sensibilities.

I believe that artists aren't just practitioners of certain traditional crafts – like painters, dancers, musicians – but rather people who approach their lives uniquely, out of the box, and with their own individual approach, expression and personal signature.

When have you discovered you have a gift or talent, expressed in a unique or unconventional way? What did you feel? How is your life affected by this realization? Do you choose to express this gift or talent more, now that it is revealed to you?

216. Writing My Book Full of Sparkles

My life has been a miracle in so many ways. Being born and not aborted was one early miracle – probably my biggest one so far! Another was being adopted by such loving parents, Tom and Nancy Nashman. They told me they chose me, and I knew they meant it. They treated me with such care, plus tons of love and support. They didn't understand my insecurities – neither did I – but they comforted me often when I felt anxious or sad.

And because I have so many events and stories that I remember and cherish, I decided to get them down on paper. As the stories kept coming to me, I realized, "I'm writing a book!" (*This* book!)

I wondered if this was the making of my memoir. I realized it's not a traditional memoir; it's more like a "self-help memoir." I asked myself how I could share my life, its ups, downs and "sparkle" moments – and at the same time, engage you, the reader. Ask you to reflect on yours. Although my life has been exciting for me, it's *your* life that means most and is most personal to you.

I've enjoyed the experience of remembering, writing and celebrating all these stories of my life! And I've made a discovery: Because I've been a flutist for over forty years, and have flutist's fingers, I'm able to type quickly. No writer's block – just fast fingers and rapid personal story downloads, almost like a stream of consciousness. This process of writing has been a true gift for me.

As I write these words, I feel as if I'm speaking through my fingers. Also, based on years of improvising my life, along with taking improv, acting, and dance classes, all have helped me to be bold. They've informed my way of being, expressing myself in real time, with little or no hesitation.

I now know that it's easier to edit later – so I simply let my life flow through my fingertips, typing my thoughts and inspirations with ease and flow. I avoid being critical or too analytical, since this can slow the creative writing process. After all, the creative juices need to flow.

I also was fortunate to take Tracey Erin Smith's Soulo theatre class intensives three times during the Covid-19 pandemic, on Zoom. She shared some very helpful strategies for unleashing thoughts onto paper, and being able to write more intuitively. I remember her saying, "First thought, best thought", which is a popular approach to improv acting, but can also apply to many other things, like writing.

Something else that immensely helped me overcome hesitation in my life was my early NLP (Neuro-Linguistic Programming) studies with one of the co-founders, Dr. Richard Bandler. He had an audio recording at the time, entitled "Hurdling Hesitation," and it really worked. Ever since listening to it, I've found hesitation and procrastination to be much less of a challenge.

Bandler has also shared the phenomenon of approaching goals: it's really fascinating that we tend to speed up as we get closer to the goal. This has helped me a lot, since along with my highly motivated personality, I've found there's a forward propulsion that happens after the initial impetus, driving me towards the completion of my goals.

I feel very fortunate now, since only rarely do I suffer creativity blocks in my life. I've had the opposite challenge: now if I were to move slowly or procrastinate, it would actually bring me stress. Being a perfectionist most of my life, in the past, before proceeding with any goal, I felt I needed to wait for that perfect moment before starting. I needed to feel completely ready, be in the right state of mind, and really want to achieve the goal.

Now, I move with speed and enthusiastic agility. This positive momentum has fueled me more than my perfectionism and procrastination of the past. Also, since I have ADD, I'm naturally spontaneous, impulsive and fast – making me best-suited to first drafts! Since I can get impatient and bored easily when it comes to details, I'm not a natural editor. I call upon the professionals to help me with this.

We all have many gifts and some are transferable. When writing this book, I found I've used my "dancing flutist's fingers." These facile fingers have played musical passages at lightning speed and have now moved me along at the speed of thought as I write. Writing at this speed has felt like I'm having a conversation with a friend: joyous, spontaneous and honest – but instead of talking, my fingers are dancing across the keyboard. What transferable skills do you use to facilitate your life? Have you been surprised by them?

217. Artists Don't Have Files; We Have Piles

For years, I was very ashamed of my "spatially disorganized" home and office. I had a lot of fresh, creative ideas, lots of papers with my latest and greatest ideas scribbled down on, and very few files, or even filing cabinets, for that matter. In a way, it was liberating to have everything laid out in an artistically disorganized fashion – and I knew where most things were. By contrast, businesspeople effortlessly pull out a drawer from their filing cabinets and locate something they're looking for in an instant, and voila, there it is, exactly where they put it.

For me, I would sift through the piles of papers, seeing if my visual/spatial memory served me well enough to remember where I'd put something. One "paper pile perk" was doing my taxes – late of course. In that pile of receipts, bills and miscellaneous scary and sometimes smelly, old papers, lived a cheque I hadn't yet cashed! And it wasn't stale dated: one accidental reward found in an artistic pile.

One day I got thoroughly fed-up with my disorganized ways. The papers were becoming unbearably overwhelming to me. It was at this point that I promised myself I'd get my life together and be more organized. What I discovered was that I just moved my piles from my desk, my working station, to the floor, out of my daily view. This cleared my workspace, so at least I could think clearly and not feel distracted by the messy pile. It was only a stop-gap measure – a sort-of solution. The piles still carried an energetic burden.

Then I decided I would give myself a break. With filing cabinets, things are put away and not seen again until the specific paper is needed. That was a daunting thought, since I often need more ready access to information on paper.

So, I've come up with a concept for myself. We artist types don't have files, but we have piles – so we feel the comfort of seeing everything spatially around us, ready to be accessed.

Since this discovery, I took up painting – and have ironically purchased two artist's cabinets, with colour-coded drawers. I put all blue paints in the blue drawer, all reds in the red drawer, and so on. Can you imagine? An artist type running her business life with piles of papers for years, and finally really taking up painting – and having two colour-coded filing cabinets for storing all the paints? I guess left-brain right-brain synchronization can be useful in many partis of our lives.

I have since made amends with my organizational inconsistencies. So long as I can find things, feel inspired, and get things done, I can create my own piles, files, or other systems – as long as they work for me!

Do you have a specific way of doing things that serves you best, even if it seems like a slightly unusual or unorthodox way of doing things? What works for you? Have you applied this system to various parts of your life? Which ones?

218. Capturing the Magical Moments

Some of my most fascinating and satisfying times have been with my camera. People often ask me if I'm a photographer, and after seeing my photos say, "You really should *be* a photographer." I find this a curious remark, since we are what we are doing from moment to moment. So, if we are taking pictures, we are photographing and are photographers in that particular moment. We don't need to be paid for it, in order to call it something we do – it doesn't have to involve money to say you do something. That is the case with my passion for taking photos. In fact, if it were my profession, I think my carefree, spontaneous, approach would change, and it would become something demanding a more serious approach.

My real passion taking photos is for the subject that catches my interest, whether it be a beautiful flower, a sunset, a fleeting moment, a sociological commentary and more. Some of my favourite photographic moments are ones that result in what people call street photography: where I capture a fleeting emotion being exchanged with people, animals or even flowers. These subjects take on a refreshing and communicative life behind the camera lens.

Although some may say we miss moments taking pictures of them, I believe we photographers really enjoy the moment – but in a more magnified and focused way, since we are literally "focused" when taking the photo. We are capturing the moment before it escapes us – before it goes away forever. This fleeting moment is what, for me, is most exciting and captivating. The photo is just the by-product of a very special and intimate relationship I've had with a moment in time – with my life, experienced through the lens of my camera.

So next time someone asks me if I'm a photographer, or suggests that I really should be one, I'll simply say, "I love taking pictures – these moments are precious, fleeting and to be celebrated, just like traveling."

I've discovered that travelling holds the same elements: no two moments are the same, you are in a here-and-now, moment-to-moment existence. It's that same delicious feeling I experience getting up close and central with photographic moments, that are here one moment, and are gone the next—a fleeting fascination of life through the lens of my camera.

Capturing magical moments on camera: What are the moments in your life that you would like to carve indelibly into your memory? How do you do it? With your camera, through conversation sharing, or in a journal? What is your definition of meaningful memories? Are these moments enjoyed more while you are experiencing them, or afterwards through discussion, photos, writing or conversations about them?

219. All I See Is Joy

In addition to being a lifelong flutist, I love painting. In a way, I have a similar approach: my brush stroke and my flute tone are smooth and tranquil. I love the process of painting and flute playing and also enjoy showing my art. In Toronto, many cafés offer opportunities to artists to hang their art – and my art has been presented in several of them. One was situated directly across the street from Toronto's Art Gallery of Ontario. Easily visible, this gallery-café is called Art Square, and has a lime-green outline of a square at its entrance. It also serves great coffee and cakes.

This being my first and only group show, what I loved was the admiration, compliments and mutual support we artists gave one another. One particular artist was fascinating to me: Her name was Jasmine Virginia, and she had amazing pieces, with crystals, sparkles, and all sorts of beads on her black square canvas. I was mesmerized by one of her exquisite pieces called "All I See is Joy." It looked like a glittering nebula. And, depending on what angle you were looking at it from, it seemed to change: certain crystals would stand out and shining brightly – definitely a magical piece. The name, "All I See is Joy" appealed to me as well.

So, there I was, hoping to sell my own art, and I ended up buying a piece I will forever love: *All I See Is Joy*. And, by the way, Jasmine was also a lead singer in a heavy metal band, where the mosh pit was part of her performance. I found her personality, talent and versatility of creative mediums so inspiring. Jasmine Virginia, a woman with so many talents!

I didn't sell any of my own art at that particular show – but I look back now with gratitude that I was part of it, since I might not have met Jasmine Virginia otherwise.

My boyfriend and I broke up for a year – and during this time, I was graced with this beautiful piece, hanging on my bedroom wall. I like to think that I look for joy and the silver-lining in life more than I dwell on life's hardships. This book, *Sparkle*, is testimony to this attitude of mine. (Incidentally, my boyfriend and I are back together.)

Have you experienced an unexpected gift at an unexpected time, when you were at an event for a difference purpose; in my case, promoting and selling my art? What was this unexpected gift? What value does it bring to your life?

220. Mom, Monet, and My Midnight Paintings

My dear mother, Nancy Nashman died on January 22, 1996, and in May 1996, I used the humble and loving inheritance from my mom to go to Paris. It was May, springtime, and my birthday month. So, I decided that it would be a special way to celebrate and honour my mom, while grieving her loss at the same time.

I literally immersed myself in French Impressionist art, one of my favorite styles, since it speaks to me in its beautiful, muted colours, and dreamy, soft expression. My two weeks in Paris were unmistakably poetic. Unfortunately, it rained every single day I was there. I've read that "pathetic fallacy" is a literary technique Shakespeare used when the weather in his plays mimicked the mood of the scene or characters. In a similar way, I experienced my own "pathetic fallacy," feeling such deep sorrow from losing my mother at such an early age. She was just sixty-three and I was thirty-two.

I went to the Musée d'Orsay, the gallery specializing in French Impressionists, many times, and tearfully gazed at the gigantic Monet paintings. I believe I actually felt the magnitude of his spirit and presence while looking at his paintings. I couldn't hold back my tears. Was my own grief causing such a strong reaction to his paintings? Or, was there a portal through my raw sensitivity at the moment I was able to feel Monet's presence? It was almost palpable.

I visited other galleries in Paris – but never had such a profound experience as that one at the Musée d'Orsay.

When I got back home, I was inspired to paint, and would do so every night at midnight. This magical hour was an elixir for my creativity. Painting without natural light, but with the energy of the midnight hush, was dreamy and trancelike.

I'd put on classical music and "danced" my paintbrush across the canvas. My unconscious process was a blend of sweeping, flowing moves along with vocalizing, dancing and encouraging myself as I painted. Each painting was intuitive, not preconceived. The paintings seemed to simply emerge. I'd blend the colours I was drawn to and simply brush the blended colours across the canvas. After that, I'd use a dry towel technique to blend the colours even more. Each night, I would finish at 1:30 am, with a completed, original piece. It wasn't until the morning that I'd get to see it in natural light.

After I had painted fifteen pieces, my boyfriend at the time encouraged me to put on a show as a tribute to my dear mother. He suggested I call it "Living Colours," and I did. I put it on at a women's club in Toronto called 21 McGill (which now is Covenant House, a not-for-profit shelter for homeless people). Funny how life and places shape-shift, bend, and mould into other things during a lifetime.

My art exhibition, "Living Colours" meant so much to me, as it was a celebration of my mother's life through inspired colours at midnight. My mother also loved to paint, so this was a beautiful way for me to pay tribute to and remember her.

The death of a loved one can definitely spin out your life. For some time, it may feel like you're in another dimension, partly because of grief and the mourning period, but also for other reasons – perhaps inexplicably mystical ones. What art, or arts, or other outlets have been a comfort to you in times of grief?

221. Inspired to Paint at the Fruit Stand

I've always loved visiting fruit stands. Their appeal is multi-sensorial. I love the brilliant colours, textures, fragrances, shapes and sizes. Even if I don't enjoy eating a particular fruit or vegetable, I may still end up buying it, since I love its artistic qualities. One example is eggplant. I abhor the taste of eggplant, yet I love its purple shade set side by side with a lemon or lime. When I get home with them, I may never eat them, but I'll use them as colour combinations for that day's palette for my paintings. I end up with "food souvenirs" from my trip to the fruit stand.

Perhaps I'm a food hoarder, since acquiring is the fun part: but storing it is like having closets full of unworn clothes. Just as I've struggled with my shopping addiction, I've tried my best to notice what happens to me at the fruit stand. I go into some sort of artistic, colour-mesmerized trance, and love it. It's from this state that I've bought way too many fruits and vegetables.

I'm happy to have discovered a new way to appreciate colour. It feels very much like choosing tubes of paint at the art supply store – but tastes better!

Have you discovered an intersection of deliciousness in your life? What is it? How have you enjoyed the combined appreciation?

222. Ecstatic Dance and Life's Delicious Moments

My life has benefited tremendously from dance and movement. I've had many transcendent experiences.

Moving through life (literally), I've experienced many different modes of bodywork and dance instruction. One of the most profound body awareness teachers I ever had the good fortune of studying with was the late Nehemia Cohen, my Alexander Technique teacher – who later developed his own version of movement practice, called the Mitzvah Technique.

Through Nehemia, I learned about physical tension I hadn't been aware of before, and how to gently allow and lift my body into postures that were natural, elongating and freeing. He even taught dancers at the National Ballet Company of Canada, as well as many other professional dancers, actors, musicians and everyday people. My air capacity and posture playing the flute greatly improved thanks to Nehemia. I remember his thick Israeli accent contrasted by his gentle and subtle touch – and the magnificent physical results his work brought to many. I also found myself feeling lighter in many ways, mood-wise, physically and spiritually.

Margi Gillis also brought her own magical approach to her modern dance classes. Her metaphor directives were so unique. Phrases like: "dance with your armpits," "open to the ceiling," and "dance the entire room with all of your body." My favourite was "breathe yourself open" – a phrase that really inspired me to dance fully and with abandon.

Another gifted dancer, artist, spiritual soul, Erica Ross conceptualized a beautiful method of her own, called "Dance Our Way Home." Her gifts of communication, listening, honouring all participants and letting their voices be heard, created both a transformational and healing movement and meditation experience. It's so difficult for me to explain, since I found her work so transcendent. Erica has written a book, *She Reflects*, which explains her practice better than I can.

And Neuromuscular-Integrative Activity (NIA) has been a movement-class addiction of mine for over twenty years. My NIA teachers have included Martha Randall and Jennifer Hicks. Martha's gentle voice and sheer gifts as a trained dancer and Black-Belt Nia Teacher/Trainer have blessed us students with refreshing, rejuvenating classes for years. Jennifer too, with her accepting ways, and her deep, whole-body listening, have brought me much joy through Nia and friendship.

I especially remember my many years studying the 5Rhythms dance practice with the late Gabriele Roth – which profoundly opened me up in ways I didn't know were possible—raw, real, alive, true, are all words I would use, describing the experience of dancing in the presence of Gabriele and her work.

The idea that we can "sweat our prayers" – one of Gabriele's signature slogans – became real to me. (She even had t-shirts with "sweat your prayers" printed on them.) I also learned that when we dance, and "let the dance dance us," we arrive at totally different experiences and points of view. It was a very transcendent and spiritual place to move into, this sense of "allowing" the dance to dance *us*. Gabriele also has many recordings under the Raven Recording label, and a book, *The Urban Shaman*, which is transcendent. There are many international 5Rhythms trainers, and I've been fortunate to study with quite a few.

What I personally took from Gabriele's work was to let our egos get out of the way, so that our souls could do the dancing. This, at first, felt to me like a very vulnerable, naked space. I was accustomed to guiding and directing my life, with my flute practising, concertizing, recording and producing. Of course, this directorial/critic approach permeated most things in my life, including dancing, up until that point.

Gabriele's 5 Rhythms practice taught me something really unique and profound. Since so much of my life had been occupied with reflection, analysis, perfectionism and inner debate, the experience I had with Gabriele's work changed me forever. Many of us, myself included, have grown up feeling awkward and embarrassed on the dance floor. Unless we knew and could effortlessly do the current cool dance moves, we weren't part of the "in" group.

With Gabriele Roth, none of this mattered. It was all about letting our inner selves guide the dance, no matter how ugly and off-putting our movements might be. Another one of Gabriele's slogans was "dance ugly and drool." Now that sounds horrible, and it is! But we have lightness and darkness in us, and expressing both makes us human. It also releases the pent-up stuff we don't want to hold on to anymore.

One of the most memorable classes I had with Gabriele was in the late '90s in Mill Valley, California, near Tiburon – one of the most beautiful places I've ever been, similar to the elegance and magic of Switzerland, Lugano, in particular.

Gabriele always loved pushing us to our authentic edge. One of her trainings was called "Mirrors," and it was one of the most ego-challenging and advanced courses she ever gave. I decided that I was up for it, or at least I thought so. In fact, it was said that many people left the training midway since it was so emotionally challenging. I stayed, but I must admit, was ready to bolt and go back to Toronto, many times.

The premise was "Being," with a capital B. After arriving, all participants would gather for the first class. Instead of the usual introductions, stating you name, where you're from, what you do, and what you want out of the training, you could not say anything but your name. It was definitely a culture-shock for me, since many of us assess, judge and pigeonhole people by their occupations and other facts that are revealed in opening introductions. This was not available to us, at Mirrors.

Another exercise was acting out an exaggerated version of ourselves. I chose to use make-up, and when I put my lipstick on, it sloppily went outside the borders of my lip line. To me, this gross exaggeration of the lipstick symbolized my self-conscious drive to be visually perfect, but not succeeding. In my attempts, I'd end up going outside the lines. But perhaps going outside the lines is actually okay. Is it what makes us unique, original and not so rigid? What if, in attempting to be perfect, we end up missing the mark, and going outside the lines of our view of perfection, because we are trying so hard? I wonder if, when we let go of the pursuit of perfection, we can attain beauty on our terms – messy, smeared, yet beautiful?

A remarkable female participant who was the girlfriend of a very famous drummer had her own exaggerated self persona. She had a sexy British accent and I gather from her act, that her beauty gave her that "trophy girlfriend" appeal. She stuffed a pillow under her skirt to give herself an exaggerated derriere. What a funny sight and a pathetic moment: she showed us how it felt to be a rock star's girlfriend – a piece of ass.

Dance has informed so much of my life. It communicates many of my life's formerly untold stories – both stories I didn't know existed within my soul, along with stories I was aware of but could only express on the dance floor. "Letting the dance dance you" has remained with me for years, and has informed my approach to life, which really is a dance, too.

Ecstatic dance honours our whole being. Have you ever experienced letting dance move you, rather than trying to get the moves right? If you haven't yet, you are in for an immersive, soul-diving, unparalleled experience of a lifetime! Have you participated in other movement classes and somatic experiences? What did you discover? Experience for the first time? What remains with you?

223. My Best Times for Creative Thinking

I've discovered that some of my best and most creative thoughts have happened in the following places:
- the shower, sauna, steam room, whirlpool
- sitting on an airplane in the window seat, looking out into the clouds
- just waking up, in the middle of night or first thing in morning
- staying up during the "night-owl" hours
- during flute practising
- during and after a run
- during swimming
- in collaborative classes, writing classes, dance classes, where there is collective energy
- during motivational seminars, since this mode of learning inspires me
- at a retreat, in a new environment
- in a fresh, simple, uncluttered hotel room

I call the above moments my "flow" moments, when there's easy access to my creativity and my soul's calling. I've also discovered that it's best to have a journal and pen whenever I am in these situations, in order to capture a creative fleeting thought that could become a book or sage advice one day!

But my most favorite place for inspired thinking is on an airplane, thousands of feet up. Somehow, the fluffy, passing clouds and my wondering mind merge. It's in these moments that I'm immersed in a sense of weightlessness, where thoughts just come to me, without trying. Effortless creatively – up in the sky! I wonder if the same happens on the moon?

Do you have your own special places that ignite your creativity and original ideas? When do you feel at your most potent and creative? What endeavours have resulted from these moments?

224. Birthday Suit Flute

I knew from the age of eight – when I first heard my cousin play a Bach Sonata in concert – that I wanted, or rather, *had to*, to become a flutist when I grew up.

Well, fast-forward to almost fifty years later, and I find myself in the middle of the Covid-19 pandemic lockdown. It's something none of us had predicted or experienced before. "Lockdown" sounded so much like being incarcerated, punished, isolated. I didn't want to feel this way, so I deliberately made different choices that allowed me to express, be creative, and feel alive.

I decided at the very beginning of this pandemic that I wanted to be as positive as possible, and to design my life creatively every day: full of inner reflection, good, healthy meals, enough sleep, nourishing walks, some light yoga, connecting with friends over the phone, painting, and of course, flute practising – alone, in the nude.

There's something very freeing about playing flute in my birthday suit. I feel like I'm expressing my naked soul, stripped away from any careerist focus or endeavour. Simply playing flute for my own pleasure, for the birds and the squirrels outside on the balcony (but through the wooden door, concealed from neighbours).

Although I chose to avoid Zoom online classes for the first three months of Covid, I eventually succumbed, and brought my naked self, in my birthday suit, to my online NIA dance classes (with the camera shut off, of course). Miraculously, I found this also to be very liberating. Being free, without clothes or any movement restrictions, was a unique and sensual experience. And the fun thing was, no one else knew I had my birthday suit on!

There definitely have been some personal perks to this whole catastrophic Covid-19 pandemic experience. Perhaps it's the silver lining of self-expression and liberation. Dancing in the nude and playing flute in my birthday suit were part of it.

Can you think of a time when you have experienced little freedoms in your life under special circumstances? What did you do? What did you learn?

225. Being Good at Something: Your Passion or Your Profession

How often have you pondered the significance of passions and proclivities? We can have a natural knack for something, but may not want to do it as a profession. I've frequently been told, "Laura, you are so good at listening to my problems, you should really consider being a therapist. You would be amazing at it." This has been said to me by friends and relatives alike, all my life.

Although this is a wonderful compliment, I've often felt like an "unpaid therapist." With extensive Neuro-Linguistic Programming (NLP) training, and a good ear for deep listening, I really could have become a full-time therapist.

But I didn't.

I chose not to occupy my days listening to constant complaining – even if I could get *financially* rich doing it. Wealth and richness have very distinctive connotations for me. Richness can be spiritual, mental, physical, along with financial. It doesn't have to only refer to money.

I feel rich within because of the life-choices I've made – although other choices might have paid my bills more effortlessly. I chose to live in a beautiful spacious apartment in a tree-lined old neighborhood in downtown Toronto. I pay rent, and to some, am wasting my money. This was a conscious choice, since I preferred to have a beautiful home I rented than a home I owned in a place I could afford – but which would have been in a much less desirable location. I chose to take public transit and not get a driver's license, and I love eating out rather than cooking. For me, it's my version of a "rich life" on my terms. I believe I can be wealthy without being financially rich.

Another passion is my love for art and painting. My paintings are organic, instinctive, and not pre-meditated. They seem to emerge from the canvas, as I blend colours together on the palette and then brush across the canvas, blending the colours right on the spot, offering a surprising outcome each time.

However, when people want to commission my work, I feel slight butterflies in my stomach. My art, my sense of colour discovery and experimentation has suddenly become a job, with expectations from a client. It's no longer just play, fun, improvisation of colours on the canvas for pure delight. I often think to myself, "What if the colours I'm commissioned to use aren't exactly what I end up using? Will they like it?"

It's so much easier to love doing and being myself *for* myself, with pleasing others as a kind of "by-product."

We all have strengths and abilities that can be applied to making a living. The sad part for many people is they've chosen to do something they're good at, but may not love doing – because it pays the bills. This common "career trap" can be a difficult hole for many to get out of. By spending more time with our special creative gifts, it's possible to experience joy, even if it's just a hobby. If others want to buy our works, that's just an added bonus.

What gifts and strengths do you use and love expressing? How are they an authentic expression of you being you? What talents have you been using, but don't like doing – but continue doing, because they come naturally to you and fuel your career?

Chapter Eleven

My *Sparkle* Wisdom

They say the teacher appears when the student is ready – and life is a great teacher. I also know, from my own experiences, that when something works for us, we often repeat it and make it an ongoing habit. I also believe that when we enjoy something, it's great to repeat it, even with things as simple as going for a walk. If we love walking, why not go for two or three short walks a day? We all have a collection of lessons, strategies and life wisdom that works for us. Here are some things I've discovered that work for me. I hope they may be helpful to you, too!

226. My Results Book

The path to self-acceptance can be challenging, for all of us. In the past, I used to make "to-do" lists – but more often than not, I didn't get all the items on the list finished. That would leave me with a sense of discouragement and, at worst, despair. I realized that although I was getting things accomplished, by the end of the day, and even by the end of the week, I didn't feel like I got much done.

Then, I had an insight. What would happen if I created a list that only featured results? These results could include things like exercising, getting up and going to bed an hour earlier, making that call or email I'd been procrastinating on, finally starting to work on my taxes, making that first step to a better diet, continuing a project I had temporarily aborted, among many other possibilities.

I soon discovered that with a results book, it's easy to review your week from the standpoint of what you *did* end up accomplishing. For example, there may be that awkward phone-call you have been putting off, or to get that pile of papers sorted, or even committing to a meditation practice and taking that first step to your own personal nirvana. By the end of the week, you can see that you actually did accomplish a lot. It just may not have felt that way throughout the week.

The results book has been such a self-esteem booster: a way to remind myself that I *am* enough and *do* enough. Too often, before the results book, I felt like I was sporadically getting things done, chasing my tail, but rarely feeling a sense of inner and outward accomplishment. Now, with the results book, I can review my day or week, and see the true evidence.

I usually get a lot more accomplished than I had thought!

When I reviewed my results book at the end of the week, I felt a sense of accomplishment and fulfillment. It is the opposite to a never-ending to-do list. With it, I could see that I'd tackled challenges in all areas of my life. I no longer arrive at the end of the week with only partly checked-off to-do list items. I arrive with results!

The results book has literally changed my life. With this, I have a new outlook on accomplishing my goals, feeling self-acceptance, and experiencing overall joy and fulfillment.

What systems or new habits have you experienced in your life that improved your self-esteem? How are you using these methods to further your life?

227. Best Advice: Passive Income

Back in the mid-90s, I took many self-development courses. I loved the sense of optimism, proactivity and group support I felt from these events.

One of my life-changing teachings came from Anthony Robbins. As a motivational speaker, with a background in NLP (Neuro-Linguistic Programming), he boosted the audience's spirits, and gave us helpful life tools and skills. His energy and magnetism have always been inspiring and truly motivating.

Tony emphasized "passive income": making money while you sleep is one of the best ways to have money work *for you*, rather than *you* working for money. Ways to do this include publishing, real estate, and "infopreneurship." Tony used to also say "design your life," rather than just getting a job. For him, "job" was the acronym "J.O.B.", meaning "just over broke." His wisdom stuck with me, and I made many CDs that worked for me while I slept!

Royalties were a rewarding way to make music and make money, that's for sure.

Later, I made a CD for newborn babies with my pianist colleague, John, entitled *Lullababy*, and it made us money while the babies *and* I slept. Funny thing is it's my most successful CD – yet most of it wasn't listened to consciously, but seeped into the subconscious minds of the little listeners while they slumbered.

One regret I have today is not having the foresight to save my money for a rainy day, and not buying real estate with my royalties. Eternally optimistic, I thought that my life would always be financially abundant. It's definitely been abundant in many ways, a deeply fulfilling and rich life. Now I also look into the future more, and imagine how today's actions will affect tomorrow's outcomes. And I save my money for a rainy day – and my future.

Sometimes in our lives we are given gems to live by. For me it was creating a residual income with music royalties. What gems have you lived by? What are some helpful or expert insights that have helped you navigate your life with more ease and flow?

228. Decluttering My Life

Like someone with a butterfly net, I've always loved to discover and catch beauty. Whether it's taking a stunning photo at sunset, finding the perfect earrings, buying fresh roses, or collecting collectibles (otherwise known as chachkas or knick-knacks) at thrift shops and antique markets, I've been there – often!

Yet I've often wondered and marveled at treasures that transform into clutter. What distinguishes beauty, in all its forms, from clutter and unneeded, unwanted treasures? I suppose being sentimental helps me collect stuff, and attach personal meaning to it. I love the unusual, rare, pretty, cute, sparkly, fancy, fascination with shiny objects of all sorts – the list goes on. Collectibles of the clutter-bug!

One action I've learned to take is decluttering my desk. By doing this regularly, it helps me to focus and think more clearly. And I need this in order to function properly. So what do I do with all the piles of paper and stuff I need to go through? I simply put those piles neatly on the floor to be dealt with later. My desk remains clear and my mind stays clear, too.

When it comes to decluttering chachkas and pretty things, I go through phases. The sentimental mood I was in when I acquired the clutter isn't the same mood I'm in when I decide I need to get rid of it. I'm sort of on a "clutter spectrum" – which, like a sliding scale, and depending on my mood, adds or subtracts clutter in my life. Some days, it is just easier to let go.

My aesthetic sensibilities are varied: Not only do I love sparse, Zen-like environments, but I also love "stuff." I love colours, textures and interesting treasures. This will always be part of me, and I have to make peace with myself as the eternal collector. To deal with my passion for remarkable things, I've devoted my spare room to house my collection of teddy bear chachkas, ornaments, and other cluttery stuff. They have a *home* in my home.

Are you an emotional, sentimental person or more logical? What are you holding on to? Often, the way our homes look reflect our internal states. Know thyself: do you see yourself as a hoarder or a personal curator of life's beautiful things? What have you learned about yourself by loving (or disliking) sentimental objects? How and what have you been able to let go of and give away? How has this changed you for the better?

229. Distilling What Is Really Important

I used to worry about many things when I was younger. Life seemed like such a huge and vast highway ahead, with so many decisions to make. Now that I'm older, and have been able to do many of things that are important to me – like concertizing, recording music, voice acting, taking dance and acting classes, painting, traveling, personal development courses, animal activism, writing, and more – I look at what is important *now*.

It seems very simple; as life progresses, it's the simple but meaningful things that take central focus for me. I love having a partner, a dog, eating vegan and caring about and advocating for all animals, as well as loving to continue playing flute, painting and writing. Contributing to others' lives with my heart and ears, through companionship is also very important to me. Learning and growing has always taken a front seat in my life, whether in self-development courses, or spending time with my wise elders.

If I were to die tomorrow, I think I'd be ready, since my life has been *my life*, my expression of self, not dictated by outside influences too much. Having said this, I don't want to die any time soon, since I'm still enjoying living my life and looking forward to more surprises and miracles to unfold. One thing for sure is I want to help the plight of animals, and my focus has been on factory-farmed animals, promoting veganism, and helping dogs get out of dogmeat trade.

When I die, I hope that I will have been able to make life better for animals and people in the best ways I can.

What is really important to you? Things can change, we can change, but often our values remain the same. We express our values in so many different ways. One of the keys to knowing what is important to you is the feeling you have when doing things. Do you feel fulfilled? Does what you're doing give you a sense of joy and authentic accomplishment? Could you do this for hours – and it never feels like work, but instead a chosen purpose? Some call this phenomenon your "dharma." What do you live for? What do you wish to leave behind as your legacy?

230. My Life in a Rollercoaster Seat: Front, Middle, Last Car

As a kid, I had my fill of thrill-seeking. From riding horses bareback at top speed – galloping dangerously by the side of a steep hill – to enjoying some of the fastest rollercoasters, I can say I've always enjoyed the ride!

On a rollercoaster, one thing I enjoyed was the differences between the front, middle or last car. Each car offered its own unique experience. The front car, for instance was the "entrepreneur" of all cars. It took the initial risk, had the first experience, while hearing the screams from passengers behind. It was the "thrill-seeker" of the rollercoaster seating.

The middle car was the careful one, experiencing the front car "rush" vicariously through the initial screams of passengers up ahead. No quick turns, just manageable ones. It also didn't experience the speed of the last car, swinging around corners faster than all the other cars – and hearing all the screams ahead before actually having the rollercoaster experience for itself.

I can say I've enjoyed all three positions on the rollercoaster. And using a rollercoaster as a metaphor, I would say that my life is a mix of all three cars. But usually, I live my life in the front car, boldly choosing to take the lead on my own ride through life. This doesn't mean that choosing to be a middle car or the very last car is less beneficial. They just give different vantage points.

Sometimes, in life, we feel the need to be more reflective and observant. Other times, we want to take the bull by the horns and go for it, no matter what. All positions are good positions.

What are your favourite cars on a rollercoaster? If your life were a rollercoaster ride, which cars have you spent the most time in? Would you like to change cars now for some new experiences and vantage points? What cars would your choose and why?

231. My Identity Shift: Extrovert to Introvert in Just One Year

I never thought I could become an introvert. All my life, I've enjoyed connecting with people, events, unique situations, and they all required me to be outside my home, communicating and connecting. When the Covid-19 pandemic arrived in 2020 in Canada, I rejigged my whole life. I transitioned from extrovert to introvert, in what felt like no time at all. What was so wonderful about this was that it was *not* an identity crisis. I was actually expanding my identity and living more of my full potential expressed inside and out.

In the '80s, as a flute student at Toronto's Royal Conservatory, and then at the University of Toronto's Faculty of Music, I was a "band nerd," practising between three to five hours a day. This was essentially quite introverted behaviour – however, I never saw myself as an introvert. Always self-reflective and self-conscious, I still was an extrovert. I would joke about my identity, being an "extroverted introvert," since I loved being sociable. My introverted side was the private, self-led and self-disciplined part of me that practised flute for hours daily.

When Covid-19 arrived, like many of us, I retreated. I went within: more self-reflective and I started practising my flute again, three to five hours a day – something I hadn't done since university, over thirty-five years ago. Navigating through technical exercises on the flute and navel-gazing were my two focuses during lockdown.

A lot of my weekly activities were cancelled, like NIA dance four times a week, daily swimming, and more. At first, I chose to avoid the "Zoom phenomenon" because I could and needed to, and I preferred to spend my time going within. My work life hadn't been digital before Covid-19, and I didn't want to hop on the popular social and business bandwagon of virtual meetings all day. I heard how exhausting they could be, and how "Zoom fatigue" was a very real phenomenon.

I also did a lot of journaling, painting, walking and some talking with close friends on the phone – but felt more drawn to self-reflection and introspection. Was I becoming an introvert, due to circumstance?

Although the daily unfolding of the pandemic was daunting, the deep breathing involved in playing the flute regulated my calm and centredness. Practising scales and other technical exercises kept my mind sharp and focused, and the sheer beauty of the music made my heart sing. I felt an inner purpose, keeping myself mentally, emotionally, physically and spiritually filled during the pandemic.

I found a sort of inner serenity, playing flute for myself. Then I started to share my music over Zoom with a global group – a sort of meditation/prayer group, most days. It was a remarkable discovery. I'd coincidentally found a group on Facebook and felt drawn to participate. As part of the group, I played my flute to intentionally send love and healing to a talented young jazz guitarist in a medically induced coma in Seattle, Washington. He was only twenty and had his whole life ahead of him. This meditation/prayer group was made up of devoted family members and friends from all over the world – including me.

I can say that only a few times in my life have I been able to say, "I played flute for a friend I didn't know". Yet, as a fellow musician, on some level, I felt I knew him. The meditation group gathered on Zoom for months every day at three o'clock. This was one of the biggest life-changing experiences I've ever had.

The power of connection – whether it be connection to ourselves, inwardly and reflectively, or outwardly to others, in a global healing group – produces an inner state that is profound and without boundaries. I've gained a sense of peace, and now have an appreciation for introverts. I became one. Just as some people are ambidextrous, I believe I have acquired the ability to be introverted, after a life of extroversion. What a gift, to be at peace, in "lockdown." It seems ironic, but being forced into a quiet, calmer place, caused me to be calmer than I've ever been.

Have you ever experienced an "identity shift"? Or perhaps a new perspective on your identity? What did it teach you? How have you and others benefited? What have you discovered about yourself and your identity?

232. Social Distancing from Myself

Is it possible to do too much navel-gazing? Well, the Covid-19 pandemic proved this true for me. At first, the pandemic offered ample time to self-reflect, ruminate and deliberate. From shutdown to lockdown, there has been plenty of time for self-examination, self-criticism, and self-discovery.

But when is too much contemplation a burden? In fact, questioning myself made life heavier than I wanted it to be during such an intense global period.

So, after a while, I decided I needed to "socially distance" from myself. What a phenomenon: to think I was taking up too much space in my own head, deliberating, worrying, questioning. I've heard a saying about thoughts taking up residence in our minds, and have no right to if they aren't paying the rent! A bit of a funny expression, but I will always remember it.

I made a conscious choice for my emotional survival. I decided to watch funny TV re-runs, like *Two-and-a-Half Men, Modern Family, Seinfeld* and many other sit-coms. This took me away from my navel-gazing and into joy and laughter.

Self-preservation can take many forms. When have you felt the need to take extra care of yourself, by nourishing yourself with self-care? Has it involved cutting out the worries and ruminations? How has reducing worries and self-consciousness given you more joy and fulfillment? What have you done to achieve this?

233. My Big Moments of Change

"Hindsight is 20/20," is an interesting expression. Before life becomes "hindsight," we can become overwhelmed by the changes we are going through, and feel them to be unbearable. At the time they're happening, life may seem dire and impossible to get through. These times are transient and transformative, but not impossible.

We usually find ways to reframe, look through a different lens, or change our perspective and move on in our lives. Some things stick with us, as old wounds that are buried deeply. It may take therapy or a conscious desire and willingness to work with these wounds, to bring them up to the surface and release them.

In my case, *my* big moments have been:
- Losing my dog, Ben, who, as a puppy, got run over by a car at our farm.
- Stopping my childhood passion of equestrian riding at age twelve, and immediately starting up flute as my new life goal.
- Experiencing many breakups, leaving me with feelings of abandonment.
- Changing flute teachers, at the recommendation of a well-intentioned one. I got emotionally attached to, and felt torn away from them when stopping
- Learning Mom had brain and lung cancer when I was only thirty-one.
- Having six close friends move out of Toronto, experiencing a breakup and Mom's diagnosis of cancer, all in the same year-feelings of overwhelm and abandonment
- Experiencing financial hardship and having to do a consumer proposal to consolidate all my debts: one step away from bankruptcy-feeling shame
- Losing my dad: my personal philosopher and friend
- Losing Ito, my lifetime dog-soulmate of sixteen years.
- My German past boyfriend, Markus, dying with MS, during Covid-19 at age fifty-four.
- Letting go of some hopes and dreams, which brought a sense of grief, mourning and resignation.

These have been some of the many big changes I've experienced in my life. It's funny how things that feel big to us resonate so deeply. Even so, it's possible to work through challenges and come out the other side – with new realizations and hope. One therapist said, "In order to get over something, often you have to move through it." This phrase seems quite general – but what I gleaned from it is that there are many possible approaches to dealing with change, challenges and life's hardships. We just need to be willing to, and to have a support network to help us through.

The good news is, despite how hard it seemed at the time, I chose to be an optimist, a problem-solver, and dedicate myself to opening up to the many possibilities to get through. I think I was saved by this and by maintaining a sense of curiosity, positive mindset and gratitude. This outlook, inspired by my adoptive parents, Nancy and Tom, has helped me so much with life's challenges.

What personal transformations have you experienced when going through your life's challenges? What approaches have helped you heal and thrive? Are there mentors who've positively guided you? What was their input and wisdom?

234. Philosopher's Walk: A Path Back Through Time

I remember walking through the beautiful University of Toronto campus, along a path called Philosopher's Walk. Situated behind the Royal Conservatory of Music, the Royal Ontario Museum, the U of T Faculty of Music, and U of T Faculty of Law, it winds its way over to the back of Trinity College. Lots of brains and creativity flow along this pathway.

Over thirty-five years ago, this was the path I took to the back door of the Faculty of Music, where I was studying the flute. As I entered the building, there was that familiar, fear-inducing smell of the building, fraught with memories that felt like doom: the inherent competitiveness of many fellow students, my own insecurity, and more. I would stop breathing for a second, my stomach would tighten, and the whole foreboding flow of feelings would overcome me.

Now, sitting on a park bench near the entrance, I'm in a different head and heart space. Over thirty years ago, I chose to carve out my own professional music life and career. I remained true to myself. I also chose not to become an orchestral flutist, but rather, to create my own music entertainment company, Montage Music, and produce and record music. I remember contemplating the name of my first business, Montage Music. I decided if I used "M" for both words, it could appeal to the sense of taste: "mmmm," as in "Mmmmontage Mmmmusic." On a certain level, I was hoping clients would find our music tasteful and yummy.

In addition, in 2002, after I had recorded several albums, I started a CD label called, Spa-la-la. The music is mostly instrumental, soothing, and can suit spa environments, whether they are businesses or at home. I also have a division of Spa-la-la, for my visual art called: "Spa-on-the-Canvas." The reason I call it this is because the paintings are very tranquil: My intention is to offer the spa experience in colours. I've even been told that merely gazing at my art causes the viewer to relax and shed their stress. By simply breathing in my art, they are calmer. *Fait accompli.*

Today, over thirty years later, here I am again, returning to the special U of T path, Philosopher's Walk. But now I am whole: I know who I am, what I stand for, and how I want to express myself authentically in my life. Gone are the fears of becoming, since I know who I am, and am daily becoming more of it.

With a contentment that comes with age, I sit on a park bench, hot cup of coffee in hand, drinking in the sights of nature and people: squirrels, birds, passers-by with dogs and babies in carriages.

I also find that I engage naturally with people on this Philosopher's Walk path, whether it be talking about the beauty of the day, common interests like our dogs, or simply "being." The invitation and ease by which I live and start conversations with passers-by is a clear sign of my personal journey of self-discovery and self-acceptance. I notice people responding openly when I offer a friendly and open approach – and it's these moments of instant and spontaneous connection that give me so much joy!

Isn't it funny how context and time can change your entire perspective on things? Can you remember a time when you'd changed, grown, or shifted your original perspective? What was this change? How have you changed, and how has this new perspective changed you?

235. Winning Lottery Numbers and Music: the Space Between the Notes

As a musician, I know that music exists not just in the notes, but also in the space, or silence, *between* the notes. When I used to play in the U of T Symphony and the Toronto Symphony Youth Orchestra, conductors would often emphasize the importance of the silent spaces or musical rests between notes. And, for me, playing the lottery has always had a curious similarity. On one hand, I've put my focus on the numbers I want to choose as the winning numbers. On the other hand, sensing the space between the numbers has also been significant to me. I look at choosing lottery numbers almost like notes of music, with rests or spaces between the notes.

This idea came over me at a time when I didn't win the lottery. I would examine and analyse the winning numbers, and in many cases, notice that the first two numbers were single digits (for example, 2, 8). Then, what followed were two double-digit numbers (for example: 15, 18) – and the final two were higher double-digits (for example, 44 and 47). So, all together, the winning number might be 2, 8, 15, 18, 44, 47. I would then study the distance *between* the numbers. (I wonder if anyone else has done this kind of studying of spaces between numbers?)

One day, I decided to buy a ticket and put my focus on this distance between numbers when choosing my potentially winning numbers. And guess what: I chose four of the six numbers correctly, and won $60. Had I chosen five I would have gotten close to $150,000! Something to think about, and work on for sure. A game of chance – and by chance, perhaps the spaces between numbers count too!

Life is made up of material and spiritual aspects. The solid and the non-solid. In what areas of your life do you depend upon the facts, and in which areas is your intuition and gut instinct your compass? When have you looked at things in an unconventional way and won or excelled? How has this perspective informed you and your way of doing life?

236. Time, Not Enough Time, Time of Your Life: You Pick

I remember when I first laid eyes on my Pomeranian, Ito. It was in Montreal in 2002 with my best friend. Although I lived in an apartment building where there were no dogs allowed, I knew I wanted to take this sweet little puppy back to Toronto with me. My friend emphatically tried to discourage me from doing this by saying, "Laura, you aren't going to have enough time to look after him. You already have four cats, and are so busy already."

In that moment, I realized that time doesn't really exist, and that we attach different meanings to this word called "time." I decided to make a distinction at that moment, for which I am totally grateful. It actually changed my life.

By transforming "not enough time" to the *"time of my life,"* I actually made the right choice: I took this ball of fluff home, and I took care of him for over sixteen years. Cherishing every moment with my soulmate, Ito made those years so meaningful and unforgettable. Had I listened to the advice of my friend, thinking having a dog would take too much time out of my life, I would have missed out on the greatest "time of my life" with the soulmate of my life, Ito.

What if someone else's "not enough time" is really how *you* want to spend *your* time? What if this results in being the "time of your life?" I'm so grateful that

I chose to listen to my own inner voice, and decided how I would experience my time by getting Ito. It was the greatest decision I have ever made.

When have you made a distinction about time, or how you spend it, and discovered you made the best choice for you? Someone else's interpretation of time well-spent may be very different than yours. Rarely do people question "not enough time" and see it as a wise choice of time well-spent. If they do, they may discover that it can result in "the time of their life."

237. Life Gets Easier as You Age

I'll never forget a therapist telling me that "anticipatory anxiety is always worse than the thing you may fear." That turned out to be true. It's strange that when I was younger, it was so easy to both visualize positive dreams for my future, but also scary thoughts of things I feared happening. This is definitely for sure: our imagination is a very powerful thing.

My therapist would say to me that most likely the thing I was fearing may never come into being, so not to worry. Time does distort, for sure. Some say there is no such thing as time: that "now" is all that exists: that life is made up of consecutive "now" moments, one after another, till we die.

If I had known years ago that when I got older, everything would seem more manageable, I wouldn't have been so self-conscious, or even cared so much about the opinion of others. I would have said and done more of what I loved when I was younger, and wouldn't have focused on others' reactions.

Now that I'm older, I try to only do and say things that are an authentic expression of myself. And it takes a lot less effort being real than being a persona you think others would like or approve of. You being you, authentically is more than good enough.

What have you discovered as you've gotten older? What wisdom have you noticed yourself developing? How has life become easier for you? What would you tell your younger self, by sharing your current wisdom?

238. Future-Pacing: an NLP Technique That Works

I've always been a list-maker and goal-setter. Somehow, knowing where I am and where I want to be helps me create a practical framework for attaining my results with more ease. When my goals are reached, through focus, discipline, consistent action and importantly, intentionally thinking, this can be very satisfying. Traditionally, for many of us, achieving goals follows a certain path – a trajectory forward from A to B, for example.

With a technique called "future-pacing," you actually visualize all the steps you need to take to arrive at your goal. As you rise above the moment you are in right now, you float above yourself and continue in this visualization forward toward your final outcome. There are many guideposts or benchmarks on the way to your final goal, and you see each of them as you are flying above them to your ultimate target. The use of your imagination is very important, and its best to do this process with your eyes closed.

The magic of "future pacing" is that once you arrive at the finish line of your goal, in your mind's eye, you simply turn around and face yourself, as you are now, at the beginning. You'll be able to see all the guideposts or benchmarks you were able to accomplish and pass through in order to get to the final goal. And you can look back at yourself now with feelings of relief and elation that the goal has been completed. You've arrived! This is such a non-traditional way of contemplating goals: from the arrival-point of your goal, looking backward to your present moment. For me, it has given me a sense of accomplishment, since I'm imagining the good already attained.

The beauty of future-pacing is feeling the result in advance of its actual achievement. This instills a sense of confidence and takes away any doubt approaching a goal. The "it's done already" feeling settles into the body and the mind, allowing more ease in its actual manifestation.

This technique is a simplified version of a Neuro-Linguistic Programming (NLP) technique, founded by Richard Bandler and interpreted by Tad James.

Have you ever used a technique like "future pacing" to arrive at your goals? IF you have, what did you discover? Was it easier to achieve your goals when you were equipped with this visualization technique? Can you think of a current goal you can apply this approach to?

239. Parachute or Process

Most of my life, I've enjoyed the phenomenon of what I call "parachuting in." I define this way of being as pointed, focused and swooping in: sort of like a hawk does with its prey. Most of the time, hawks look free, boundless and graceful high up in the sky. Then, suddenly they see something they want and they swoop down with pointed accuracy.

I often experience my life this way. I've never been one to chomp away at projects, in a process-oriented way for a long period of time. Quite frankly, I've never had the patience for it. Perhaps having ADD has contributed to this proclivity.

What I've found beneficial and enjoyable is allowing time to flow with ease. I use my intuition a lot too. This gives me a sense of freedom and autonomy – and then when a creative impulse arrives, like a hawk, I sweep down and go for it.

Another image that has often come to mind is a hot-air balloon that becomes a sudden parachute. In my mind's eye, I see the balloon effortlessly floating in the blue sky. Then, when an impulse comes over me, I see it transform into a parachute, with sharp focus on a creative endeavour. Perhaps this is the way of many artist-types. Some say you can't plan for a creative moment – you just need to be open to them, and create a mental/emotion/spiritual space for these sudden impulses.

Many people function daily in a "process orientation," where they chip away at a goal, step by step, until the goal is reached. Each day, mini goals are achieved and this offers great satisfaction. However, because of my ADD and impatience, I like to just *do* things, rather than plan or rehearse too much. Somehow, just "doing" brings an immediacy that is both exhilarating and satisfying for me.

Just recently, I've learned how to also appreciate and even enjoy a more "process-based" orientation. Writing this book has been both a very inspired and inspiring undertaking. It's also built up inside me the ability to be both creatively juicy and inspired, while writing daily – expressing my creative impulse while being in the writing process. It hasn't felt like a chore or a pedantic process, but rather a daily ritual that I look forward to. In a way, it's a "disciplined unfolding" or "download" of creative inspiration.

I'm happy to say that now I can integrate "parachuting in" with "process orientation" and fully enjoy the richness of both.

Are you a process-oriented person or more of an impulsive, parachuter? Have you been able to integrate both parts? How do you do it? How has it helped you to get things done?

240. Living Life Backwards: from My Eulogy to Now

When I was in my twenties and thirties, I had a crazy thought. I wondered if I'd ever get to travel when I was at retirement age. I pondered over whether future circumstances would hinder my ability to travel.

So, with money from my CD royalties, I ventured off to many places: New York, California, Florida, New Mexico, Hawaii, Europe, the Caribbean and Asia. Some of my favourite trips included taking my Pomeranian dog, Ito, to Grenada, Florida and New York, and going on my own to Bangkok, Thailand. Visiting the elephants in the Elephant Nature Park in Chiang Mai, Thailand was a dream come true-and playing flute in the open field while they grazed on long grasses was surreal for me. There really is nothing quite like experiencing life in other countries and cultures.

I'm so glad I had the foresight, since now, as I sit here writing, I'm in the middle of more than a year-long global pandemic-Covid-19. Travel is restricted to the essential, and there are shutdowns and lockdowns galore. Writing this book, *Sparkle*, has occupied my "traveling within," reflecting upon the meaning of life, my life and other things. I actually have time to settle and ponder: a rare occurrence, due to the unprecedented times with the pandemic.

I've also written my eulogy: imagining what I would want to hear people say at my funeral. It's an unusual perspective to come from, but I find it helps me to reaffirm my values wholeheartedly. Day by day, I continue to design my life according to this eulogy.

Interestingly, I've discovered new things about myself and my relationship to people, places and things. It has helped me to home in on what really matters to me, and how I choose to live my life in accordance with these values and goals.

Many petty things fall by the wayside for me as I consider what matters most to me in my life, and how I can express it most authentically. One thing for sure is not worrying about what others think of me, but being myself, no matter what.

As the saying goes, "What people think of me is none of my business." I like reminding myself of this, since sadly, so much of my life was caught up in worrying about what people thought of me. Now, I chose to be the best version of myself and that's enough.

What are some of the most important values you live your life by? What discoveries have you made along the way? How would you like to be remembered when you are gone?

241. Driving, Thriving, Being In-Synch with Seniors

We all go through stages of our lives, some easier than others. I definitely have experienced the "driving" phase, when I pushed myself, by forcing and trying so hard to get life to work that it hurt me. I was a self-critical – often self-loathing perfectionist with insecurity as my invisible middle name.

Now that I am older, after going through many life-changing experiences – like losing my mom at an early age and a multitude of romantic breakups – I've arrived at myself, as I was always meant to be. I'm much more content with myself: more authentic, expressive, creative and thriving. Reaching midlife, I wasn't as concerned about what people thought. I decided that what I cared about most was being the best version of myself. Now, in my fifties, life has become a lot easier.

I also notice that my appreciation of elders helps me to just "be," by modelling after their state of ease, contentedness and sense of arrival in their lives. Thanks to the many retirement-home concerts where I give flute performances each year, I am blessed to experience a very special population: the elderly. First hand, I get to witness so many of them, and so many are living in a such a gentle state of contentment and "beingness." Witnessing them in this state has had such a profound impact on me. I like to remind myself of them often as I progress in my own aging process and years.

There is something very beautiful about being content simply by being your true self. As Shakespeare said: "To thine own self be true." It couldn't have been said any better!

Have you been influenced by a certain age-group? Can you remember the first time you realized this? What do you admire the most about them? Have you modelled some of their behaviours and mindsets into your own life? How has this transformed you?

242. The Mysterious Meanings of Time

I've always been someone who struggled with being on time. Somehow, I was often late by five to ten minutes for things, *consistently*. I would ask myself why I'd persist with this easily solvable problem. After some careful consideration, I realized that I loved the adrenalin high, euphoric state I would go into as I hurried to be somewhere on time, knowing I was probably going to be late. I would jump into cabs, run at top speed, and feel my heart flutter as I hurried to my destination—always a few minutes late. This pattern continued consistently for years. After a while, I really wanted to conquer this bad habit. I was ready.

When I took one of my first NLP (Neuro-Linguistic Programming) classes, I discovered that people have different ways of viewing time: Some people are "through time," while others are "in time" or "on time." For me, I think I experienced time in a state of "in time": living the moment *in the moment*, not anticipating the next moment by being ready for it, preparing for it, or even thinking about it.

The downside of living "in time" has caused me to be late so much of the time. Living with passion is a great way to live, but living in the moment sometimes caused me to lose track of time. I didn't always plan for enough time to be on time for the next moment.

As a result, people told me that I came across disrespectfully when I arrived late for appointments or meetings. It was then that I decided to change my ways. I wasn't purposely trying to be disrespectful – I was just so absorbed in what I was caught up doing that I either lost track of the time, or underestimated the time I needed to get to an appointment.

Now, I am an "on time" person – in fact, a bit early these days. I have a very close friend from Germany, where punctuality is a sign of respect. (Germans don't view tardiness as polite.) I also made a little inside joke with myself, warning myself that being on time for a German is only one second away from being late. I decided that it's best to be at least five to ten minutes early, to avoid unexpected delays that could cause lateness.

Being on time has made such a huge difference for me. I'm more respectful now, honouring other people's time. That familiar old feeling of flying to my appointments in a euphoric rush has left me forever. Arriving on time works for everyone.

How do you view and interact with time? Are you usually "in time," "through time" or "on time?" Has it been the same throughout your life, or has it changed over the years? What has helped you with your relationship with time?

243. Being Myself, Since Everyone Else Is Taken

I have always loved the Oscar Wilde quote, "Be yourself, since everyone else is taken." It's a cute reminder of our uniqueness. What's even more amazing to me is to realize that there was never anyone quite like *you* or *me* before, and there *never* will be someone exactly like either of us again. That realization makes me gulp.

So many of us have been aware of our potential for greatness, yet have let inner and outer critics in our lives discourage, dissuade and extinguish that spark within us.

Yet, life is so short.

A friend of mine, an author, actor/comedienne whom I adore, named Frannie, shared a lot of wisdom with us on her "Facebook Love" live broadcasts. One particular gem is something that palliative nurses hear so often from their dying patients: "They wished they hadn't cared so much about what others thought of them."

Isn't this a profound realization? I've often thought that since many of us are self-conscious, doesn't it make sense that other people are not as concerned about us since they're focused on their own image and what others think about *them*? So, rationally-speaking, most people are too busy worrying about what others think about them to bother judging or criticizing us!

We can ease up on judging ourselves and just *be* ourselves.

Fortunately, most of us are not in a palliative state, so we can set ourselves free and lose our self-consciousness. By doing so, life can become a lot lighter, more joyous and we can be our most authentic selves.

What is one quote or axiom that has impacted you the most? How has it changed how you think and live your life? Have you created any axioms of your own that help keep you on track for yourself?

244. "Now" Is "Won" Spelled Backwards

"Winning" in life takes on so many different meanings and connotations. Everyone has their own personal definition. I used to think that being chosen as first flutist, winning equestrian and music competitions, being popular, and other outward manifestations, meant I had won. But what had I really won?

I've also discovered that my past, present and future can also factor in on how I feel about life's challenges. A sense of inner triumph comes from letting go of the past, with its shame and guilt, since the past is over. And not worrying about the future, since it hasn't arrived yet. In fact, some spiritual gurus have said that we have nothing but the present, since the past and future don't exist.

A lightbulb went on for me, with the realization that all we have is the present. This perspective has given me the understanding that "winning" for me is staying present, from moment to moment, observing, being, doing – and staying open and authentic to myself and others.

In a way, by viewing "Now" as "Won" spelled backwards, it helps to see how they are one and the same. We win our race with ourselves by actually *stopping* the race – by stopping to smell the fragrant flowers of life, both literally and figuratively. Also, by being aware of the rich unfolding of each ever-present moment.

Now, more and more, I'm conscious of the choice I have, to show up for each and every moment, fully present. With this mindset, it's easier to triumph over the past and its woes, along with conquering anticipatory anxiety over the future.

"Now" is "Won" spelled backwards: These words complement each other well, and remind me to include both in my life, every single day.

When have you experienced yourself being most present? What were you doing that brought you into the present moment with ease and flow? Have you overcome your regrets of the past and your worry about the future? What do you have to do, think, and be, to create more of this awareness in your everyday life? Are there specific practices, rituals, mindsets you use to achieve this?

245. My Important Lists

It's funny how lists can be such an important part of our lives: to-do lists, shopping lists, and more. But the two lists that matter most to me are the list of what I love about my beloved (and giving this list to him), and a list of what I love about myself (and humbly reminding myself daily). I cherish both.

You see, when I was a little girl, I was an avid list-maker. Somehow, by making lists I thought I had a better sense of both the purpose and structure of my life. I literally kept lists on everything from making my bed to how much I jogged each day. I was also a fastidious note-taker. At flute masterclasses, even one of my master teachers, who was a prominent flutist in the New York Philharmonic, asked me to send her my notes from her class, since she knew I took such copious, detailed notes. I took that as a big compliment, photocopied them and sent them to New York.

Another one of my most significant lists is the one that expresses my gratitude. Like many people, I have a gratitude journal – a helpful tool to keep my life in the grateful lane rather than the complaining lane. It resets my happiness dial if I've become upset about something and have gone off course. I've discovered that the more I focus on what I am grateful for, the more that irritants fall by the wayside.

My father used to always say to me, "Laura, what you focus on expands, so watch what you give your attention to." He was right. Dad also emphasized the development of a positive mental attitude and reminded me to notice and put a stop to "stinkin thinkin." My gratitude journal has also been a wonderful tool and reminder about all of my life's good stuff.

I've found that by making lists of what I love about my beloved and myself, it returns me to a state of positivity, appreciation and self-acceptance.

Do you have lists? What kind are most helpful to you? Why? Do you have a gratitude journal? What are you most grateful for?

246. The Breaking News, or *Your* Breaking News

I've often pondered the significance of the breaking news. It seems to do a really great job selling newspapers, and gets people tuned into radio and TV programming. All media does a great job at one thing: They succeed at getting the public's attention. Unfortunately, it's often bad news. I wish that the breaking news could also be uplifting, good news stories. But I guess that wouldn't shock people enough, or make them feel compelled to keep tuning in or reading the news.

The news took on a whole new meaning the year my boyfriend broke up with me. I decided to make my new life without him *my* breaking news each day – but not bad news like most news outlets. I chose to focus on the everyday news of *my* life: what I was doing, what was significant in my new life without him, and how I could learn from the relationship, grow, and not only survive, but truly thrive.

And I did.

The two rules I gave myself were no alcohol for six months, and no television for six months. Television "programming" was not the type of programming I was interested in being sucked into. By shutting this form of media down, it forced me to look within, reflect and be creative. It was a time for me to be productive and thoughtful, rather than escape into the tv or drink my sorrows away. I've never been an alcoholic, but I believe that drinking can be a crutch, and I didn't want to go there. I also watched my diet, and didn't allow myself to indulge in overeating too many comfort foods. I wanted to be present to myself, what I was feeling and who I was becoming.

This was an exciting, transformative time. I was getting to know myself again.

After a year off, my ex-boyfriend and I met for a few dinners, and decided to reunite. It had been a year dedicated to personal growth, friendships, asking myself how I had contributed to the breakdown of our relationship, and getting to know myself a lot better.

By tuning into myself and my *own* breaking news and daily current events, I remained focused on my life and didn't get distracted by global news I couldn't influence on a large scale. This choice created a clear canvas to paint the life I wanted – and the bonus was our relationship reunion!

When have you made your breaking news more important than the news on TV or the news of others' lives? What did you discover when you focused on your own life with dedication and commitment? Have you kept this habit of focusing on your own life more than the news or current events? What have you noticed about the quality of your life?

247. Speak from the Scars Instead of the Wounds

A quote from a clergy-member – that I learned in one of Tracey Erin Smith's Soulo Theatre classes – made a big impact on me. "Speak from your scars instead of your wounds." There's a huge distinction between scars and wounds.

For me, scars are the learning, the sealing up of the wound, the arrival at understanding; whereas wounds are the fresh, new, open emotional cuts that we need to work through. Some people may focus too much on the wounds themselves – as opposed to the transformations we can allow ourselves to go through, in order to better understand what occurred, grieve, mourn, overcome and triumph over them.

The Hero's Journey (as proposed by Joseph Campbell) is a very powerful concept. It takes you through the many stages of life, with learning and growing and becoming someone new and transformed, at the other end of your life's challenging journeys: more evolved, having a better sense of self, and being able to help others move through their challenges, too. You are the living example of your own growth.

We all have wounds and scars in our lives. It's how we move and live through them that helps us to learn and grow. My classes with Tracey Erin Smith have been instrumental in the process of looking at my life's stories, and sharing them with a new, transformed, perspective in the form of solo (or "Soulo") performances. During the Covid-19 pandemic, I was fortunate in being able to participate in three Soulo classes, along with performing three one-woman shows on Zoom: "Turkey Talk," a piece about veganism; "Lookalike," a piece about finding some of my birth-family at age fifty-three; and "I Call Him Ito," about my long-time soulmate and best friend, my Pomeranian, Ito.

I've been fortunate to have had so many mentors and teachers who've shown me different perspectives and ways to think and live. Tracey Erin Smith definitely has been one of them.

Who have been your greatest teachers when it comes to living and speaking from your scars or wounds? If you could change an unresolved wound into a scar today, which one would it be? How would you reframe it to make it a scar, full of wisdom and insight?

248. Life's Moving Sidewalks

Have you ever had the experience of getting on and off the moving sidewalks at the airport? What a strange sensation it is, going from a regular walking gait to hopping on an already-moving foundation.

In a way, life can be that way too, both metaphorically and literally. I have noticed this phenomenon most when doing voice-over recordings in the studio. I've worked with many engineers – but the most efficient one I've worked with will both record and edit my mistakes during the same recording session, right on the spot. What a brain optimizer! We've all heard about the value of exercising the brain with such things as chess, sudoku, crosswords and word searches – and now, voice-over recordings! It sure has kept me on my toes and tongue!

In the studio, if I make a mistake with pronouncing a word, my engineer will play back the recording to the word I needed to re-record. I have to literally "jump in," almost like hopping onto a moving train: smoothly, and without any abruptness. I have to speak at the same tempo and volume as the word before. This is my "moving train" recording exercise!

In a way, isn't this how life can be? It's like a moving train of thoughts And actions, life itself. To flow with life, it's taken me many years to discover and try to master the "merging with" action. This means being present, focused, aware, and just simply "going with life," as I jump onto the moving train of life.

In the past, I would navel-gaze a lot, would question the "train," and miss jumping on at the right moment. More and more, as I get older, I realize it's safe to simply trust my experience and instincts, and boldly jump on *life's train*, at the right time and place.

Have you discovered moments in your life when you felt as if you were being called to jump onto the "moving train"? How did you feel? Did this build confidence within you? What else did you experience? How has it informed your life?

249. Raising My Standards, Lowering My Stress

Isn't it funny how raising our standards gives us a sense of higher self-worth? Is it possible to combine the raising of standards with the lowering of stress?

I discovered one day that by raising my personal standards, (what I expected from myself), I was also able to lower my stress at the same time. I thought about it for a while and realized that when I'm operating at my fullest potential, believing in myself, this actually brings my stress down, since I'm in the natural flow of life.

I also found that the opposite was true: When I lower my standards in how I think about myself, words I use and actions I take, this actually can increase my stress levels, and slow down my progress and ultimately affect my inner fulfillment.

So, although it isn't a perfectionistic approach, it is an authentic approach. I'm being true to myself with my thoughts, words and actions. It definitely requires conscious awareness, since it's easy to slip into patterns of limiting beliefs, speaking negatively and not taking action on what I know is possible.

It has taken me years to really register the fact that when I believe in myself, and live my life with self-honesty at a high standard, I can do my life with much less stress.

And, it's made me a whole lot more happy!

Have you discovered things about your standards for yourself and their relationship to your stress? When do you feel most empowered and least stressed? What are some ways you lower your stress? What do you tell yourself, and do?

250. The Difference Between Choice and Decision

Some decisions in life feel heavy, such as which house or condo to buy, or whether to buy at all. As a renter for over thirty years, I've never been drawn to the need to buy. I was so fortunate with an apartment that has always felt like a house, in a safe area, on a tree-lined street with a ravine nearby. It's very spacious, and I don't have to be concerned with shoveling snow, raking leaves, fixing the furnace, the roof, or anything else. In a way, it's big enough to call a house, but minus the costly repairs and maintenance of owning a house.

For my needs and values, I think I made a wise decision.

When I look at decisions, I see them as pointed trajectories of choice. They don't have to be limiting: "This is it." I believe choices are simply decisions made at a certain point of time, at a certain place, for a certain purpose.

The nice thing about decisions is they can be changed. Our choices are as unlimited as are we. We can make a decision that works for us today, and later make a new decision that serves us better in the future.

This is similar to my "committing out" concept: acknowledging that there's value choosing to change your mind and *not* do something. Different decisions serve us at different times. As with making declarations when committing to something or someone, "committing out" is also a solid, finite declaration. It carries weight, and is helpful to declare with a witness present. You can more easily walk away, knowing you ended it with conviction.

Is it easy for you to make decisions? When it isn't, what criteria do you go by to make it? What have you noticed about choices and decisions in your life? Have you ever made a "commitment out" of something you once committed to? Did you have a witness? How did this affect you, declaring your "commitment out?"

251. Hitting the Bullseye on the First Try

I believe that we can shoot for so-called perfection in our lives: whether it's selecting a home, finding a loving partner, choosing the perfect vocation, life's work, or pretty much anything else. It's our "bullseye": aiming for what we want and knowing when we have it.

One thing I've discovered is that sometimes we hit the bullseye on the very first shot. This may feel like it's too good to be true – but good things can actually happen on the first attempt. And if we hit the bullseye with our first "dart," we can stop right there. We got what we wanted. It was easy, and we can celebrate.

What about high-school sweethearts? We all know people who end up marrying their very first love. What other life experiences turn out on the very first try?

I believe that too many of us keep shooting for the right home, the right person, the right job, and miss noticing we already have them. Wanting what we have is another often-overlooked thing.

Some of us think it's necessary to spend a lot of time thinking and speculating about choices, leading to a "paralysis by analysis." We don't need to be in chronic self-doubt and over-analysis when it comes to making decisions. It's a pattern a lot of us have gotten into, since it's human nature to keep searching, assuming there's always something greener on the other side of the fence.

But what if the life you have, the person you're with, and the choices you've made *are* the right choices, right here, right now? Can you be content?

If not, are you allowing yourself to focus on your "bullseyes" with conviction and determination, and aiming with confidence? When you get it on your first try, know it's yours – and don't hesitate.

Can you think of a time when you hit the bullseye on the very first try? Did you think it was a fluke, or merely good luck? How can you make hitting the bullseye on the first try a tool you can call upon whenever you wish?

252. Monetizing the Happiness Formula, and Other Things

For many years, I've embraced the idea of living the "big life," full out: living spontaneously, boundlessly, intuitively. Somehow, the magic of life unfolding moment to moment, day to day, week to week, and year to year, has been my biggest pleasure.

I love the organic process of life: meeting people, sharing life, lessons and experiences, and then moving on – like a spiritual nomad. I've gravitated toward open-minded people, whether the big motivational speaker/gurus, or those who advocate doing what you love and the money follows, along with contributing to others' lives.

These days, during the pandemic, I've noticed a large number of people are monetizing their formulas for happiness and fulfillment. Everywhere you look, people have online "how-to" courses. More and more online communities are cropping up everyday.

As a technology-adverse person, I've never really liked sitting in front of the computer. I prefer living life in *real* time, in nature and with beauty, not in front of a screen. But when I did some acting and dance classes online, I discovered I've developed a love/hate relationship with the ever-burgeoning digital space. Zoom is all the rage, standing in for face-to-face life.

Online courses, monthly memberships, and other offerings are popular these days – and all of us are each other's students and teachers.

The digital space: definitely the way of the future, but I haven't caught up with the future yet. I'm still living in real time in a real, non-digital way, most of the time. I really hope that the balance between on-line and off-line will find a balance in me one of these days.

As a personal social experiment, when my computer died a few years ago, I chose to only use my iPhone, and not use a computer for over a year. This was such a liberating experience: less screen-time, more real life in real time.

Have you discovered a love/hate relationship with digital communications and learning? How have you been impacted during the pandemic with more or less time in front of your computer? What happened, and perhaps changed in you? What did you discover?

253. Looking Back at a Younger You

I've often experienced moments in my life when I wished I could have had the wisdom of a sage, but I was either too young or too inexperienced. As the saying goes, "Youth is wasted on the young."

Looking back at many of the wonderful lessons you've learned so far, what would you share with your younger self, perhaps when you were a teen, when you were in your twenties or thirties?

In the same way, jumping forward to ten, twenty or thirty years into your future, how would your older self advise you to deal with your present moments now?

Time is a funny thing; it is said that it doesn't even exist, that it is merely a construct. How have you treated yourself after learning lessons later in life that you wish you had known much earlier? Are you gentle with yourself – forgiving, generous, parental – or something else? Are you willing to be more compassionate with yourself?

254. Experiencing *vs.* Suffering

I believe that we think and speak our lives into being or becoming. It's only a small but very important distinction to say, "I'm experiencing some challenges," rather than "I'm suffering." "Experiencing" denotes something that is fluid and changing; whereas "suffering" seems like a state of being, and is much heavier energetically. When I've used the word "suffering," I've felt more like a victim, rather than my inner warrior, experiencing challenges, deepening my awareness, solving my problems and transforming my life.

Whenever I catch myself using the word "suffering," I stop in my tracks and correct it with "experiencing." It can even apply to how we discuss illnesses. I remember years ago a "body electric" practitioner advocated the use of such phrases as "I am experiencing symptoms of cancer," rather than either "I have cancer," or "I am suffering with cancer." In that moment, it all made sense. There is great power in words and how they land in our minds and bodies, energetically. I could now understand the subtle distinctions and connotations of words and phrases.

When friends speak about challenges in their lives and they use the word "suffer," I offer the suggestion of "experience" instead. It seems to really work for all of us in making the situation more supple and changeable.

Are there words or phrases you use to empower you when dealing with a challenge? How do they compare to the words and phrases you were using before? Words are power. What are your power words?

255. The Rings of Your Tree-Trunk Essence

Like tree trunks with their age-rings, we contain all of our experiences in our cellular memory, along with our subconscious and unconscious minds.

I like to think of my past, present and future all being one, given that time is just a construct, and we have become accustomed to thinking of it linearly on a forward-moving continuum.

What if we could perceive our own rings as something very sacred and personal to ourselves, not to be invaded by energies, people, data that we have not invited in? This could really impact upon our inner strength, by not allowing influences into our consciousness that doesn't serve our highest selves.

This is how I see the global news on TV, when watching becomes more than just knowing the headlines and having an opinion about them. When it infiltrates our lives, like insects infesting a tree trunk, I believe it isn't helpful to our overall well-being. I'm not advocating for "Pollyanna" living, but rather to be in control of the information we ingest. News is like nutrition: it's food for thought. But a steady diet of "fast-food news" can be unhealthy, to our minds, bodies and souls.

I believe we must monitor what we allow into our lives and selves, and be very careful to guard against toxins – not just nutritional but emotional, intellectual, spiritual. I am hypervigilant about not letting bad news, or uninvited and unwelcome stuff, into my life: my own personal "tree-trunk" rings.

Have you ever shifted your perception about how you choose to digest the news, people and life itself? What did you discover? What do you consider to be "good nutrition," from all standpoints: food, mindset, news, people, and ideas?

256. It's How They Make You Feel

There's an expression that describes the significance of people in our lives. It isn't what people *do*, but how they make you *feel* that makes them memorable. It may be something they said, how they listened and empathized, or a particular gem of wisdom that has stuck with you for years.

When I think back to some of the people who've really made a loving impact on my life, I think of:

- Dad: "Geez, Laura, I don't know how you do it. You amaze me." His sheer enthusiasm and sense of wonder about the way I live and do my life has stayed with me as a loving vote of confidence. His vote of confidence throughout my life has given me strength and belief in myself.
- Mom: "Just schedule fifteen minutes a day to worry, and no more." When I was a chronic worrier, Mom helped me by suggesting time management for my worries, too. This helped me to harness my strength and budget worrying-time, so it wouldn't take over my entire day.
- Colin, my partner: "It will be okay. You just watch. We'll get through this." These simple but deeply loving words have carried me through challenging moments in my life.
- William Bennett, master flutist: "Keep doing what you are doing." To have my most favorite flutist/mentor believe in me is beyond encouraging.
- John, my friend and pianist: "I don't know how you do it. You just keep inventing yourself. I've never met anyone like you." This makes my heart sing.
- Nehemia, my Alexander Technique teacher: "Allow and lift." Learning how to feel life in a more physically lifted, lighter way changed everything for me. Physical has informed my mind and emotions with more lightness and agility.
- Gabriele Roth, *Urban Shaman* author and 5Rythms Founder: "sweat your prayers," and "dance ugly and drool." These phrases brought authenticity to self-expression through movement. It's not about looking pretty and doing the moves right. It's really about letting the movements move us, expressing and releasing, and simply being all we are. I realized I could take this learning from the dance floor to day-to-day life.
- Dr. K, my therapist: "Anticipatory anxiety is often worse than what you are fearing happening. And often what you are fearing never comes to being as

you've imagined it." I've reminded myself of his wisdom many times in my life, and it has greatly softened my fears and anxieties.

Are there people in your life who've impacted you positively with what they've said to you? Who were they? What did they say? What do you say to yourself that provides you with belief in you, hope for the future and a full life everyday?

257. Daily Doing *vs.* Being

I've been exploring inner peace, and have come to understand that I need balance between doing, being, and having.

I'm not a natural morning person, yet most mornings when I wake up with the birds, I'm always relieved that I did. For me, forest sounds, birds, squirrels, and all the sounds of nature are my preferred music – I love them more than the sound of musical instruments or singers. Somehow, nature is my quintessential music.

So, when I first wake up, I review what I want to do with my day. If I don't have any pressing activities, I often find myself listless and self-critical, because I haven't made it my goal to have a to-do list. At the same time, I love and live for spontaneity, to show up for life and meet it moment to moment, in all its adventure and surprises.

My life has been a balancing act: balancing the sense of purpose and activities with sheer spontaneity, flow and auspicious moments. I have a sort of mantra that I allow life in, and let it present me with miracles, surprises and unrehearsed moments. I attempt to balance my life between these two states every day.

When you think about balance in your life, how do you create it? What ingredients do you like? What are your biggest challenges when focusing on "being" vs. "doing"? For creative types, "being" is part of the doing. For example, playing an instrument or painting. But for others, where work is work, and hobbies are something else, how do you differentiate between being and doing?

258. Curiosity: Are You a Cat or Dog Person?

It's often said that there are two types of people, when it comes to animals: cat people and dog people. Since I've had both cats and dogs, I can say that I love both. However, I do tend to think that dogs embody more extroverted, expressive, obedient, natures. Cats, although friendly, too, can be exceptionally independent and introverted, and purr to the "beat of their own drummer."

One thing I've noticed among dog people is their willingness to talk and connect with other dog-owners. Are the dog owners sociable people to begin with, or have their dogs brought them out of their shells? Maybe both.

When it comes to cat people, among my cat-owner friends, I've noticed that there is a quiet sensitivity to their subtle gestures. They have a connection to their pet that's private – not like the collective, sociable experience of dog people.

One habit that broke the so-called rules about dog and cats was getting my Maine Coon cat, Tigger to kiss Ito, my Pomeranian on the ears before bed. At first, Tigger wasn't up for the challenge, and by the looks of Ito, he was feeling quite unsure. After the trepidation subsided, Tigger had a nightly ritual of licking my Pomeranian's ears, while he allowed it, looking cautiously at him from the corner of his eye. No fights ensued, but instead a cozy night's sleep for all of us.

When I had four cats and one dog, I loved seeing how they all got along. One particular memory that has stayed with me is coming home and looking up at my bedroom window. There were three of my cats and Ito, my dog, imitating their posture, sitting together looking out the window at me. This was truly a remarkable and unforgettable pet experience.

Would you consider yourself a cat or dog person? Or another animal? What has your connection with animals taught you? Have you embodied some of their habits and ways of being?

259. The Sweet Spot: Finding the Flow

As a lifetime perfectionist, I've experienced intense self-judgment, but also self-approval when I'm satisfied with my accomplishments. One thing that I realized is that when I have a timer on my creative endeavours – such as creative writing, practising flute or painting – I go into an automatic "Zen-like" state.

I've thought about this, and came up with the realization that when we don't give ourselves extra time to ruminate – going over and over something in our heads, or on paper, or practising an instrument – we actually are in a state of "allowing," not "forcing." We're in the flow. Life is easeful and without stress.

I've experienced this state often: even when writing *Sparkle*. I simply sat down and wrote: no editing, no inner critic, just the truth of my soul. What a truly liberating feeling, especially for someone like me who has battled perfectionistic proclivities most of my life! I've also experienced this sublime state when practising flute: finding a place between fastidious perfectionist repetitions and simply playing, without physical or mental tension. I love the sweet spot, my flow.

When have you noticed yourself in the "zone" of effortless being? How have you incorporated this mindset into your life? What have you overcome?

260. Pandemic Perks and Pearls of Wisdom

I've never experienced anything quite like the 2020 Covid-19 pandemic. On a personal level, it stripped me (like many others) of my habitual livelihood, and caused me to go within, and to reflect, very deeply.

I've always been a navel-gazer, but this period of time turned me into a deep diver into my own soul, and my own purpose. It raised many existential questions.

Was my old life over for good? If so, what would I do next? What had I always done, that I could still do? Who am I now after this global shock to the system? Am I changed, and how do I see myself being in the world now? What have I lost, what have I gained, and what is left to explore and investigate?

Some of the Pandemic Perks were:
- Adopting introverted habits (although I was always an extrovert), such as writing a book and reading more.
- Becoming more comfortable being with myself. Getting to know myself better.
- Letting go of favourite habits, like swimming and dancing and replacing these with new habits. I also discovered that I wasn't as attached to the old ways as I thought I was. That was liberating – feeling resilient and renewed.
- More walks, more nature, more simplicity.
- Renewing my love for the flute and practising daily, because I wanted to.
- Doing three Soulo classes on Zoom with Tracey Erin Smith. A deep dive into my soul, for sure, plus a sense of likeminded online community.
- Journaling and creative writing became a big part of my days-resulting in this book, *Sparkle*.
- Looking deeply and discovering what is really important to me, before, during and after the pandemic.
- Appreciating what I do have.
- Celebrating my friendships with calls and texts.
- Quality time with my furry friend, Kito.
- Making friends with neighbours through simple waves on daily walks
- Being in the present moment more than I'd ever been.

Pearls of Wisdom:
- I can emotionally survive a pandemic.
- Life is fragile, moment to moment.
- Cherish the moments and *carpe diem*.
- Simple living is beautiful living.
- Nature is a healer.
- Time expands and contracts, depending on our perspective.
- A positive attitude during tough times, and all times really can help.
- People become more of who they are during a pandemic.
- Compassion and empathy help us share peace.
- Exercise, good rest, nutritional meals help a lot.

What "Pandemic Perks and Pearls of Wisdom" did you discover going through the Covid-19 pandemic? What did you discover about yourself? What surprised you? Are there habits you adopted that you are continuing to use? What do you appreciate more? Who have you become?

Appendix

Loving the Animals: Famous Quotes

I love the quotes of George Bernard Shaw:
- Animals are my friends, and I don't eat my friends.
- I choose not to make a graveyard of my body with the rotting corpses of dead animals.
- A man of my spiritual intensity does not eat corpses.

Also, Albert Einstein said:
- Nothing will benefit human health and increase the chances for survival of life on Earth as much as the evolution to a vegetarian diet.
- If a man aspires towards a righteous life, his first act of abstinence is from injury to animals.
- Any society which does not insist upon respect for all life must necessarily decay. The indifference, callousness and contempt that so many people exhibit toward animals is evil first because it results in great suffering in animals, and second because it results in an incalculably great impoverishment of the human spirit.

Leo Tolstoy had much to say about animal cruelty:
- Compassion towards animals is so natural to us, that only through conditioning could we become callous towards their suffering and death.
- How can we hope that peace and prosperity will reign on Earth, if our bodies are living tombs, in which murdered animals are buried?
- Kindness is incompatible with steak.
- The hypocrisy of people who cannot kill animals, but who do not give up their consumption of them, is great and inexcusable.
- A society which treats animals badly, will always be poor and criminal.
- The joy which a person will derive from kindness and compassion towards animals, will compensate a hundredfold for the pleasures one would be deprived of, were they to give up hunting and meat consumption.

- One should not turn a blind eye to the fact that, by consuming meat, they demand the killing of a living being for the sake of luxury and taste.
- If you saw children torturing a kitten or a bird for fun, you would stop them and teach them compassion towards living creatures, while you yourself would go hunting, shooting pigeons, horse-riding and you would sit to a lunch, for which several living creatures were killed. Is this blatant contradiction not obvious and not enough to stop people?
- The killing and eating of animals occurs because people are convinced, that animals were created by God to be used by man, and that there is nothing wrong with killing animals. But this is false. In whatever books it is written that it is not a sin to kill animals, it is written in the hearts of all of us, more clearly than in books, that an animal deserves compassion in the same way a human does, and we all know this, but we silence our conscience.
- By killing animals for food, a person suppresses in himself the higher spiritual sentiments – compassion and mercy for other living creatures, similar to him – and, stifling himself, he hardens his heart.
- Don't be disturbed, when upon refusing to eat meat, all of your loved ones begin to attack, judge, mock you. If eating meat was an indifferent act, meat-eaters would not be attacking vegetarianism; they are annoyed because in our time they are already aware of their sin, but still cannot free themselves of it.
- When you feel pain at the sight of the suffering of another being, do not give in to the initial urge to hide from the sight of suffering and flee from the victim, but, on the contrary, rush to the victim and look for a way to help them.
- As long as there are slaughterhouses, there will be battlefields.

What have you done in your life that exposed you to a truth that was hard for you to witness or bear? How did it affect you? Did it change you? How?

Manufactured by Amazon.ca
Bolton, ON